Sandra Ntonya was raised in Malawi, Africa. She is the third born in a family of six, to a ruthless father known to the masses as 'Idi Amin', due to his brutality. Growing up, she thought freedom was just a fairy tale. Full of dreams and yearning for change, in her early twenties, Sandra embarked upon a journey to England with her then-husband and son, whose severe disabilities dismantled the marriage and she was left to fend alone for her and her son's survival. She has since lived in Manchester with her beloved son, Alfred, and an amazing community. When the clouds are full of rain, they pour themselves upon the earth… sad it would be if they held back. Likewise, when Sandra's life was bursting with experience of scandal, abuse, to rubbing shoulders with the rich and well-heeled, she retains nothing but reveals it all, to the fullest.

Gripping and revelatory, there was a new path waiting for her inner fire to arise. Her journey becomes a wonderful meditation on being humanised and a hooker justified. As your eyes open to the truth, you hear the chains breaking away to freedom and delight in how the worldly-wise beauty queen brought African sunshine, smiles and warmth to the friends and lovers in the grey North of England. Now she boldly says, "Keep calm and kinky on. I love it when my clients wait their turn, in an orderly queue… better still, just join in."

Proudly, I dedicate this book to myself and with deepest gratitude to my legions of fans across the globe. The right people hear you differently. With support and warmth, you sent me hugs across the miles and whispered to me to fight on. Thank you for loving me as a 'justified hooker'.

Sandra Ntonya

CONFESSIONS OF A JUSTIFIED HOOKER

An Autobiography

AUSTIN MACAULEY PUBLISHERS™
LONDON • CAMBRIDGE • NEW YORK • SHARJAH

Copyright © Sandra Ntonya (2019)

The right of Sandra Ntonya to be identified as author of this work has been asserted by her in accordance with section 77 and 78 of the Copyright, Designs and Patents Act 1988.

All rights reserved. No part of this publication may be reproduced, stored in a retrieval system, or transmitted in any form or by any means, electronic, mechanical, photocopying, recording, or otherwise, without the prior permission of the publishers.

Any person who commits any unauthorised act in relation to this publication may be liable to criminal prosecution and civil claims for damages.

A CIP catalogue record for this title is available from the British Library.

ISBN 9781528931779 (Paperback)
ISBN 9781528966801 (ePub e-book)

www.austinmacauley.com

First Published (2019)
Austin Macauley Publishers Ltd
25 Canada Square
Canary Wharf
London
E14 5LQ

When someone understands you, they are your tribe and balance. After years of benefiting from each other and unpacking our mysteries, I thank my clients, with whom I have had such enchanting moments with sweet fillings… some of which would be ruined if put into words. Together, we survived the darkness in this tangled web. Thank you for riding with me all these years and showing me repeatedly that I matter. Keep calm and kinky on. It is a *business* doing *pleasure* with you.

Foreword

This is the moment of truth and I am not here to be cautious or careful, because nothing is sacred anymore. Who feels it, knows it, so who is to decide what the fabric of my life ought to be? When the concealed is revealed, of many things that piled up over the years, I realise that there is no more dignity to preserve; nonetheless, a life, a journey, to share. Altering anything… to suit anyone… would tragically change the fabric of my journey and that is a sacrifice I am simply not going to make. No one has a say in my healing process. My own mind and evidence are my backbone.

The depths you will find in these pages are my words, my account, my life story. I lay it all bare and share it now, uninterrupted and unhindered, because it is time to tell the truth of my life and to reveal the struggles I have experienced. This book is a monumental token of my victories… a liberating experience that will echo my life forever. Some of the things you will read will be familiar to you, some not. Some you will have read in the papers, but most will be new to you.

There are times in my life, as you will discover in these pages, that were harrowing and horrific. Strap in, for there are times that were joyous, wild and exhilarating too. There are scandalous, sordid and graphic stories too. I won't apologise for that. But there are tales of great tenderness and love, especially for my boy, and I won't apologise for those either. You might ask why they would share the pages of the same book. Why should graphic accounts be present in the same book as stories of my son's childhood?

The answer is simple: in life, we cannot choose only to recall the fairy tales we have lived through and not the tragic realities or vice versa. Even for a moment, we cannot detach ourselves from our cluttered experiences. They all weave together and overlap. And we are the products of every one of them. Like a mosaic, we both make each other, and his presence reminded me that there was no time to be weak. When you factor it all in, more than an escort, I am a mother. To erase from my journey, the seed of my wisdom, the one person I procreated, would be incredibly painful. It is him who continues to shape me up into a strong and courageous warrior. Revealing layers of myself, a beautiful part of me emerged because of him. More than a son, Alfred is a force to be reckoned with.

After years of slogging through the swamps of sadness, the wounds have given me wisdom and the scars continue to remind me that we have survived and there is hope. Having done all, to create a possible world for us, no matter how bad or magnificent, memories are the only things that don't change.

Thrilled to share with you from how I got into sex work and why I haven't got out of it, this book, above all, will chronicle those plentiful wounds, those desperate experiences in a challenging, ever-changing world – whilst showing the wonderful exhilaration that comes from coming through all that, coming out the other side a stronger and more complete person.

Please remember too, that this autobiography is my own story, written by my hand and it chronicles my life, coloured by my perspective. Confessions are truths. There is a price to pay for exposing truths. There will be those who will contest the contents of this book and seek to challenge my right to publish them even. But I rise and grow stronger at every attempt to intimidate me. No two people will see the same things in the same way. Perspective is subjective and that is enormously valuable; such is the rich tapestry of the world. This is my stitch in that great work.

***

As one dear reader, James Singini, simply put it: "Sometimes discouraged, but not defeated, this is a compelling true story of a mother's struggles in survival and hope against all odds. So tragic, yet her extraordinary dedication so inspiring, it is enveloped in a glow of love and gratitude. Its insights so moving and intense, it will live with me for a long time. Thank you, Sandra, for sharing with us a life with much gravity."

Simon Kelly, a profile in courage and my regular client for nine years, whilst working for the global pharmaceutical company. We became inseparable as I continued to meet him for sex after he became a self-employed Chemical Regulatory Expert. He worked all over the country and his best moments were when I accompanied him by train and stayed the nights. Great memories I will hoard forever. After reading this book on his dying bed at the Manchester Royal Infirmary (MHSRIP), he said, "It's interesting; worth reading; I was fully absorbed in what seems like an immigrant's love letter and appreciation to Britain. She provokes some deep topics and got my attention through and through. It serves as a great reminder of what truly makes Britain great. It is the continuity of that touching gratitude that stamps Sandra's character and gives her account a high moral tone. It's a fascinating read and emotionally raw to those of us who are deeply concerned about fairness, justice and protecting the frontline services. This book is incredible, extraordinary and essential. I wish her and Alfred every future success."

Another bookworm, Paul Harrison, highly recommends it because it highlights so much more. "A truly brilliant book on so many levels, not fiction and not average, it resonated a bit deeper than I expected it to. A mother crushed down but not destroyed, her gratitude and grit are to be admired. A proud lioness will never abandon her cub. This is beautiful and undoubtedly one of my best reads yet. I went through varying emotions in reading it. There is a sadness in their life that is somewhat beautiful. It made me gasp at the reality of modern-day Britain. I only wish there could be a sequel."

Wendy Heywood, a great neighbour and an outstandingly generous gem, said… "Living on their street, I have had the pleasure of knowing Sandra and Alfred personally. This is an astounding true story of phenomenal humans with life lessons for us all. Several times, the authorities let her down terribly, but her strength and determination are so inspiring, she continued to keep her head up high and do the best for her son. She has fought many battles and conquered each one with a positive attitude. I wish I knew her in her dark days, I would have wiped the tears from her eyes. Above all, I wish them both a very bright future."

Chapter 1
"I Don't Call This Thing a Child"

Always in a rage, screaming harsh and hurtful words to my face just to wreck my broken heart a little bit more, his constant words were, "I don't call this thing a child… I can't father a disabled child." As though it was my choice to opt-in to the various forms of abnormalities that our son had. Alfred had underlying congenital issues, which gave me cause for concern, such as his spinal malformations and inability to rotate his head, roll over or even stand independently. I put it down to a developmental delay. Perhaps I was in denial of this sad reality. To my husband, this was reason enough to burst into violence and interrogate me with the most painful words of blame. Each time, I died a little inside.

He ignored my pleas, until one day, he chased us away.

After residing in Britain for nine months, it was March 2003; the nightmare before Alfred's third birthday. At the end of a gruelling day – the messes, confusion, and tantrums – it was a point of sheer mental and physical exhaustion, and so I decided to have an early night as soon as our son fell asleep. I was used to having my sleep disturbed from diligently supervising him and meeting his demands, but this time, the sudden disturbance came from my husband. It was the night that changed everything. I lay in bed, almost asleep and he burst in the bedroom with raw anger, pulling the covers off me. He said, "I want to talk to you." Then he demanded that I sit upright, but I told him not to worry, he had my attention. If someone pulled the fire alarm constantly, you would eventually start ignoring it, right? My heart was racing and instantly, I knew it was going to be one of those 'It's-Your-Fault' moments… Again.

It is a fierce world, and no one knows when evil will strike. He was constantly yelling and shouting about the *undesirable being* I bore with him. A child not worthy of being called his son. "I don't call this thing a child. Only a witch has this sort of child! It's your fault! It should have gone in a septic tank!"

Nothing hurts more than love. It can frighten and frustrate us. Nothing breaks more than a heart. It began to occur to me that pain is the hallmark of love, and that all the fairy tales are but a wicked lie. But still, it is better to have loved than not.

Alfred was crying as I screamed with pain, but my husband didn't stop beating me. My son was just a frail child, and with one arm my husband pushed him to one side as I begged him to stop. In pain and desperation, I remember screaming, "You've popped my eye!" hoping he would get scared or at least take mercy on me. He paused to look at me, and when he still saw signs of life, still saw that both my eyes were intact, he beat me even more. What had I done wrong to deserve such brutality from the person I thought would stand by me?

He wounded me that night. My husband already had his first son with another woman, with no disabilities, so he used him as evidence; that it was impossible his genes could be at fault.

Alfred watched on as I was severely beaten, but I did not for a moment question his existence. He was simply there - his existence was the crime. He needed me now more than ever before. To this day, I count it miraculous that I am still alive following the brutality of the attack that left me limping on in agony for weeks.

Nobody with an ounce of love hurts the person they love. No parents should fight this way about their child. No child should witness this absolute evil and yes, more than a decade later I am shattered in tears, because writing this nightmare breaks my heart. As with every relationship, you learn to nurture and embrace some differences, but how could I, when my husband's spirit was rooted in hate and mine rooted in immense love for our child. That difference became too huge for us to even room together.

I was always panicking because the sight of our disabled child provided him with a 'perfect' excuse for the ranting outbursts. Did I have to beg him to accept our son's existence? It shattered me, but I was not crushed. My heart was ripped out of my chest but what remained in my soul was the love for my son which intensified each time I looked into his innocent eyes or held him close to me. He was not my shield, but at times it was the only feeling of comfort, if not a sense of bonding I had. My life was hidden in his, and his in mine. It was too dangerous to cry myself to sleep in case the monster attacked me again. I was in agony, horrified and deserted. With no defence to switch on, I shed so many tears; I was deeply wounded and sad. Curled up like a ball, I watched the night roll into day. I imagined how in the world some parents stick together when they hear news they never expected about their baby, whatever the diagnosis. Weeping uncontrollably, I longed for a supportive husband who would have held me tight in his loving arms and tell me, "We will be okay." Where is that love that makes one feel safe and free? Blind to my sorrow and pain, he walked past me a few times throughout the night; his cold heart was not melting. Where there is no conscience, there is no soul.

If he could inflict this level of violence and suffering repeatedly, because of the ideology that he was the *head of the house*, then this volatile and dangerous man did not deserve us.

Horror all over me, on Heathcote Road; it was a long night of anguish. My lip was bruised, I could taste my own blood. I felt like the mountains had fallen on me. My husband got up early and unashamedly left with one command: "When I come back tonight, tell me why you gave me this thing of a child."

It was an unbearable warning that I was to expect more slaughtering that night. For goodness' sake, take me to a place where my heart doesn't hurt so much… I didn't deserve this. Did I have to wait for him to make up his mind about our own child? You can't choose who will hurt you, but you can choose to leave.

When does struggle end… when does freedom start? I experienced the horrors of being in an abusive marriage. With infinite sadness, my turbulent pregnancy comes to mind because even then, he was careless and cruel. When you consider that babies can hear their mother's voice, heartbeat… and cries, the trauma that this little boy survived in utero is truly horrifying… before encountering this life of more horrors. If anyone deserves peace and serenity, it's Alfred and I was desperate to give it at all costs.

What was left of me was all I had, but at least I had that. I was without a penny and clueless about what life had in store for me, in a country wherein I had only resided for less than a year. I didn't know what to plan or where to go from that point. No possessions, I owned nothing. Apart from what I am, and what I can give, I had nothing but our passports, endorsed with a rubber stamp; engraved with prohibition of employment and benefits. Life does not always afford us the luxury of infinite choices.

I considered the birds in the air: they do not plant, harvest or store food in barns, yet they survive … We will survive.

It was, yet again, a sorrowful night, but we survived, and it was a greater depth and beauty to see a new day. As hard as I weep, I hope even more that a new journey begins. In almost unbearable pain, it felt like a privilege to simply be alive. We are all battling for life and I was spared for another day; to create a new path and start another chapter. It was a new mercy; a new faith… a new hope. It may sound radical, but I never take a new day for granted.

It was the first day of the rest of my life.

When you don't know what to do; all you must do is discover what to do. Arise! You cannot be half asleep during a battle. I walked to my friend Mary's house, whom I had known for only a few weeks. She had been heavily pregnant when I first met her, but when she came to answer the door, I realised she had given birth just a few days before – a son. Upon seeing my bruised face, she expressed a mix of shock, anguish and grief that my own child had inadvertently put my life on the line.

There are many pains in life, but the biggest is staying stuck where you don't belong, until you bend out of shape. Do what is good for you always. True heroes save themselves. Only you, can break out of the oppression.

I faced a gut-wrenching choice, and, no matter the cost to my heart, there was no deciding who was more important, my husband or our son.

Why look for a reason to stay, when love doesn't stand a chance? Why cling on, to lose yourself until there is nothing left of you? No matter how much it breaks your heart, at some point, step off the rollercoaster; recognise that the journey has ended and accept other paths. Yes! Sometimes we are forced into the next chapter of our life. Release…let go. Leave no life or love behind. Just let go. Don't be ashamed, afraid or wallow in self-pity. It will be daunting as you walk through that valley… You begin to wonder what even carried you there in the first place. Rise from your ashes, wipe your tears, gather yourself up and keep pressing on because none of us by worrying can add a single hour to our lifespan. It was a dire situation, but to be fair to my heart, I never looked back at the man who meant us harm.

Every challenge changes a life, so nothing could have prepared me. In a twinkle of an eye, our dreams for a more hopeful future can be filtered out and muddled by an overwhelming array of gruesome dreams.

Like me, Mary was also a socially isolated-struggling immigrant new to the UK, hardly making ends meet. She was in a bad episode of depression; her boyfriend was angry that she had not aborted their baby. "I don't want a mixed-race baby," he said. And moved in with another black woman. Despite it all, her love took us in, she nourished and sheltered us. Our paths crossed at a serendipitous time. She resumed her cleaning job a few hours a day and I looked after her son and Alfred.

Every end is a new beginning and it is wonderfully odd that there is no design for survival. Mary lived in a studio flat above a kebab shop on Hyde Road in Gracious, one of the busiest roads in the city. It cost £30 a week, plus £10 for gas and electric. A little bag containing a few clothes was all I had. Bruised, black-eyed and distraught, still I felt elation, merely at the thought of shutting my eyes and falling asleep in safety. Mary shared the bed with her new-born son, while Alfred and I slept on the floor beside her bed in the tiny room. We chatted away until very late at night until we slept soundly. Strong in mind, gentle in spirit, she kept us warm for a few weeks. To be constantly woken up by her crying baby was miles safer than the thought of being woken up and torn apart by that brute.

Fuel poverty is brutal. It's alienating and isolating. Despite it being a studio flat, it was uninsulated and there was an expensive prepayment meter we couldn't afford. I wasn't surprised when Alfred ended up in hospital one bitingly cold day, despite wearing multiple layers of clothing even when indoors. Facing the extra costs of caring for Alfred affected our health and wellbeing daily. Next time you boil a kettle, just remember that there are some throughout the country who can't afford to, having to make do with what little they have, making a choice between whether to heat or to eat, even if they are lucky enough to choose. At times, I felt hopeless in my helplessness. I felt like such a failure and had nothing to give back, but I kept the faith.

There was no television and no toys, so the fire engine and ambulance sirens along with all the traffic kept Alfred busy looking out of the glass all day. It was not a window, just a pane of glass that didn't open; a good thing because it was situated so low that had it opened, it would certainly have been extremely dangerous. It just meant that to get fresh air we had to open the door.

The stairs in the building were so steep that one day, upon realising that I was carrying Alfred up and down them all the time, a man in another room said to me, "Buzz my flat each time you are down there, and I will come and carry him up for you."

"You have an aerial in there," he went on. "I will give you my telly. You need it more and I don't watch much of it anyway. Leave your door open while I get it." He wheeled it through with the stand and plugged it in, something different in the way of entertainment for Alfred, apart from the window. It was so comforting and humbling to know there are people as kind as that man. He was jobless and didn't have enough for himself, but it was a self-sacrificing, loving gesture.

I had an appointment with the health visitor that week at my husband's house, the house I had fled that terrible night. I rang the health visitor that was due to meet me that afternoon to notify them of my current address.

Upon arrival, he had cause for concern. The flat was in such poor condition, it put our health and safety at risk.

"What if there was a fire?" he asked, clearly worried. "How would you get Alfred down the stairs?" Throughout the appointment itself, he did not sit down once. After a while, we were moved to a ground floor council flat which was specially adapted for Alfred's disabilities. The Family Fund, a charity organisation for the disabled, assisted me with some household goods.

Finally, our own castle! This was an enormous first step to stability.

Chapter 2
A Tribute to a Member of Parliament

A sad day descended on my life as I woke up to the distressing news that the Father of the House of Commons, the labour politician who served as a Member of Parliament (MP), had died aged eighty-six. Such a brilliant light extinguished… There are no words powerful enough to express my devastation.

Sir had served for Gracious Constituency until the time of his death. His illness didn't negatively impact on his passion and commitment to his constituents. He remained devoted to the end. May his legacy stand eternal!

As tributes to this iconic man flooded in from many politicians and his constituents, one would have to be hard pressed to argue with their opinion of him. Regardless of the political stripes, he was a highly respectable politician missed on all sides of politics.

It must be difficult trying to explain to an Inuit what a tree looks like. It has never seen one. But is it difficult to simply appreciate and acknowledge someone who has changed your life? From the abundance of the heart, the mouth speaks. If gratitude is abundant in your heart, it will pour out and it shows. When your words go beyond your heart, then they are hollow words.

We like to think we have our life mapped out and with so many chances. One day you will wake up and discover that the pillar and beacon you are most thankful to is no longer with you. Even if tomorrow was promised to us, don't save until tomorrow what you can say today. That affectionate pouring out of the heart and soul, don't hide it, don't hold back because one day it will be too late; it will be painful to wish you had reached out earlier. That sincere apology, that gratitude, that hug, that encouragement, that word of hope and comfort, if it is abundant in your heart, express it in words or actions. Don't hold it back from the person it is due.

Dying is not the tragedy. We are all edging closer to it. The broken hearts and the broken dreams that survive the death… those are the real tragedies. My heart was broken. The way he handled everything was beyond incredible and I took great comfort in that he was aware, throughout the journey, how immensely grateful I was. For fighting a good fight – wholeheartedly – to help keep my son in this great country which has unlocked the fullness of his potential. He will forever be cherished in my heart. This MP was not running his personal race for his own gold medal. This MP was not motivated by selfish ambition. He wished to serve the electorate wholeheartedly and did just that until the end of his race, to the finish line.

As soon as Alfred woke up, I pointed to Sir on the television's breaking news and asked him if he remembered this man. Then, with tears rolling down my cheeks, I told him the reason for my sadness. He has a good memory, but he does not understand death. According to Alfred, every person who has died has gone to team up with his greatest superstar Michael Jackson. They will be breakdancing without him and it's not fair! He asked me if I was crying because I felt jealous too. Before long, he was blasting out to Michael Jackson on full volume and danced like it were a contest.

My grief was so deep I felt like the world should have stopped spinning out of respect – even if just for a moment. In respect, honour and thanksgiving, I lit a candle all day, in his memory and honour, to reflect on the magnitude of his dedication.

Years ago, one encounter with Sir changed my life for better, forever. As I found myself dug deep down, he threw the rope of rescue. I first approached him one evening during his open surgeries, after my husband ruthlessly attempted to get Alfred and I deported, upon discovering that OUR SON had many impairments due to his chromosome abnormality. It was my fault. I disgraced him. He was ashamed of us and wrote us off... completely.

My first meeting with the overwhelmingly humble MP was rather philosophical yet dramatic; the pleasure was all mine. My neighbour accompanied me but felt she also had a pressing issue to raise, so I told her to go first. She moaned to him that her doctor was not changing her medications as she required, so she was under stress. He told her to go back to her doctor because his surgeries were not for medical examinations. They weren't that kind of surgeries! It wasn't until I laughed heartily that she realised she should have gone to her doctor.

In that emotional moment, as I unfolded my story and introduced him to my son first, Alfred's health complications meant that he could not even walk due to a floppy muscle condition. He had no pushchair. I had to carry him most of the time, but he carried my strength and faith all the time. He could not speak, and at that time, his condition was yet undiagnosed. The days were gruelling, but I had to stay strong for my son.

Very accessible and genuine, he had his ears on incline and was revolted at what he heard. Overwhelmed by the unbearable weight of sadness, tears down my face, my heart wept. Looking at Alfred, he knew instantly that we needed help. If the NHS is the vine, Alfred is the branch. He wouldn't have made it without it. Cutting the branch from its vine is detrimental. He could not fathom how a father would be so brutal and demand our deportation, to withdraw all medical support of a fragile baby with complex health needs at his most desperate hour, solely because he considered his child 'ugly and disabled'.

This meeting was my first step up the ladder of a new hope. As he penned everything down, he was always kind and attentive, yet still threw in some jokes appropriately. You've got to love the spirit of the British, even in the dark times. Watching the constitutional series of Prime Minister's Questions on Wednesday will keep you abreast with the antics of the political parties. You can cry and laugh through them because they manage to address dire situations with great humour... and a dollop of sarcasm, and still get the job done.

My neighbour could not fathom what she heard. She knew I had an immigration issue, but the full details immensely broke her heart.

On our walk home, it took us a while to break the silence. The first thing she said was, "I realise just how lucky I am and how good I have it. I must stop worrying over silly things. I get stressed over buying the wrong sanitary pads. If they don't have wings, my day is ruined!" As we giggled it out, the healing within her brightened my moment. There is nothing like a good dose of perspective. Visit an intensive hospital ward and you will be thankful that your bones and organs remain inside your body for the time being.

On our second meeting, during which time my child was undergoing an assessment for a proposed statement of special educational needs, in accordance with section 324 of the Education Act 1996. They took into consideration all the evidence and advice from educational, medical (audiologist, physiotherapist, speech and language therapist, genetics and Winnicott centre, psychological) Children, Families and Social Care Team and a Disabled Children's Team's officer.

As we awaited further consideration from the Home Office, the National Health Service did not consider that this child was an immigrant awaiting a decision. They put the border issues aside.

They looked away from the immigration rubber stamp in a passport. What they saw was a desperate child with complex health needs and did what was morally right.

We are not poor in thanks and I have schooled Alfred as best as I can to understand the deep debt of gratitude that we owe Britain for preserving him. It's amazing how the undying gratitude grew in him and 'thank you' has been tattooed on the palm of his hand and in his heart. When you reach the highest level of gratitude – perpetual gratitude – your words, thoughts and actions are of love and kindness. He had no choice but to grow to feel and understand emotions. He knows it's okay to be sad, angry and discouraged and he also knows the strength to overcome hardships and pain. He may not understand fully why I raised him the way I did, but one thing he understands is gratitude. Be it just picking up some litter, to keep Britain tidy, he does so with genuine passion. He gives something back. His friends have often told him, "You don't have to do that Alfred, you know!" but he wants to.

Although a Member of Parliament cannot cancel an order for removal or deportation, Sir's involvement to address my concerns directly to the Home Secretary and update him each time I had new and compelling information, mounts up to my freedom today. My immigration and citizenship case awaited further consideration for ten years before it was finally decided upon.

He was my only string of hope, and it was a decade of real difficulty, living life on the edge. Hope was everything. He knew my circumstances like the palm of his hand, and he dedicated himself to the case with compassion. Whether his stance was anti-immigration or pro-deportation, I did not know. I just needed help and his caring heart spoke out. Whether he had a track record of any involvement in asylum and immigration issues before, I did not know, but his compassion and love were compelling.

An icon in the community, many people spoke highly of him and my neighbour commented on what a thoroughly decent and compassionate MP he was, and suggested I meet him. Also, it was gold standard and reassuring to me that he was a man who condemned and spoke out against the horrible crimes against humanity. People of integrity take it with them wherever they go, and he undeniably had the heart to support the defenceless immigrants trying to make it in a restricted world.

He seemed more in touch with the situation in Palestine and simply detested what had become of Israel and proved that you can challenge Israel's policies without being anti-Semitic. Despite the failed attempt of some to assassinate his character, his unapologetic views and the very words that caused them to despise him will be given prominence and magnified by academics and historians, because they have never been devoid of truth and power, if not already. We cannot relate to some hurdles, but we can at least spare a thought to appreciate the harsh experiences of others.

In standing up to truth and justice, his bravery to speak out against evil assured me he would detest my husband's brutality. Whatever way you look at it, he was rooted and grounded in what he believed, and his moral compass led him right. He represented us magnificently.

Unlike other immigrants who shamelessly cite the laws that unlock the jigsaw of their immigration case – hence they boast entitlement. I humbly recognised that Britain did not have to save my son. It didn't owe us anything. There was no entitlement, but it exercised its discretion in our favour and had compassion for a defenceless child. Gratitude begins when entitlement ends. Entitlement is a selfish concept. It dishonours. It is downright arrogant and creates hostility towards the host culture. Where there is entitlement, there is simply no gratitude. Realistically, you are entitled to nothing... be grateful for whatever you have. Many are poor in thanks, but I feel indebted to Britain, for giving me hope, reassurance, and a chance to dream. It is becoming more and more evident that those who boast entitlement will not want to integrate and that is like trying to mix oil and water.

The MP updated the Secretary of State, of the rare and critical circumstance. He proved that the mark of a compassionate society is that it looks after those that are vulnerable. Sadness in his eyes, he was stunned, shocked and aghast, that a father of a child with complex health needs could be intensely evil... terribly wicked as to cut the vital medical treatment, to punish the child for being born that way and further punish the mother for bearing him such a child. Having a disabled child was an offence for which I was penalised. It made me an object of scorn by the man I expected would stand by me and hold each other's hand to love our boy.

Rest in peace, Sir! You were a truly inspirational person who went so much further than simply the extra mile. You stood the test of time and showed your humanism, hence my love and admiration for you is huge. Your incredibly selfless character and truth will always ring out across the community because you left a legacy of hope, kindness and colour that will forever be shared and remembered. You touched so many lives and became a pillar of many memories, whilst bringing us the ability to see the future.

The community has been solid Labour for many years. The by-election campaign in the area was a constant reminder that indeed this man was no more, and it was time for another to fill his big boots. When it is time to replace, change, substitute or succeed, do we want another of the same kind or another of a different kind? I longed for another of the same kind.

Some independent candidates had no ties with the community, nevertheless, they promised to continue the late Sir's work and live up to his legacy.

Personally, when the leaflet detailing the list of candidates was first posted through my door, I found the contenders list, by any standards, 'worrying'. It needed more representation of people from more backgrounds. I am not one for diversity for diversity's sake because it is foolish, bigoted and hurts those who work hard to achieve equality, but surely, in Britain, based on merit, another race must have deserved inclusion.

How was it impossible to not understand the message portrayed in this? That multiculturalism and cosmetic diversity had sadly gone on the rampage, so much so that the scales tipped to one ethnicity, in an election as crucial as this. At least someone with unwavering principles and unshakable opinions came forward with brilliance whilst others, who could barely stomach it, cringed in their closet.

If it's true that the nearest is the dearest, the constituents must have wanted a local candidate, but the candidates were quick to quash this myth by comparing football royalty such as Sir Alex Ferguson, Pep Guardiola and José Mourinho who were not native but had been embraced by the city of Manchester.

Some courageous candidates boldly declared that they would tackle the dangerous confrontation between the West and the Muslim world which threatens us today. Now that is a crucial topic which many spineless, lightweight politicians shy away from. It is that cowardice of political correctness that Britain as a society is falling and crumbling upon itself.

We live in hope, that the hardworking people of Gracious will not be forgotten, that there will be change and development and that the community will not remain the same, with the most deprived ten percent of the constituencies in the country.

Chapter 3
Fifteen Years Absent

It was a ten-year plea to the Home Office to exercise their discretion to allow us to remain, with the help of my late 'iconic' MP, and other good Samaritans. Because of his passing, a month prior to my ex-husband's return, I took matters into my own hands…to ring the alarm bell. He returned to England after fifteen years absence, to benefit from the British citizenship of the child he had abandoned. This was the hardest pill to swallow and it would have seriously frustrated Sir, who did everything in his power to stop our deportation. He detested my ex-husband for ill-treating us. He would have protected us with dragon fire and spat him out of the country with venom, had he still been alive.

I was not starting a fire. I was building a resistance. I wrote a petition which was met by a loud and clear response from the outraged community, far and wide and was overwhelmed at how people shared my burden of the frustration. Their horror and compassion were shining more and more each day as people signed and reposted it to maintain momentum. There was an outpouring of love from everyone who was resolutely against this man's expectation. The stone he brutally rejected cannot be the cornerstone of his wellbeing today.

Everyone who signed was revealing their unity in standing against his application to the Home Office for citizenship on the grounds of a rejected son. I was strengthened yet humbled at the wondrous love and unity people heartily demonstrated.

Those who were not content reached out to me personally because it was beyond a petition. It was a cry for help, a plea to the public to fight for what is right and demonstrate what Britain stands for… fairness, social justice and compassion where it's due.

Throughout his childhood, Alfred never had the privilege of a happy-birthday card from his dad, because, sadly, he didn't meet his impossible *standards.* I was both mother and father. One day, Lauren, a support worker who took him out weekly for respite, asked me, "How long is Alfred's dad in jail?" I assumed that Alfred had told Lauren this and was fascinated at how he came up with that. Then I pieced the puzzle together. A few children in our neighbourhood had their dads absent due to serving jail terms, so he just figured that could be the reason he has no father around, because I never talked about him. Sometimes distressed, I wish I could set fire to the page where I fell in love with this lunatic, but hear, hear, he gave me a very special boy and that stands. Eventually, I told him the bitter truth that his father was not in prison, but he never wanted him because of his disabilities. He was not quality enough, for his father to love him. I still remember his first response to this was just 'oh', as he shrugged his shoulders.

For my son, I went through his distressing diagnosis of autism and severe learning difficulties and a chromosome abnormality (1p36 deletion) alone whilst enduring hardships of a visa that prohibited employment and state benefits, endless medical appointments and the process of Special Education Needs Statements for Camberwell Park Primary now at Melland High School.

Chapter 4
The Insignificant Becomes Significant

Learning that your child has disabilities is devastating and it's even more poignant when the person who must stand by you, erases the child. I have not felt any more hurt in my whole life.

Real men don't run away from fatherhood. They witness and watch over their child, to encourage and show them that they are worthy of all they bring into this world. I stood alone and bore the pain of watching Alfred push through his disabilities and ailments.

He failed to do the bare minimum and still thought he could swim his way back in. It is merciful that memories have no eraser. I was not screaming vengeance for his irrelevance in the universe; however, when you cause so much grief the stars tremble, life comes at you fast. His day of reckoning had come, and he made a spectacle of himself.

Bearing in mind that fifteen years prior... he had vanished as soon as the idea of responsibility arose, for a child he procreated. Having borrowed money from various lenders, he returned to Malawi, for his own benefit, for a fresh start to a world with no commitment or responsibility. I accepted that he was not going to be there for us anymore. Gallivanting in fun and frolics... as I was single-handedly having an unimaginably difficult time. Until, that is, one day he got infected with HIV/AIDS...

In his fifteen years' absence, we never disrupted him in any manner. But he inconvenienced me twice. First, demanding the divorce certificate, despite refusing to sign the papers. I ignored him. In fairness to my heart, I still feast my eyes on the certificate dated 14th February. Artistic timing by the civil courts!

The second contact was to insult me after he saw some pictures of my *disgracefully ugly imbecile on social media and I ought to be ashamed of myself.* This was our son, Alfred, whom he described in such a hateful way.

He remarried and had two children. After the online petition in 2017, his current wife – who by then was separated from him – contacted me to express her shock and disgust, because although she was married to him for ten years and had two sons with him, she had not been made aware of Alfred's existence. She feared what else he hid from her if he had managed to conceal a child for over a decade. I thought they would be safe if their two kids were in perfect health, they were desirable beings and he may just love them.

"You are absolutely right about the passport; that is all that makes Alfred valid in his eyes. If he truly loved your boy, he would never have kept him secret from us for a decade. He hid him in shame, and I had no idea that my boys have another brother, until I saw that petition. Never a word or even a rumour about Alfred and my heart goes out to you, I am very sorry. We separated last year. The boys were caught up in the HIV virus too, and I have been in a turmoil. He did not tell us he was travelling to Britain, until, your petition revealed the circumstances and I signed. Please don't let him exploit your child like that. I stand as a witness and a grieving mother;" she revealed.

In solidarity and goodwill, she sent Alfred three African print shirts which were truly appreciated.

***

I couldn't believe this was happening! It was early 2017, just when we had finally started to heal from the horrific ordeals and established our own ways of restoration, this man turned up in Britain, weak and wobbly with HIV/AIDS, to reopen our wounds and knock us right back down. His plan was to prolong his life, in Britain, using Alfred's citizenship, on the National Health Service, using Alfred's passport. The insignificant child had NOW become significant.

He returned in a whole new world where he saw a strong woman in real life for the first time. Strong, despite the abuse he inflicted upon us. How dare we move on and prosper without him! It made his blood boil. He hoped to find us in ruins, permanently tormented and wanted to pick up right where he left off. I moved through the wounds and he no longer had control over anything in my life. He couldn't cope with the change and didn't know how to react.

Beware you all, there is always someone who hopes that you remain stranded and that you give up on life. I was not only emotionally stronger and mature; I was ready to grind him under my stilettos. He discovered a woman empowered, unshackled, the wild he would never tame… and, my god, I don't regret what I have become.

Abusers do not own the strength of those who survive them.

It was staggering how he was never regretful or remorseful for the immense pain he had put us through. The mere fact that he blatantly continued to say I was not the first woman to be beaten by a man, nor will I be the last, was alarming. "You made a big deal out of nothing just to get sympathy from the white people, now you got it through my child; I want the passports." How barbaric and backward, for a man who wanted to now fit in a civilised Western society! It was strategic and ugly that the only reason he had made contact upon arrival was to demand our British passports for citizenship and sustenance with the best medication on the National Health Service.

The way the NHS design and deliver care is phenomenal, with human decency and dignity at the core. I have so much love for its perspective. Ignorantly and arrogantly, others call it 'useless and unsafe'. The uneducated hubris is astounding. To some of us, it is the spine… the vine. The NHS rewrote our life to say the least.

In other [rich] countries, due to the high price of insulin, certain people come close to death, go a few days without it, whilst they save up, take loans out, go severely in debt because their health has a seamless correlation with class, economics and access. Some even die because they cannot afford to buy it.

The erased child was now his cornerstone. The insignificant child had now become significant. The 'ugly and disabled' son that he rejected with every fibre of his being, was now needed because… for his struggles… because he was now riddled with HIV/AIDS and yearned for a route to use the NHS. He had conveniently forgotten how he intended to withdraw medical access from Alfred at a crucial stage. Fifteen years prior, his intention to throw us to the wolves was there, but he just missed. Others showed us honour and saved us just in time. Fifteen years prior, he decided that his son meant nothing to him. That was bad enough but who would have predicted that he would come back, for is convenience, to decide what he meant to us?

Yes you! Remember when you had us, and we were not enough? Remember when you considered yourself a genius for accomplishing the total abandoning of your parental responsibilities, passing those on, along with the consequent huge, yet essential, struggle to raise Alfred? You missed out on raising a phenomenal, and loving genius... yes, the same word, there is only one genius in this family.

The tables had not only been turned, but ours had been set before him, with all the essentials on it. We defied the odds and were moving through to thriving. This time, he was crawling, and we were flying.

It was blatantly obvious that he was not here to bind up the fractures and heal the deep wounds he had inflicted, and we didn't need him to. All he did was brought us health and social detriments... more pain, reminding me of the hurt he had laid upon us in previous years. Always loitering near my house, his presence created a sense of threat.

After writing us off, he was here to exploit us, and I was not bowing down to his invasion and bullying. He had not walked a mile in the upbringing and the challenges of raising a special child. After sixteen years of single parenting with zero physical, mental, emotional and financial support from him, he knew absolutely nothing about his own child and reuniting with him was not on the agenda. The gods must be crazy, I thought, to even allow his return, let alone to justify his expectation to lean on the child he had abandoned.

Clearly on a temporary visa which was running out, he was desperate round the clock. His demands for the passports turned to a raft of threats, that he would cut and dismember me. His insanely immoral relatives; the aids and comforters of the enemy, were all screaming that I wouldn't be in England if it weren't for him and perpetuating their ruthless idea that I was expected to cater to his needs, despite throwing us over a cliff.

This nightmare was happening just a month after the passing away of Sir. Having leapt to our defence and paving way for us to stand and be free, he would have protected us with dragon fire. Had he gone too soon? (Of course.) What would he have said of this man's return? (Presumably words that cannot be printed here, but even for such a gentleman as Sir; would have been perfectly appropriate.) The tumour we thought had gone had come back.

When you break free from your abusers, a level of fire and fury arises automatically. Still lamenting over his death, I had a powerful idea. He fought his good fight for us, and I had to continue in that strength.

Who fell off a cliff now?

Chapter 5
Eighteen on 8 March 2018

Everybody at school and the neighbourhood knew how Alfred wanted so much to turn eighteen. He had his own vision of what eighteen looks like. It was crazy. I was celebrating on so many levels... embracing how a beautiful part of me emerged because of him. So proud of what he had become, I was remembering the journey we embarked, how it brought us here, to this time and place, also the struggles, turmoil and the many blessings. As a mother, my favourite moment is when I am defined by the boy whom I raised into an awesome man he is now.

"How many more days, Mum?" To make my life easier, I made an advent calendar for him to count down to 8 March 2018. He was astonished when I turned up at his school with three huge cakes enough for the whole school to partake his moment. That was all he wanted: to share with his people. Meanwhile, his father had other plans as he was racing against time. He became increasingly desperate as his visiting visa was running out and he saw an opportunity since he thought Alfred turning into an adult meant that I no longer had a say. Waiting at the school gates to have access to his impressionable mind, he took some desperate measures of preying on his vulnerability, with a new phone, to bribe him into surrendering his passport with a promise of Heaven on Earth. Alfred did not return home and missed out on everything that I had planned after school including the surprises the neighbours had for him. His father 'kidnapped' him for hours and promised him the world. "Give me your passport for a cruise. Look at your cheap phone. I have a better one for you; your mother hates you. No wonder she never got you a better phone; look at what I have for you."

Such unfaithfulness and cowardice.

Distraught, my rage meter was broken. I felt so physically sick of what might happen to him and couldn't make sense of the chaos that was erupting on this day. A man had never walked a mile, no... make that a metre, in raising this child, so he knew nothing about him, nor did he care that he was putting at risk the substantial progress that Great Britain had installed in this boy for many years. Driven by self-seeking guile, he was ready to bribe him into stealing the passport to apply for citizenship. This man now wishing to portray himself as the perfect father was ignorant of Alfred's struggles, pains and obviously the law. Although Alfred was legally an adult on this day, he was a vulnerable adult who does not have the mental capacity to make certain (specific) decisions and is at risk of harm and abuse, be it physical, emotional and/or financial abuse. He abused him before; that was then. I made it clear that I was not going to bow down to his demands nor allow him to mess up the path I had now straightened. Where my son has no ability, I am his ability and will always support him at his weakest.

It was getting late and a search to find him intensified, it was an exasperating day. When I finally got through to his phone, his father answered. Trembling, I fell apart with worry because I knew there was no limit to his ugly and vindictive bigotry; to see to it that I suffer. He previously warned me that he would deal with me within forty days. His voice choked me to a point I could barely speak. In a haughty, snide tone, he said, "Alfred is now a man. He will come back whatever time he wants; he says he loves me and doesn't want me to go back to Malawi, it's his right to give him his passport." He switched off his phone before I responded. He made it abundantly clear what he wanted. We had not just become strangers again. He was irrelevant to me.

How could this insignificant man, who was absent for almost the entirety of his son's life, contributing absolutely nothing, not a damn thing... had nothing to prove he even knew his own son... want to make use of his citizenship? So calculative and sinister, on this day he was somewhere taking countless pictures for the sole purpose of proving to the Home Office that they had a relationship... so he must remain in Britain on family ties. His desperate attempt to take the "rosy pictures of fatherhood" was beyond pathetic. We had not a single tie with him so why should he be afforded this gleam of hope to get through his visa?

After having his way taking the photographs, he spat Alfred out... horrendously dumped him on the bus stop to Gracious. A Good Samaritan, Phil recognised him, and together they got on the last bus just after midnight and walked him home, to ensure he was safe. This made me weep, both with happiness and rage on numerous levels.

It was devastating that he had effectively created unrest, halted my big plans on a big day and was desperate to make things so painful and difficult for us once again; as if the storms he put us through sixteen years before were not enough, now he wanted to wreak havoc upon all the progress Alfred had made.

It was a desperately sad situation and an extremely distressing time for everyone involved with Alfred. The school worked tirelessly beyond belief and urgently made a referral to the adult social care to raise a safeguarding concern to protect him from the psychological and emotional abuse. Everything had now taken its toll on him. He seemed emotionally disconnected from the world. He had changed and appeared confused, but he received great support.

Chapter 6
Meet Alfred

Dear Alfred, my inspiring and brave son
I am proud of many things in my life, nothing beats being your mum. Tragically, your father saw an incomplete person... he abandoned and failed you in every way, my heart weeps. You were truly unique and undeserving of his love; I tremble when I recall how he tortured you, my beautiful boy. I couldn't do more to make him love you and I am sorry for the pain. I was hurting too! We walked alone in a journey that seemed long and bleak, at least we had each other. The odds were stacked against us... Nonetheless, in the face of rejection and sufferings, we built ourselves off what was left of us. Together we went through that ring of fire and came out the other side. It burned like hell but still we powered through the grim times. You are absolutely, exactly enough, just as you are, I promise. You are destined for great things so shine on, your future in Great Britain is crystal clear and bright; not even his rejection will stain it.

A pillar of the struggles and a motivation of life, you have always been a special boy and raising you was a pathway deeper into myself, because your influence in my life gives me strength to go on and be a better person. Whilst trying to survive in a foreign land, my primary passion was to love and protect you, and I did what had to be done. I always knew that the test ahead would not be easy, and it couldn't be done half-heartedly; so, I had to endure all the hardships. Nothing could have prepared me for the whirlwind and fiery darts, but proudly and with good reason I had to be relentlessly strong and courageous.

Every moment of every day, I was rooted and grounded in faith and steadfast hope, hence my feet never slipped. In my desperate desire to give you a hope and a future, we had to survive, somehow... and yes, sometimes I put myself in harm's way to make our living. It was a tunnel of obstacles and mountains to climb, but for you and with you, I remained strong and courageous. With inward pain, sometimes I became dismayed, sometimes I hesitated, but through it all, you never stopped shaping me. Through it all, you built your character and I built mine and we mastered how to be strong alone. Even though the darkest hours seemed endless, and my strength almost ran out, I always kept the faith and discovered the things that really matter. In the darkest moments, your love was still shining through. Your little voice in my heart kept me going on and on. Other times, when I was in terrifying predicaments, I tried to mask it, but you clearly saw the sorrow behind my smile. When I was silent, you heard my words. That love was the purest bittersweet moments in my life. My head was under so much water, there were times you watched me dissolve in a puddle of tears but still I never retreated. I rose above it. I kept fighting, for us.

In our chain of constant struggles, you have touched many hearts along the way, especially mine. Today, stand tall because I give you the curtsy, a deep, ever so respectful and, above all, loving curtsy. Thank you for keeping me humble.

Continue to take the highway and maintain your character. Be kinder, more courageous and continue to see the world with hopeful eyes. This book is a vital reflection of our life of many sorrows, afflictions and much gratitude, yet also, it is an exhibition of the full circle of life. I wrote, because no one will remember our memories and silent voice. I wrote because our story will be used as a reminder of how unique this life experience is.

The hurdles we had to leap were higher and harder to cross. Still we are more than conquerors. Stay humble. Stay loyal. The tide has changed. The hardest part is behind us.

Thank you, Alfred, not just for simply being you. Not just my wonderful son, but my special gift. My hero. I hope for you a future full of people who treat you as lovingly as you should be treated. Continue to believe in yourself as you move on to Manchester College, your road to more possibilities. Go for it! Go with power, run your race and achieve everything great that you are. Lean on your faith and have nothing to be ashamed of; more rather… be proud!

One day…

Love always, your biggest cheerleader!

Mum.

***

Phrases or terminology used to describe disabled people have altered over the years and differ in countries with others causing offence and segregation. 'Handicapped', 'people with different abilities', 'people of determination' have emerged recently, although the able-bodied are bound to make waves about it and argue that they have 'determination' too.

Whatever the preferred term, others say the phrase 'disability' is wrong, but however it is renamed and reframed, in my own experience of caring for Alfred, the anguish of watching him struggle with everyday things is distressing... or rather it could be... but I won't let that happen... for either of us. It is precisely because of these times, these shared experiences, that our hearts are strong... and as one. He wants to be a productive member of society as anyone else. He is extraordinarily determined, but he is disabled. His downright stubbornness and determination are because there is a gene in him that always defies the odds. His limitations frustrate him when he desires to get a task done. In anger when he clearly knows what he wants, and I don't understand his intentions, he bangs his head, punches the wall and that pain is so painful for any mother to watch. I refuse to call autism a gift, but a barrier my son must overcome.

Autism is a highly variable neurodevelopmental disorder which affects the way Alfred communicates, interacts and processes information. It is highly inheritable, but the cause includes both environmental factors and genetic susceptibility. With Alfred, his symptoms became established by the age of three with impaired social interaction, verbal and non-verbal communication, restricted and repetitive behaviour.

Despite limited speech, it does not limit the richness and diversity of ways of understanding and interacting with him. He is seen and heard because many have wonderfully developed their own ways and 'language' to communicate with him because he mixes sign language and a little verbal. It takes kindness and patience to try to understand him and he has a lot of that around this marvellous community.

Alfred never wants to share his world with me, but in those rare moments that he reluctantly allows me access to his territory and therapeutic programmes, I see awe and wonder and all the details I would otherwise have missed. When recognised and valued, autistic people are tremendous, hardworking and loyal assets to a society. As others say autism can be a gift, it's a life-changing diagnosis and a tough one at that, with every spectrum being completely different.

Indeed, it can make one passionate and committed to the detail of one subject for a long time without the anxiety that can come along with that.

I have never treated him differently or allowed anyone else to treat him differently because of his disability. I empowered him and let him to grow. I have seen the amazing things he can do, and he is the most loving, giving and compassionate soul I have ever met, and I believe this is due to his autism.

He's made the most of his unique traits because the community has been flexible towards behaviour and social needs. Many have not frowned at his harmless yet unavoidable autistic behaviours. Surely, he has had to confront barriers but through his enthusiasm and creativity, with better understanding and support from society, he shines.

Back in Malawi… mutilated, sliced with a blunt razor blade underneath his tongue, Alfred was subjected to a barbaric traditional ritual known as *litata*. It is carried out without anaesthetic, to "cure" a delayed speech and supposedly remove the demon causing developmental delay. It was a dark moment, he fainted for a moment, with unimaginable pain. I dread to think how many more painful rituals they would have forcefully inflicted upon him.

A freethinker with an enquiring mind, an adventurer and discoverer… but with the worst problem-solving skills, when he sees me paying for anything, whatsoever, he says to the seller, "Keep change," and I must always request my change back. He does not have maths and money skills, but everyone can keep the change anyway because that sounds cool.

Many people find him amazing, intriguing and intelligent in a unique package… and they are right.

The 'how' is unthinkable, the 'why' is terrifying, but there is always the arrogant and rotten apple in the community who will mock and ridicule him for being disabled; yes, they made it extremely difficult by bullying him relentlessly including telling him he is a loser due to his struggles and a condition he has no control over. "I hope that Alfred be the last person you have misjudged and abused verbally or physically. I wish he could have been spared that. You did not witness my tears, but you saw how sad he was after being bullied. Please stop bullying today."

One winter day, a bully called Donald had threatened to stab Alfred and the police turned a blind eye to it, because according to them I was wasting their time and resources. So, the brave and special community stood by us, reassured us and were in solidarity with us whilst others warned the perpetrator via social media that they had their eyes on him. If there is a fire, it doesn't matter who sounds the alarm. People went knocking on his door and told him that he lacks a spine, integrity and compassion. They demanded to know why he wanted to prove his 'strength' on a disabled boy who could not defend himself. There is always the rotten apple who thinks disabled people must be isolated, harassed and bullied. But there is strength in numbers when many oppose bullying and take care of each other. Love reigns and that is the spirit of Gracious. Without love, humanity can never survive. Strong warriors, their biggest weapon is unity, and no one got away with hurting Alfie or even intimidating him.

Watching your child injure themselves by head banging, eye poking and skin picking is heart-breaking and the family distress I was going through only multiplied the pain. Watching your child try so hard but get increasingly frustrated when he is not able to verbally squeeze out his thoughts is worse still.

After many years of trials, eventually accepting that your child will never be able to ride a bicycle because of his difficulties is more than upsetting. It's only a bicycle, nevertheless a constant reminder of what holds him back.

Since his childhood, Alfred has always had car keys with him. Now nineteen, this remains an essential, treasured belonging which was bought from the damaged cars scrapyard, they are his "livelihood". At an early age, the school was concerned for the health and safety of other kids, but a risk assessment gave him the benefit of the doubt. He functioned with joy when he had them with him. One day, my friend's new partner attempted to rob them from the chair when Alfred went to the kitchen to make them a drink. As he put them in the pocket, Lulu shouted to him, "Don't you dare! Those keys are his world. Put them back." Now they are almost surgically attached.

When he was in primary school, with our household living on less than £30 a week, a teacher once mentioned how Alfred would only have a bite of his sandwich because he shares a little bite with all the classmates. I decided to make enough sandwiches for the whole class every day and that joy seemed to complete his life. When the bell rang for break time, all the children, regardless of what they had brought from home, looked forward to Alfred's distribution. It was only bread, butter and jam but it was from a poverty-stricken home. I didn't feel much poorer for it. Sacrifice enriches our life. After a year, it was time to move class, but the next teacher did not welcome the idea. That was a big blow for both of us. A routine that had become so natural was prematurely cut off.

With an incurable curiosity, he is resistant to change and hates to be interrupted. Routine is his cornerstone. His compulsive behaviours include arranging objects in stacks or sometimes lines, displaying many forms of repetitive and restricted behaviour, meaning patience was a virtue I needed. His ritualistic behaviour of unchanging menus (corned beef and mashed potatoes), dressing rituals and unvarying patterns of daily activities were all little tests of that patience. I learned that a little understanding goes a long way, and I went to all the training sessions that were offered via the school, the best one being the 'parent survival course'. Unfamiliar cultures raise children differently and it was important to know the legal framework of the rights and responsibilities of a parent and to share ideas about our children and how to cope.

Teenage life and the social difficulties he experienced have been the hardest part for me, because he was having a tug of war with himself: fighting with the hormones, trying to fit in and to be the cool one.

Although he has been through a lot of challenges already – branded an 'infidel of misfortune' by his father – overall, the people of Gracious have been supportive beyond belief. To those who have felt my pain and assuaged that pain, and they are many, who have loved and protected and him from harm, I can never thank you enough for restoring my faith in humanity. Whatever has been missing, stolen and broken by his father, there has been a great restoration from you all, which gave me joy and strength as though you all understood how broken he was. His friends' fathers got used to being called 'Dad' by him. Everyone's nana was his nana. I couldn't keep up. They understood that he had a very inherent belief that we are all created from the same energy and are thus related. "Michael Jackson says it doesn't matter if you're black or white," was his justification.

A disability may define you, but it will not confine you if you are surrounded with wondrous love. It takes a whole village to raise a child. It does not matter which village. Indeed, it has taken Gracious as a community to raise Alfred. Although rejected by his own father, I take great comfort in how much he is loved by the community. He is the living evidence that love, not blood, is thicker than water. Your own flesh and blood can walk away, turn their back on you, forsake you, but love is the spirit he has found. It is a privilege to live in this community, amongst such people… and this story should be an inspiration to all. Families are found where you build them; therefore, build wisely.

Making and maintaining friendships often proves to be difficult for those with autism, but with Alfred, he is continuously looking for different ways to express his love for people. This makes him an absolute legend in the community because he brings people together due to his original, gentle and funny principles which have been a source of wonderful humour to many. People celebrate his kind, sweet and funny ways. To the kids, he is funny and entertaining; to the old and very old, he never fails to have them in stitches. Like an outreach worker, he finds a need and meets that need with love, compassion and kindness.

Always cheeky yet an absolute gent with a unique sense of humour, Alfred's video games collect dust because he would much rather sit on the doorstep with the neighbour who once told him they have cancer, just so he can ask them how they are doing and to catch up on the latest gossip. One lady, Janet, said to me that she pulled through her chemotherapy because Alfred always knocked on her door with a big grin and made a huge difference. He steps into each day like he belongs, because he knows that there is room for him. The way he supports people at tough times and brings pleasure to their lives never ceases to amaze me. The choice he makes at school to assist the tube-fed kids at break time instead of playing out with the rest says how passionate he is about his artistry. It's quite remarkable… and for the writer of these words…

The world can be a beautiful place if we want it to be. I am proud and with good reason, to say it has been an absolute honour to share Alfred's light with so many. If only we could inject the world with even one drop of his amazingness! We have a lot to learn from him. I was officially raising the kindest human.

So, folks I ask, is this a disability? I never question his unique abilities.

Chapter 7
Mum Loves You

I am his mum yet there are times when we needed to understand each other, but I struggled to. Others always stepped in with kindness and compassion, to make our life easier. Just because we are mother, and son doesn't mean we have always 'liked' each other. We had some parallel thoughts, but those meltdowns didn't mean I loved him any less. I cherish him with my entire being.

His silence is always a symbol that he is either brewing something strange or special, I never can tell. Damn right he keeps me on my toes. When I am planning one thing, he is seriously planning how to contradict it, but two can play at that game.

Parenting a child with autism forever challenges your mental astuteness; I could not afford to lose my thinking cap. The last time I light-heartedly said, "get lost", he literally took me at my word and did just that. He went missing and was found on a train to *eBay*. There were times when I had just one nerve left, and he still got on it; I would cry and laugh at the same time. When I would say push, he would pull. When I said pull, he pushed, just to wind me up that little bit extra as if that was what he was programmed to do. But deep down, everyone can agree that he is loving, caring and the essence of love. Totally interesting and sometimes mysterious, I will never judge a mind that I cannot myself envision. Christmas carols are on his playlist all year long… "Do they know it's Christmas time at all?"

Despite massive challenges in his restrictive world, he never allowed his disability to dictate his life. His hypersensitivity means although he enjoys wearing street staples and hoodies, they must all be a specific feel and fabric.

However, sadly, his autism has always meant that I, his mother, am never really granted that glimpse into his world. A hug was never within my grasp. Usually, I must force myself into his being, if I must. He does hugs with others, except Mum. Since childhood, he has always given a Mother's Day card which they made at school, to the childless woman across the road, who had several miscarriages. Above all, to Alfred, whom I hope one day will be proud of me, I thank him for the teamwork (never) and the tantrums that constantly tested my patience and courage.

Despite his 'I-can-do-it-myself' stubbornness, constant risk assessments must be done, routines and *rules* must be upheld for our sanity because change can be a real crisis with autism. Part of Alfred's condition is thinking aloud, so I have been delighted to hear some utterly beautiful thoughts of me, which he fails to express otherwise, but also, I had to hear some hard truths, and some of his rebellious plans, of which I had to shout, "Alfred, don't you dare!"

He loves Lord Sugar who hires and fires on his 'Apprentice' TV show and hope is: 'Lord Sugar, you come to my school, tell all the teachers they are fired, then we can all do what we want but don't fire the dinner ladies.'

Trauma does not always bridge; sometimes it attempts to drive people further apart. Sticking together does not mean being glued together so we set each other free because we had an idea of what works and what doesn't. We allowed each other to make mistakes and I allowed him to take risks and possibly fail. That was the route to reflection and growth. We are all learners. Seeking help is not weakness but strength. Hurting is not being damaged, just human. I grew, gained and learned through pain and loss. I may never find an answer nor piece together the jigsaw, but I have never shied away from speaking about it to school and health professionals to help me try to process consequences. Although severely disabled, I gave him some freedom whilst allowing him to make mistakes.

The schools have always been aware of the terribly difficult situation and have always been tremendously supportive, because I have never shied away from making them understand the situation and context. Even though he is wholeheartedly great in school and the loveliest of creatures they have known, they have never reduced my struggle to 'just one of those things'. Everyone gets the best of Alfred. I must force myself into his life because he doesn't want to share his experiences. It can be funny yet also terrifyingly sad.

I take great comfort when his teachers and support workers and networks have always emphasised how immensely proud, he is of me. What the terror produced in him; he chooses to love me in silence because in silence there is no rejection. Having endured so much pain, this was his *classy* way to cope with the intense rejection felt. It makes me smile. Also, it makes me cry.

Since his childhood, I can't enjoy the TV programme he's enjoying. Upon seeing a smile on my face, he will either change the channel or switch it off. I am not allowed to like a song he likes: "Find your own song, Mum; this one is mine."

We can't share the seat. He points me to the spare seat. "Space over there, Mum." I have never held his hand to cross a busy road. He will brush it off. It's hilarious, sometimes painful. It gets frustrating when enough is enough, especially in public when I am trying to preserve his own safety.

Be a fly on the wall and catch a glimpse of how his mind works, to better understand the complexities. In the end, deeply moved, you will either shed the odd tear, laugh yourself to tears or just give me one big hug to make up for some alarming and extraordinary experiences. The sooner I realised that my life is changed, but it's still mine to live, instead of "why me!", the sooner I believed "why not me?".

It can be incredibly difficult to process and heal the hidden wounds of trauma. It can take months, years or even a lifetime. He may have been only a little child, but his gentle heart experienced the terror. Who is to decide on anyone's healing process and demand them to let the past die? Take as much time as it takes to restore the wound. He has been vulnerable since the day he was born, and it would be cruel of me to expect his mind to respond quickly and efficiently. I hate to live in the past, but this past lives with me.

Always striving for his father's love but never receiving; I have memories of a sweet, loving, little boy, crawling to his father… naturally because he loved and trusted him, but he pushed him away with disgust and slammed doors in his face. I have painful memories of a sweet, loving son who yearned to be Daddy's boy. He yearned to be embraced but he didn't qualify for his father's love. Being disabled hurts. Alfred didn't wait for love to be mutual. He loved first. He loved more. He held out his heart to his father and watched him turn his back on him.

Just when he needed extra love, attention and understanding, I watched my son be rejected and the pain I felt was immeasurable. My tear ducts stand no chance at this soul-crashing memory of a toddler tortured.

Betrayal leaves a terrifying taste and it is truly saddening that the confidence in a parent may take him forever, because some pain never leaves you. It doesn't have to be the latest trauma. Abandonment and abuse, in any form, is traumatising. Coming to terms with the tension between the deep world within him and the dark world out there was startling. Evil is real and his delicate mind was racing to defend himself from a parent. With these insecurities, Alfred learned how to love me with more caution. That was his safety mechanism. Tears down my cheeks, as I open my vein, I write. It is grand because herein, I find some closure and most importantly, I find the measure of my life.

No one deserves this kind of anguish. Although my goal was always to meet his unique needs in a way that honours who he is, he carries the significant and lifelong burden of a parent betraying his trust as his protector. He tries to decide who deserves him. In me, he found a vent for that hurt and rejection. Some wounds take longer to heal, and he unleashed his frustration on me. It saddened me. I may never know the various effects this trauma must cause, but the noble woman in me feels his grief and will always be sympathetic… by his side. Even I didn't make it through unscathed.

To reach some depth, go to the roots. Hear-me-out when I wish that his father never came back after fifteen years' absence – to break us again whilst we were slowly gaining ground and busy fixing ourselves.

How could I make my son believe that there was truly a safe space? As painful as it is, I will never stop convincing my son that he is enough, and I make sure that he feels loved and safe. Each day helps me progress my understanding of his protective shell. Each day sheds some light on his reactions and the ramifications of autism, abuse, rejection, and trauma.

Every action brings a reaction, the barbaric actions clearly took its toll on him and deprived me of hugs from my own child. A part of him separated itself from me and he was cold. My own child was scared to show me love and he then protected himself, attempted to make himself secure in a challenging way. Other than just smoothing over the differences or bury them into the depths of this darkness, through learning, I am growing and changing as a person. I am open to translating ideas, research and different possibilities into action. Learning is a process that continues throughout life, but it requires humility. Instead of clinging on to me that much more, he withdrew from me.

Everyone has a little story. Unique and full of dreams. Every family has their own needs, some are more complex because past experiences have led to battles of depression, anxiety and even shrink in fear.

It is safe to say the community has been his escape whilst my work has been an escape from the whirlwind of life. But what about us together? There was a gulf between us but most importantly, there was an essence of love which binds us.

It was a full-time job continually calculating tensions that might escalate his tantrums, sometimes in the horrifyingly funny ways. Give children some freedoms. Allow them to make mistakes and never judge a child on everything they do wrong. It destroys their self-esteem whilst ruining your relationship.

Chapter 8
Gracious City

Abandon the unnecessary and be moved by love and the unity in diversity. Others call it grime, the hopeless place, the ghetto… Look deep into the hearts; it's filled with so much warmth and love. When people have so little, they give more of themselves, including the most precious commodity, time. Unite or perish, we were each other's only hope. Be moved at how pain and adversity bring us together in want of hope. Life is a highway; let's merge. The biggest part of the solution is within us… our communities. I have always relied on the goodwill of a place called Gracious, where we have lived since arriving in Britain. Inclusivity goes a long way. Its residents…strong, vibrant, brave for themselves and for others because the least protected always have each other's backs.

Here, every brother has a keeper, and dealers can't afford snitches. It's a 'loyal job' and their motto is "don't deal if you aren't loyal". Their typical day is roll, roll, roll a joint, twist it at the end, light it up, take a puff, and pass it to a friend. For safety, it just needs to be legalised at this point.

Gracious is a community that doesn't sleep nor slumber, everyone seems so hyperactive and full of energy. Whoever puts those happy vibes in its water supply does some wonders. They say laughter is the best medicine. Deep laughter or deep pain, this is where everyone has some cracking stories up their sleeves. Humour and sharing, are their tools for survival. This is where you see the astonishingly generous gestures. There is always someone with a big heart, sharing their roast dinner or a hearty hot pot. Lives are enriched with perpetual kindness. Every day, those with cannabis genetics share a spliff, booze, and other horrific 'indulgences' … from the rising of the sun, to the going down (if the sun goes down at all!). Hilarious family feuds and juicy gossips, I have witnessed some Oscar-worthy theatrical performances… the stories are endless. This is where it all happens.

To most Mancunians, Gracious is just a place to pass through to and from work. Some aspiring residents may even feel embarrassed to live in this part of the city which is home to a mostly middle-class population. Many eyes have rolled at the mention of it due to its economic deprivation. Oh, the 'shit hole', the 'no-go-area' as though it's so grimy, and everyone is predisposed to committing crime. Statistically, there is some violence, but there is more to it than meets the eye. The desire to alleviate the sufferings of others is right here and many depend on the strangeness of kindness. Everyone is someone's advocate and source of hope.

Having done all that a mother could do, to stand and to create a possible world for the two of us, I stood my ground when his utterly pathetic father turned up fifteen years later.

After all the wrangling and surviving domestic violence, we tried to take the rejection with grace as we started our own chapter, but there is no shame in admitting that other than bringing us together, the terror that happened to us, radically changed him, but not in ways you would expect. This shattered us because we were equally broken. Besides the rejection, breaking our bond and creating a gulf was a double blow tragedy… the most painful damage.

It could have been a rough, lifelong struggle, but it was no use crying over spilt milk, so, a breakthrough happened naturally with no express terms. For survival, it was vital that we established our own resilience to navigate through these storms.

We didn't have to search for hope. It was there. The biggest surprise in this art and adaptation was letting go. Never underestimate the power of adaptation. He found his own path to solace in the community whilst my new path was waiting for my courage to arise, for me to shine. We didn't hide away from life. We found channels that brought us joy and embraced them. I was happy. Most importantly, Alfred was very happy.

The community was full of Alfie's Angels, Alfie's Army, Alfie's Advocates; he was the amazing superhero who would disturb the universe, just to test these defensive strategies.

Real people make real sacrifices, and that is the incredible way of survival here. In the end, when the helpless still find a way to help, love prevails. Having an army of people deeply and truly care for your child who is seemingly different to the world is beautiful and an instantaneous love and appreciation from me. When the police systematically disadvantage underrepresented postcodes, and protect the privileged ones, is it that they can't help but stereotype?

That preconceived idea is lazy and harmful. Please don't mark everyone as unruly. We are not all dysfunctional families who need to be treated like a disease, yet we have suffered the most terrible injustices. The perpetrators got off scot-free and remained employed.

You would be hard-pressed to find anyone who dislikes Alfie and I don't think it possible to appreciate the community even more. Always keep an open mind and you will truly explore what others bring to the table. Their living is in their giving. They are born for the sake of others. Whilst you are out there having road rages, they are merely there to love and serve mankind. They exert effort in actively trying to realise the needs of others in the society around them. In a world awash with pain and tears, love still happens all the time… we are just too preoccupied to see it.

Whilst I shared his uniqueness with those who cared, they didn't have to tread carefully. They just included him. Kingsley took him to the gym. DJ Forbes got him mixing the music and took him to his events because music is his passion. Sue, the hoarder, took him to the car boot sales every Sunday. Alan named his parrot Alfie. Except that it swore a lot, some words which would never find their way out of Alfred's mouth but still it's lovely. People saw him for the lovely little boy that he was. Was this path laid out beforehand; to make the crooked place straight and dry out my tears? Inclusion is powerful and this is the story I was meant to tell.

Despite it all, Alfred and I have been extremely fortunate to be surrounded by much love, we were no longer foreigners. It is a place where Alfred has grown, developed, become an adult and felt safe. Many in the neighbourhood have advocated for him and cared so much about him to ensure he is not stigmatised or left behind. He gets the love and attention that was withheld from him by the man who should have loved him most. People engage with neighbours. It's a multicultural place and they have a sense of community. What others call a 'dilution' of Englishness is, in fact, a diversification of Englishness here, hence why assimilation has seen greater success than other parts. If like me and Alfred you are that immigrant who participates, appreciates and values the sphere of British culture and traditions, rather than convert it – you will thrive and flourish. We didn't adapt to the unique environment. We integrated into the awesome community.

Admittedly, there is a burning social injustice. Many have been stuck in a cycle of poverty because they have been reliant on handouts from generation to generation, hence feeling hopeless and helpless. Credit scores are in shambles and there is extra security in the superstores, to help protect their meat and potatoes from dodgy shoplifters, but there is a wealth of love around here… alas! The lack of money is the root of much 'evil'. There's no doubt this neighbourhood is very much in transition and there are still lots to do. Walking the streets recently, there's now a new momentum with fresh arrivals, new houses and apartments. The public transport is brilliant. Buses work well due to being frequent, cheap and efficient. New public buildings are preparing to open; construction sites are crawling with yellow-vested workers and dumper trucks; there's a buzz about the place which seems at odds with economic hardships because the positive, tolerant spirits make a strong and vibrant community. No sooner has something been knocked down than there's a new structure in its place. On the main roads, supermarkets and gyms have sprung up. You're more likely to meet your neighbour or an old friend in the car park of one of the major supermarkets. It is being revamped in many ways and becoming an attractive proposition to newcomers moving in.

Gracious market has been incredible. The greatest gift you can give a child with autism is acceptance. Friends and family isolated and chastised us but this community did not. They never looked at him as a strange creature and judged his capacity by his looks, as some do. They saw how keen, always determined and even desperate he was to contribute to society and reveal his gift. He started off with just going there to help them close the shutters, because that was his fascination. With that huge courage and character, a few stalls on the market made some adjustments for him and helped him to volunteer a few times a week after school and at the weekend. He worked so hard, as they celebrated his differences and helped him find his niche and let him flourish. They focused on his ability and not disability, with love and understanding. His passion and drive to work are incredibly evident. I feel so lucky to live in a community where they embrace diversity, a community that never failed him but gave him a chance to shine. From all ages and races, there is no street you will walk with him and not hear someone shout, "Hi Alfie!"

Moving even the coldest of hearts, Alfie has an infectious personality and strong sense of humour… He is everybody's neighbour, always entertaining, questioning things and always on his way to save someone… and he takes his curiosity very seriously.

Don't Litter; Keep Britain Tidy. He is all business all the time, dislikes fly-tippers and always thrives to leave the environment better than he found it. Every bin man knows him because he wants to help. Of course, they have tried to stop him for many years; he doesn't understand why. He has the obsession of checking every window screen to ensure each car had a tax disk. Eventually, there was no requirement to display the disks. It infuriated him, he felt redundant and it drove me insane! His idea of himself... in his world... is the reality. The best part is that he doesn't even try to be funny; he's just living life.

You can only connect with him through love. Nothing else can reach him. One stall owner gave him a Manchester United shirt. Others from the vegetable stall gave him a Manchester City shirt. Up until today, he wears one on top of the other and I realise he may never decide which one goes. It's CITY-UNITED for him. Demanding him to make up his mind was fiddling with his mind, so everyone appreciates that he is a supporter of both.

This was the most amazing ratio I have ever seen. As though they knew that they were binding up the wounds! That son, who was rejected and detested so much by his own father, was embraced so much by the community. It was a glorious restoration.

Even with a chromosome missing, a chromosome broken, LOVE doesn't count chromosomes here. He is complete, with nothing missing, nothing broken. We love him as he is. What an embrace to experience!

I did not give my son up to the community. Interestingly and lovingly, they gave themselves up for him. Many sacrificed their time and resources they hardly have. It has been very difficult, but he is a gift to and an asset to the community. There was Anna-Maria, an English lady a few streets away, with a beautifully tender heart. She lost her only son many years ago and spiralled into depression, her own presence suffocated her, and she sometimes had suicidal thoughts. When she met Alfred, she found a son and in no time, he had his own room in her house. With the sweetest of temperaments, she took time to teach him and appreciated that he needs extra patience and understanding, to help him shine. We always encouraged courtesy, manners and responsibility. But still, he thrived on pranks. That urge to do something inadvisable every now and again. If he is smiling, it's because he is planning something so gloriously evil. If you see him giggling, damn right, it's because he has already done it!

The school and the local authority were aware of her in his life because she turned up at many events and there was no stopping her. Her responsibility was prematurely cut off from her when she lost her son. She was bursting with love and aching to care for a child, timing is art. Everything she would have loved to do for her son, she did with Alfred. There was no stopping her! Seeing and watching them, with a tear in my eye of many emotions, usually, my heart melted but there were times when I got envious, because my son cherished her wholeheartedly, preferred to stay at hers many times, to catch up on their beloved series. Then I remembered the amazing ratio: He was rejected much. He is loved much. Even I loved him enough to share his love and uniqueness with those who had his best interests at heart. From caravan breaks to car boot sales, they were just inseparable.

To the local Tesco, who offered him a great start, his first work experience via Melland High School, you gave him an opportunity in a welcoming culture and environment. Thank you for taking on a young man with learning difficulties and for giving him the support he deserves. You saw a different ability, not a disability. You saw a boy hungry to learn new skills, with an incentive to work and prosper. At the end of the work experience, you acknowledged his awesome work with a £20 voucher, which he presumed was everlasting. He threw a major temper tantrum when he learned that he had used it all on the sandwiches. That was bad news! Nonetheless, he learned the fruit of labour and just wanted another job!

Today, I shop in Tesco with pride and I urge the community far and wide to join me in praise for a remarkable workforce that gives opportunity to all; by involving and integrating unique abilities. Any firm that erases the stigma of disablement and reveres grit and determination is to be magnified.

He then went on work experience, under close supervision, on Seddon Homes building site next to his school. Their awareness and understanding are truly outstanding.

My heart goes out to those who do not get their diagnosis until adulthood, because it has an impact on their adult life too. Alfred has been very lucky to have had his diagnosis since childhood, so his educational background has been ideal for his condition, although many a time I have clumsily scrambled through to learn the hard way, that which works and that which doesn't, continually calculating on how to avoid tensions that might escalate his tantrums.

Although some support has been slashed due to the government cuts to public services, now eighteen, he is still receiving the essential support due to the considerate people around him. The glass is always half full. As a mother of a disabled person, I have learnt so much. I have laughed. I have cried. I have been overwhelmed by how people with nothing or very little have offered massive help. I have made friends for life that I would never have made if it wasn't for Alfred.

To all those who have stepped in emotionally, physically and financially, to help our mentally and physically challenged children, you make a difference to the lives of others by donating to noble causes, especially the trusted organisations that give wings that the disabled people need in order to soar high and have quality of life. Love and peace to the donors, employees, volunteers and all their precious recipients. Thank you for understanding what we go through and feel. It is a lot of stress to worry about a child with special needs, and what the future has in store for them or what will happen when we are gone. All the wonderful programmes that have helped to teach Alfred skills that promote independence and allow him time away from home, to feel some freedom in a safe setting, have given me the hope that every parent need. You are a great help to those in need.

NHS
CAMBERWELL PARK SPECIALIST PRIMARY SCHOOL
MELLAND HIGH SCHOOL
CHILDREN'S SOCIAL SERVICES

The world's most incredible bridges are people. Everything you did showed that you cared. You are the terrific team I would love to give the world's biggest hug to. Because of you, it was never a lonely journey. You are all amazing and words don't do my gratitude justice. This superb team wrapped up the gift of life for Alfred, giving him the privilege to access education with specialist support in the classroom, although he has severe learning difficulties. From his initial stages, I had excellent support and *YouTube* was a useful tool wherefrom I learned sign language, because that was the best way he communicated and made himself understood. I care and I will care enough to learn everything needed to make his life easy. Nothing hurt more than watching my son harm himself with frustration because he could not properly convey his thoughts and feelings… He spoke a language I did not understand YET. Frustrated and angry too, my heart couldn't take the emotions and sadness. I ended up with tears and silent sobbing, feeling that I had failed miserably. Then together, we invented a new kindness and connected things in our strange little world; that was the highest intelligence… to understand what he was unable to say. It was an intimate revolution of a mother and son.

Apart from being isolated, I was chastised by many 'friends' for not forcing Alfred to speak, implying that I was celebrating an impairment. That lack of consideration angered me and sometimes brought me to tears. Love dedicates and adapts communication skills to make a difference. I was never too busy to give my son 'time'. It was not nailing that held me on to him; it was my love. An impairment cannot be celebrated but the fruits of love can be; patience and kindness embrace all odds, so I focused on what he could do, not what he couldn't. Other families don't realise how privileged they are, until they have a glimpse of how hard some families have it.

Behind every student's Individualised Education Plan lies an excellent team of teachers and assessors. They find that little gem in a child and give them positive reinforcement.

It has been an amazing journey shared with a team that continues to uphold the British tradition of 'Every Child Matters'. I am eternally grateful for the incredible support Alfred received from Camberwell Park Specialist Primary School, the foundation and anchor of his virtuous character, confidence and childhood. They celebrated Alfred's unique and uncommon ways, focused on the genius in him and never let his disability dictate his life.

Melland High School staff and its medical team stood by him through his transition through puberty and into adulthood. He was surrounded by a talented and passionate team who shaped him up. The love and support we received is unparalleled. You are appreciated and valued. It has been challenging and I thank each one of you for using your expertise and allowing Alfred the chance to grow and flourish into the man I am in awe and incredibly proud of today. There are times when I was visibly upset and cried due to his very challenging behaviour, but the continuous support from the amazing staff throughout the years no doubt made special needs parenting possible. They have been my rock under difficult circumstances. Words cannot be uttered. Consistently understanding, welcoming and kind, you did not opt for the effortless way out. True teachers are continuously challenged on their patience, compassion and kindness in exceptional, sometimes frustrating situations! You understand vulnerability and trauma and if it wasn't for your relentless dedication, to secure Alfred's wellbeing, I would have seriously broken down during my pain and suffering. Your concern and positive ethical conduct seeded in you add a lot to my appreciation of who you are and what you do for us every day. Nicola, Julie, Danny, Gill, Mr Barlow... EVERYONE at Melland, for your tireless efforts. By saving Alfred from destruction, you saved me. You took every step to make our experience an amazing one. Watching my son perform at the assemblies was consistently and unwaveringly the best part of my time on this earth. I grinned and cried at the same time. What a credit to their profession!

When his favourite teacher was expecting a child, he was on his best behaviour for a few months because he wanted the child to be named Alfred. "Teacher's child has to be a good boy, Mum; I'm being good." When the child was called Noah, he said, "Mum, the teacher says that baby cries too much. I'm glad it's not called Alfred."

Because of my journey shared with Camberwell Park Primary School and Melland High School, I appeal to all parents of any child in any school, please do not disrespect and look down on teachers. Whatever your status, career, or wealth, we can appreciate that teachers have a critical role and share so much with our children; from the energy to create, to staying inspired. When I count my blessings, those who helped to shape Alfred's life every step of the way, are paramount. With extra patience and tact, teachers do a tremendous job to ensure our children are safe. If not them, to put on the pedestal, then who is worthy of our honour and respect? Surely not the Kardashians!

There is a level of dedication that money cannot buy, and it comes through beyond the classrooms. I saw how endlessly frustrated the teachers became, seeing that their popular student, always dedicated and delightful with a beaming smile, now feeling alienated and frightened, his mother distressed. Our confidence was rooted in the trust of those who understand their vital role, and yet there was only so much they could do when the relevant agencies... the Adult Social Services, the Home Office, the Police were slow to the rescue. It was a paralysing situation because this man was aiming at destroying and making a mockery of everything that had been done for a child with complex health needs.

If we truly believe that the children are the front, the centre and the future, we can agree that teachers are the cornerstone to lay out an excellent quality of education. By design, parents, guardians and teachers are meant to complement each other to bring out the best in a child. Other than looking narrowly down at them, we can look up at them with trust and respect and acknowledge their labour and effort. Let us empower them and fuel their passion.

Some people have such a strong desire to do great good. Have you ever had an appointment that has gone so well, you cry? The health professionals have listened without judgement, discussed preventions because they care, spoken without prejudice, helped without entitlement, understood without pretension and loved you without conditions. Dr Ann Ferguson, Consultant Paediatrician, your thoroughness gave me a solid assurance that my child was in good hands. I celebrate your challenging work. I appreciate every second of your absolute best care, in our best interest and wish you all the best in your retirement as Alfred moves on to the next level. I want you to know that you have been an asset to the NHS. I end this with a curtsy, and I am certain that Alfred ends it with a bow.

I am eternally grateful for the dedicated National Health Service which does Britain proud, making every single day better, stronger and great. Nursing Alfred through many years of complex needs, their agenda is to make lives better, without leaving people in lifelong debt. No cutting corners at the expense of Alfred's health, they never turned their back on us. They treated access to healthcare as a human right. Despite being under enormous pressure, it is the best healthcare system in the world. The joint effort, care and perseverance that go into providing quality healthcare have made my boy the man that he is today. The continuing support they give him with their skill and expertise means life.

Replying to that email or returning that call simply made that day a much better one. Magic happens when you know that these people care, are aware and conscious of your health worries.

I owe a debt of thanks to all the skilled and unskilled (yet just as passionate) volunteers who made a difference in Alfred's life and went the extra mile to help secure his welfare and wellbeing. I celebrate your hard work, patience and perseverance. The support workers who gave him some hours of respite each week, treated us with kindness without expecting gratitude. I honour you all.

My heart goes out to the distraught family of the British tourist who died unnecessarily on a safari trip in Egypt, 2017, after his life support was turned off because his family could not pay a £7,000 medical bill. His care was ended because "the travel insurance was null and void". "It was not updated accordingly," said the man in the room. "You pay now, or I switch off the machines." And he did just that. A tragic case of a life cut short at the push of a button, because when the funding stopped, the medical treatment stopped.

02/04/12 at 10:05 AM
Dear Professor, JCS

Struggling to come to terms with my toddler's disabilities, striving to cope with economic hardships as well as the tremendous pressure of caring for a disabled child can be physically and emotionally draining. Dealing with pressures for deportations made it worse, yet you were there to help when I was asked to leave Britain with my severely disabled child. In my distress and exhausted confusion, I wanted to leave him behind, only because I love him beyond measure, and I could not bear the thought of him returning 'home' and facing hardship. His father left him because he hated him. I wanted to leave him because I loved him too much to take him back to the gutters. Britain is adequately furnished with every good thing necessary for a child with special needs to be able to live a normal ordinary life, although he is disabled. Which loving mother would want to take with her a child like mine from a country that ensures that all aspects of a child's needs are considered and met?

I wish to express my gratitude for taking time to write a report on Alfred's condition dated 21 March 2008, as requested by the Home Office, which they considered, in the best interests of a child. Once again, you will say you were just doing your job. Still I want you to know that your job has given my child hope for a better future, to continue to receive an education in a specialist support school which provides a safe, fun and happy learning environment, to increase his opportunities and reach his full potential and to continue to receive the much-needed medical help.

You are outstanding beyond measure!
Sandra

Monday, 9 February 2009, 9:14
Dear W Davis,

Driven by empathy and duty in all that they pursued, I can only express my gratitude for the dedication of your staff from the Disabled Children's Team, Leslie and Jenny, to be precise.

Because of Jenny's intervention, the tensions I had with Alfred every night taking him to his bed is now a thing of the past. The devastation of taking him in the house when he gets off the school bus has been resolved. A beloved educator who be sharing her talents and passion, helped me in managing these behaviours to overcome the stressful challenges I have had with Alfred for a long time. I realise even more, just how much I needed a nurse like her involved. Life is certainly better. Please pass on my appreciation and as she moves on to other families, may she keep up this excellent work!

Sandra

Chapter 9
Acquitted on All Counts

Lessening family distress is key to parenting a disabled child. However, when you are constantly under attack, mocked, ridiculed and locked out of the social circle and the vicious waves of family and friends sweep over you like an ocean, it's disheartening.

Amongst my fellow Africans, it was nothing about me – everything about them. Those who agreed that Alfred's disabilities were not entirely my fault, said they could help me get rid of him, to relieve myself and have a fun life. To even suggest such was terrifyingly wrong and harrowing, to say the least.

They embraced ever mean-spirited, false and dangerous assumptions about me. They are prone to feelings of intense jealousy including when one buys a new kitchen utensil. They drew a deep dividing line from me. I was relentlessly bullied, 'convicted' of being a witch and on the verge of being ripped apart, for giving birth to a child with disabilities. They insisted that god's wrath and severe discipline fell on me because of my disobedience. It was a primitive, institutional embodiment of hypocrisy, with everyone thinking of themselves holy and more superior than everyone else. Primitive dogma and superstitions are still deeply entrenched. They believed that Alfred was a painful consequence for not praying adequately, and god was out to punish me because of my sins.

Your promise to keep confidentiality does not end when the friendship ends. In fact, that is when your honour comes into play. But these tensions meant there was always someone being named and shamed, it was startlingly scandalous.

As I juggled to care for my son, on the other hand, I was an outcast, and Alfred was the only child who was excluded from their social circle. Each day, building a wall around us, they made it clear that we did not pass the purity test to fit in their midst. They cast stones at me and boasted that their children have no deformities, because they did something so right and I did something so wrong; I deserved what I got. They passed with flying colours and earned themselves an immaculately perfect child. I was made to feel like there was a historical, contextual interpretation of 'scripture condemns disability'.

Nothing more than sanctimonious folks, they get too high and mighty, and pretend that they have some secret key that is not available to the rest of us. With more insults than logic, they assume that atheists are immoral by default. What I saw and experienced speaks volumes of their morals and why I have a low opinion of religious bedbugs. I will not be kind about it: they were the source of my unimaginable pain. They send me thoughts and prayers whilst displaying a shocking lack of compassion. No wonder they are making the world less safe and poisoning everything.

How much sin does it take to be a sinner and by whose standards do they call themselves holy? I had stones cast at me whilst they claimed to be squeaky clean. Their very souls are malformed, in harmony with their theories. Hypocrisy is a real epidemic.

For what it's worth, if they want to hold true the doctrines and convictions outlined in the texts, perhaps they should stop the cherry-picking of scriptures, to suit their theories. They have decided that there is fury 'up there', and that eternal hellfire awaits everyone but them.

They looked for vulnerabilities to exploit me. They listened, not to understand… but to gain something from me and make me indebted to them. My emotions didn't matter, unless they benefited in some way.

At this rate, with irreconcilable differences, I had reached my tolerance level of hypocrisy and I no longer had the strength to put up and be there for callous people. Sometimes we must remove people in our life without warning and be at peace with our decision. We are getting too old to perpetually explain what they already know they are doing wrong. They are not only hectic but hazardous. This was my way into freedom. I was only a decision away from a different life, yet it took so long to realise that simply being who I am is service. It changed everything. I have never felt more liberated and satisfied. No one can truly hurt your feelings unless you allow them to. People will always have their thoughts and opinions but love yourself enough to not care.

As much as they pushed their philosophies down my throat, no longer was I folded, moulded and distorted to fit into their idealism. We live in a rational world and can exist without 'heavenly' rules and standards written down in a book or engraved on stone… and still be fair, diverse and loving, with good values and filled with respect. Religious folks will never understand this as they are too occupied with building a tower to reach Heaven. Look at the world today! When one believes that killing is a step closer to Heaven that is mental retardation. On the verge of being damaged by religious programs and its frustrated folks, when you survive the cults, conflicts and confusion, you have a newfound appreciation for life, and you safeguard your peace at all costs.

The world is full of judges, none of whom are qualified. Tangled in a web of greed and betrayal. Shackled with desperation and lies. Who said the church was the highest moral entity on the planet, and is it unreasonable to assume so? Whilst they prayed unceasingly for my downfall, I received support and great understanding from some truly phenomenal atheists who showed up and showed love. When I was drowning in pain, they held my hand and dried my tears. They choose love, compassion and inclusiveness over judgement and condemnation. We worked together to heal and grow and had some healthy debates too. In solidarity, they told me: "You are not alone."

Thoughts and prayers don't cut the watermelon. I needed help. My thoughtful neighbours showed concern and checked on us. I did likewise. "I am going to the shop. Do you need anything?" or "I am going for a walk; can Alfred keep me company while you have a little rest?" with a gracious smile on their faces. He would quickly put his shoes on, because he couldn't wait to go out. When they drop him off, he says thank you in sign language and asks if they can go again tomorrow. "Be good for your mum and I will see you tomorrow." The following day, that atheist fulfils that promise.

Meanwhile, the ruthless, religious weirdos are still harbouring hate and debating the definition of love until they are blue in the face. They are wearing a mask, and now the world has a glimpse of what's underneath that mask. They tell you how much you don't adhere to the ideal image of a good person. They knock on doors, standing on street corners, ready to run a background check, to decide whether to offer you things in Heaven that are forbidden on earth. Perpetually seeking to frighten people about hell and judgment. Pick one and be consistent! You don't get to be both a Christian and a judge. Give the gavel back to god.

She was a hard-core religious woman who followed the code to the core; she never cleaned or cooked on the Sabbath because it was a holy day reserved for prayers, yet she lacked love. On the morning of 11 September 2009, a four-year-old girl named Kath, walking together with her mother down Parkhouse Street in Openshaw,

Manchester, on her way to the doctor's surgery, was hit by Erica, a woman whom I called a friend. The little girl later died from her injuries in hospital, just over an hour after the accident. What a tragedy to befall the young little angel!

At the scene of the tragic accident, a learner driver named Erica – who originated from Nigeria – was driving unsupervised. She alleged that I was present in the car, supervising her driving, which I was not. As luck would have it, witnesses at the scene and CCTV evidence from a charity shop in Stockport proved exactly where I was at that time. She was later jailed for ten months after admitting to causing death by dangerous driving and was banned from driving for five years. She had a son who was the same age as Alfred, but she decided I was the one suitable for jail as though I had nothing to lose. In her eyes, I was the outcast who didn't deserve even a drop of freedom. In such a despicable tragedy, my name came to her mind as the scapegoat who would get her out of trouble. It was a very difficult time for me as the prosecution prepared their case and evidence.

Her mother escaped with injuries to her knee. I was present in court to see this case through. It was judged to be the second most serious category for an offence of this kind. The sentencing judge said of Erica, "Your remorse was slow in coming. You have sought to blame others and impugn their integrity." Her defending lawyer maintained that Erica was a 'committed Christian' who understood the enormous pain felt by Kath's family since her husband and daughter had been killed in Nigeria.

Alfred and I have often laid flowers at the scene for Kath. Continue to rest in peace, little angel.

I think I was expected to conform to their belief that my child was a curse and was not worthy of love, and it was an abomination to cherish him as I did. My effort, labour and performance in disciplining a disabled child determined how they treated me. I was always working on something to suit their environment of blame and it was always at the expense of my peace and joy. They were masters of stealing my joy. I found myself always wondering if I was good enough for them until one day, I did myself a favour and wondered instead about whether they were good enough for me and Alfred, with their bigoted mindset regarding disabilities and their twisted views? Clearly not.

Adversity is not all bad – you know who your friends are. Others helped me in difficult times, others left me in difficult times and others put me in difficult times. They were all crucial to my growth, the handful who stood by me at my rock-bottom time, the true ones, will always occupy a special place in my heart. Mary, you did not slam the door on us, when I knocked to seek refuge after my husband chased us away. Pamela and Roger, Lucy and Peter. It was not socially acceptable to admit to liking me, but you sacrificed and helped me in grim times. I live in hope that one day you will stand with me in celebration, as I honour your unfailing love.

It all stems from bigotry but there is certainly a stigma imposed upon both the disabled child and the mother, which followed me relentlessly. I was detested in the most harrowing way. Regardless of how hard I tried to fight the prejudice, the culture and belief system was permanently riddled with blame and abuse against me. Being around certain 'friends' would be the worst attribute of a mother. How could I justify that? I realised that the only way upward and forward was to disassociate myself from the world I once called 'my people, my roots'. What a sorry world! I was segregated by my own. The disease of a bigoted mind and the misfortunes of its world... Those who have your best interests at heart and enhance your purpose are your people, your tribe. They feel you and they hear you differently.

After pushing through so much judgement, it was expedient that I changed and switched lanes and withdrew myself from the toxic people and culture that no longer served us. There is a difference between giving up and knowing when you have had enough. I was sick of this vile game. I recreated my world with my son, around those who believed differently. Even when there is no common ground and no matters upon which we agree, we tend to stick to people for the sake of our roots, but in the long run, it may harm us to do so. Beware of roots; seek happiness. It was a new horizon for us, idyllic that people in the community took us by the hand and accepted me as I am and Alfred as he was, with our feebleness and fears. When you are not poor in thanks, to a country that has done so much, you integrate effortlessly. The Africans often called it being a 'choc-ice', when blacks socialised with whites: the English, the westernised. Unlike some I know, who have frequently alarmed me, I have never been that racist African mother who has warned my son: "Be careful of these people." Which people are 'these people'? The white people had given us a roof. My most unpopular opinion is this... "If these people are really that evil, we can pack and go back whence we came from – and get some peace." Often, we teach innocent children to be racist and give them no room for assimilation, robbing them of genuine friends and love.

Was it my fault? For a few years, the accusations and blame consumed me so much that they caused guilt and self-recrimination. I started to think I may have been at fault somewhere, somehow. Did my turbulent pregnancy harm my baby? Perhaps from a birth defect, because he was born under very difficult circumstances? Perhaps it was a result of early trauma? Did someone drop him without my knowledge, considering back in Malawi, a baby is in the care of a wide range of friends and family? I had so many unanswered and unasked questions. The paediatrician requested an MRI brain scan whose results came back normal.

After years of undergoing different tests, science finally proved that I was not to blame. It felt like an acquittal of a serious crime of which I was accused. A professor in medical genetics at the Manchester centre for genomic medicine, St Mary's Hospital, found the underlying cause. Alfred's blood tests revealed a rare chromosome abnormality known as '1p36 deletion syndrome'. It is a genetic condition that results from a small amount of genetic material that is missing from the tip of the short (p) arm of chromosome 1.

It was explained by science. Others wanted to explain it by religion; just to terrorise me and make me feel guilty for being human. "You were not praying often enough... look at us!"

1p36 deletion syndrome stands for the following: 1 is the chromosome number that has deleted DNA; p is the short arm of the chromosome (shortest length of DNA above the centromere) that contains designated area; 36 that is missing DNA. DNA missing from area 1p36 is responsible for the broad range of symptoms and the severity is likely related to which areas and how much DNA is missing in 1p36. It affects one in five thousand children.

Depending on the chromosome deletion sizes, signs and symptoms vary from one child to another, in general with moderate to severe learning disabilities. All patients demonstrate a developmental delay with poor or absent speech. Though it is not a progressive condition, Alfred is expected to learn new things as time goes on. There has been constant developmental progress in his behaviour disorder. Now aged eighteen, with profound mental retardation, his intellectual disabilities remain severe. His distinct craniofacial/skeletal features have remained, but as a mother, I have never questioned his existence and unlike some, I have never opted to give him up to be cared for by others.

He is not his diagnosis. He is my handsome boy, my only child and in him I am well pleased. Born in the rural area of Malawi,

Ekwendeni, my love for him was indescribable from the moment I set my eyes on him. When he was placed in my arms, it was joy unspeakable. It was Alfred. It was the beginning of a new journey. Two scans during pregnancy revealed I was carrying a girl, but it didn't change anything when they told me it was a boy. It just added more surprise to the bundle of joy. I realise that he has not manifested some of the conditions commonly observed in people with this rare chromosome abnormality such as epilepsy and cardiac anomalies. It could have been worse, but his recent cardiovascular scan showed no malformations and he will continue to be under observation for this as well as his kidneys and thyroid.

The chromosomal anomaly further explained his past developmental delay, flat-shaped head and low muscle tone. Because congenital heart defects and differences in the kidneys may be associated with this disorder, they will be checked regularly, and his thyroid function is checked every three to five years, as thyroid problems may occur with increased frequency. Be it a correlation or causation, I have personally linked his Obsessive-Compulsive Disorder (OCD) to this very rare genetic disorder. Early on, I didn't know what any of this meant for the future, but one thing that was certain was the importance of staying in the right place. That was everything. Words fail me when I try to express my gratitude for the help and support, I have received, aimed at reducing the severity of the symptoms of this chromosome disorder via consultations with experts in the medical, surgical and behavioural fields. If it wasn't for the National Health Service, where would we be?

The professor was awesome in explaining this diagnosis and we discussed how this chromosome deletion comes about. It was not my doing, even though I was beaten, mocked and suffered with blame. It was not my fault. Usually, it arises by chance in an affected child and neither parent carries the deletion. Just occasionally, one parent may carry a chromosome rearrangement, which predisposes to the deletion, and for this reason, I was offered to have my own chromosomes checked. However, I am not planning further children. Alfred is my first and last, so I decided not to have my chromosomes checked. The bulk of the research into the condition confirmed that most deletions are maternally derived, so I will just wear the cap if it fits.

They were kind enough to say they are happy to test any of my brothers and sister if they so wished, although the risks of them being linked are likely to be low. Should Alfred himself come to have children in the future, there would be a one in two chance that each of his children would inherit the same condition. This is distressing for every mum. There is no cure for 1p36 deletion syndrome but often there are treatments for the health and developmental issues that go along with it, so having support for this rare condition is a breakthrough.

The blame and unnecessary cruelty I were subjected to, from family and so-called 'friends', no doubt created some of the most painful moments I have had to endure in my life. But it is incredibly amazing how the community and the school have been so supportive throughout our journey and helped us overcome the obstacles.

Chapter 10
Social Services – Blameless

I have been known to Children's Social Services for many years because I found myself in situations where I had to prove myself a good parent, not because I had done anything wrong or put Alfred in danger, abused or neglected him. The spiteful lies all came from the nest of hypocrites who assumed that parenting a special needs child meant I had to be segregated and sad. When they saw me dressed up and laughing, that was an abomination.

It was chaotic evil amongst my fellow Africans in the community. So much hostility, they are either jealous of your success or envious of your luck. It's as if the volume knob of envy was turned all the way up and jammed there permanently. If they are not spitting venom, they are venom. They continually chip away your life if you don't put a solid hedge of protection around it. The social circle is simple because it's either you went to school with somebody or at least knew of them back in Africa, but this interlink is only used for gossip rather than positivity. Everything reeks from a place of envy, as though everyone is angry that the other person made it to Europe too. Great Britain is always, and sometimes devastatingly, the country to die for. Others have lost count the number of times they have attempted to reach here. Some have lost their lives while getting here.

In a concerted effort to destroy me, as a result of my sex work. they frequently rang up child protection agencies with unfounded statements, With everything going on in the world at large; rather than use their *knowledge, intelligence and common sense* for the greater good, they reached a whole new level of intellectual decay by starting an utterly rudimentary online petition; demanding change and adding emphasis on what an African woman/mother must and must not do in the diaspora. The petition had no basis in the real world and was a sadistic set-up to threaten me into submission. Rarely reaching its desired end, it was condemned by an outraged public… and taken down within a week.

Determined to shred me, they brought allegations of neglect. As humans, we should he frightened of this moral policing and pure hate. The idea that my child's welfare even mattered to them, was laughable and downright offensive. My lifestyle was taboo and bursting some blood vessels over. God damned right I am a hooker and a masterpiece in my own right! That dick won't suck itself… Those balls won't lick themselves. Everyone is needed. We can all be the best at different things, and that is my zone of excellence.

Living life on my own terms, I was so comfortable with who I became, so much it made many uncomfortable. They were comfortable identifying and addressing me as 'that girl with the disabled child'. It made them feel superior to me. To them, I had no name. That was my name. I was expected to be miserable, sad and they thrived on my brokenness.

Upon each feeble accusation, which was usually just insults with no logic, I endured some scrutiny by the local authority examined, in the best interest of my child. They found no basis for the malicious accusations of recklessness and risk to Alfred. Trust this mum. I have never neglected my son, nor was he at risk. Their accusations were a dog's breakfast of confusion.

Each time, I was found blameless and it is merciful that they did not come with a preconceived idea of who I am, but I gave them insight into the kind of mother that I am. Not once has being a sex worker ever hindered my parenting skills. If they had judged me on hearsay that would have been pitiful and detrimental because no one could have done a better job for Alfred than me. No one will give him the benefit of the doubt that I do and protect his wellbeing with fierceness as I do. I am his advocate and cheerleader.

Those who genuinely cared for Alfred have been astounding in their support. I was overwhelmed by their testimonies, confirming that there is nothing imaginable that I would allow to take priority before my son. Life put me to the test many times, but I will never disrespect the place he holds in my life.

Not all adversity is bad. From all the slander, I am finally, proudly, living my truth and resolutely against anybody dictating to me what I should do with my body. When there are new frontiers, the haters suddenly show up from everywhere and they hated me even more.

Despite what the naysayers predicted… and even prayed for, I made it this far. To everyone who assumed I wouldn't make it, thank you for keeping me humble. Sharing my life has been more enthralling than I hoped it would be.

My case was unique due to my job. It required a broad mind to assess my case and not base their decision on the Ten Commandments. It was easier for the Authorities to speculate and assume the worst of me than believe me; nevertheless, other than opting for the easy way out, they worked professionally and tirelessly.

Robin is a remarkable and outstanding social worker with tact and understanding, from the Central Assessment Team and an asset to the services, because he is always alive and alert to safeguard children round the clock. He listens attentively to the child without judging and casting stones at the parent.

Apart from finding no damaging evidence or even a suspicion… because I was a responsible mother doing her due diligence and exercising my duty of care to my beloved son, they realised that the accusations were not only wholly untrue but a wholly unnecessary and gross misrepresentation of reality.

When I was featured on the front pages of the tabloid newspaper for two consecutive weeks, the African community… well… the Misery Club, crawled out from the depths of hell and sharpened their swords to attack me. They seemed to suffer a stroke because my existence was known and now chronicled. They felt extinguished and feared that my territory was enlarged!

My life is a gift to share with the world and a broad mind must not be wasted. I am unapologetically, Sandra, and I am not going to negotiate anything different. If I give you heart palpitations, dizziness, and a shortness of breath, TOO BAD. I sit on my throne, unbothered.

The number of offended people was astonishing. It summed up nothing but envy and hypocrisy amongst the African immigrants, a downright venomous culture rife with conflict. No one could put facts before their slandering of me to Children's Social Services. It's an endless tug of war when you believe the Earth is round and others still think it is flat.

However, despite the malicious intent and the frailty of their accusations, the Local Authority still investigated every allegation and left no stone unturned, therefore fulfilling their duty to safeguard Alfred. Social workers are not ignorant of the haters' devices – they know that one step up the ladder depresses others. They know that when malice is on the loose, they are faced with such helter-skelter cases where enemies come in many ways. Nevertheless, their concern to ensure his safety warmed my heart. That's what makes Great Britain great.

It was devastating because these social workers could have been elsewhere, meeting the needs of another vulnerable child in real danger, but they were distracted by issues reeking from a place of malice and envy, which were prevalent amongst immigrants.

The plotlines continued to get intense when they noticed that tables had started to turn in my favour. As I ascended, they descended, and it angered them that I was no longer the borrower who was always put to shame when I couldn't repay them. It was an exhibition that a borrower loses their dignity and is always a slave to the lender, so they loved that I was their vassal, always stranded and desperate for a few pounds to top up my prepayment gas meter. The more earnest and intense my desire to pay back, the more I failed, because that last penny was for food or gas or electric. The burden of debt is slavery. Finally, I was independent, and they couldn't handle it. Finally, I was no longer the tail, no longer beneath.

As hard as they despised me, I was secretly their role model and their own fascination scared them. I established dominance just by being truthful to myself and the passion I brought to every task. Everything was falling into place... that was a uniqueness they wished to absorb. Strangely enough, those who laughed and slandered me the most attempted to do the same work but failed miserably. Be careful trying to do what I do because you might slide and hurt yourself.

If I went skydiving and my main parachute didn't open, I know who would pray that the reserve parachute didn't function too. If it did function, I know who would say, "shame the reserve parachute worked." If people could kill with a thought, we would have all died a thousand times... well, make that a million for me.

These venomous snakes would have preferred that I endure the domestic violence to stay married, just as they do and say as they do: "If he beats me, I can't blame him." Not only did I protect myself from the mental, physical and sexual abuse in the marriage, but I also protected my vulnerable son from witnessing more violence and abuse of his mother. When I cried, he cried too. It still haunts me when I remember what he saw.

If you ever have doubts about the purpose and the meaning of life, remember that I have been demonised and vilified. Mocked, and trolled. I rose defiant and spat out the hate they wanted me to swallow.

We are here now. The eternal now. The only reality we truly have. All else is either memory or imagination. Lamenting over the past only wastes more time.

Know that every discomfort in life is temporary and perhaps an opportunity to be grateful for the challenge. No season remains the same. I hope you find some clarity and peace and come through on the other side, a stronger and complete person.

For daringly being a visible sex worker, I endured much scrutiny and judgement, whilst others reported me to the police for breaking the African convention and living life on my own terms. I had defiled my body, the temple of god, and that was a grave offence against the almighty and the church. Before them, I was reckoned the most sinful and endured with their terribly exaggerated views and endless slander. They prayed unceasingly, for everything horrific; that I experience some hell down here, before I reach actual hell up there.

As well as killing people with albinism, Malawi has the biggest threat and gross violation of LGBTQ rights; the prejudice is rife. Those who come out, literally risk their life. In a climate of hate and hypocrisy, those crying out for acceptance cannot be heard because of the narrow-minded religious leaders; they value only their power and sprout off scriptures which are there to feed hate… to reaffirm their stance on homosexuality. It is despicable that the nation glorifies the perspectives of men and religion because having societal tunnel vision is praised. They are not just intolerant. They are dangerous. I have nothing but love and solidarity for the LGBTQ and I am behind their fight for rights.

Ironically, the country has lost a lot of (supposedly celibate) priests to HIV/AIDS. This speaks volumes of the hypocrisy. Even for the deeply closeted gays, their life and liberty are at risk because any persons engaging in consensual same-sex activities triggers a fourteen-year jail term with excruciatingly painful labour. Yes, it is so incredibly hard to imagine that being gay buys jail time… Domestic violence and child abuse do not. Religion is directly responsible for the culture of stigma and discrimination. Many were hoping that the penal laws on homosexuality would apply to an escort too…

Constrained by nothing more than ignorance, religious leaders feel entitled to decide people's rights and unashamedly justify this toxic control purely based on: "Thus sayeth the Lord… the end is nigh…" (We have been hearing this since we were kids.) Usually, it is just an excuse to refuse to let people be and to deny progression in society. Full of greed and thirsty for glory, in the end, you wonder who the barbarians really are.

A marriage can be a dark, fierce journey of isolation and manipulation, when you are literally trained how to be torn down by a man whilst meeting his desires. Ultimately, you must put yourself in pain for your husbands' pleasure and you are endorsed as fit to give free domestic and sexual services. Others were seemingly okay with this, but I was not. I was tired of disappointing people when even my best was not good enough. I was deemed a rebel and radical; for losing the art of being an African wife. Basically, she surrenders her existence, all in the service of her dictatorial man. She does not talk back and has no choice for her future, unable to spread her wings, an object whose duty and sole purpose is to know her place by being submissive and having no character. Living in constant fear until nothing else remains, she is barely in her life story. The track record of pain and misery doesn't lie. I was under a rock far too long. I take back my strength as I tell my truth.

Like most sex-workers, for some discernible reason, I managed to keep my identity a guarded secret for a long time, until my Adult Work escort profiles were circulated on social media, by my family. My private gallery with a fuck ton of porn went viral! That meant what was seen couldn't be unseen and there was no more dignity to preserve. It was inconceivable betrayal, no wonder they predicted suicide and that was probably their aim, to wreck my life on all conceivable levels. The mastermind behind the vile plan to wreck me was my spiteful sister who has never loved me from childhood. The tug of wars are all the memories I have of her, nevertheless, nothing more than a con artist, when she was convicted and imprisoned for two years for serious fraud, I was the only one who reached never forsook her.

Never regret any acts of love and kindness.

Judgemental to the core, she was deeply religious and deeply desirous to join my work but threw in the towel after a few bookings. Was she too well-behaved to be interesting? Well, at least she was brave enough to try. To be the artist that I am, one must have some explosiveness and depth. A spine is an essential requirement if you are to perform your duties admirably… as I do. She and the other haters now look on from a distance and admire the courage I have. Often, people get angry when someone possesses a quality, they wish themselves to have. Scales aren't equal but that's just life. Also, be careful trying to do what I do, because your steps may slide.

I have seen the terrors of betrayal, and the cost is steep... I am still unpacking some things.

To their shock and disgust, following their catastrophic plan, I rose again and unleashed the free spirit in me. I was not afraid nor ashamed. I discovered a space within me – something great came out of the job and the person I had been hiding. The more out into the open my luscious dark side came, the brighter I shone. Instead of sorry, I was roaring, and they were flabbergasted by how I bounced back, because what they meant for evil turned around for my good. They took me to the next level of my life, now their biggest threat was themselves. They were angry, if not haunted by their own cruelty.

Enough people were against me, but who does this to their own sister? Worse still, although they called it dirty cash, the begging ball was always quick to come out. I refused to be the 'useful fool'.

Their malice fuelled me to greatness. Admittedly, I spread my wings a little bit too much; my thrills knew no bounds. But that's what you do when you are reclaiming your time and taking back control. Also, when those you trusted to shield you, invest their energy in trying to maul you, the impact is undeniably huge. For a long time, my hands were tied, freedom was not allowed; it corroded my life. No wonder they don't recognise me now... they are still in panic overdrive!

Once dependant on humanitarian assistance because of the rubber-stamp in my passport, prohibiting employment and recourse to public funds, I based some decisions on how much I needed the money, but I ended up with an interesting life of erotic encounters and doing exactly what I was destined to do – bringing joy to people's lives by bringing their fantasies to life, with many pleasures unspoken, yet heard. As I embraced my new territory, full-blown, not only did lust and love meet between my sheets, but it was my platform to give love, because an ocean of loneliness, anxiety and depression swells in many hearts.

Be vigilant; some people are in a sinking ship and they just want someone to sink with them – the narcissists and naysayers. Cut some people from your life when there is a new frequency and a new chapter begins. When you finally overtake your many years of struggling, beware who you keep around you. Some people can't cope with identifying you as the person who is now happy and healed. There is always someone putting traps on your doorstep. OLD IS NOT GOLD if they can't cope with your elevation.

I recreated my world and found a new courage, refuelling my appetite for constant redesigning and restructuring. Instead of deleting my online profiles, I enhanced and sprinkled them with more promises of wondrous and wild experiences they won't soon forget. Having blurred my face for confidentiality for so long, I eventually showed off my powerfully captivating smile and wonderful persona. That original voice when I answered their call sealed the deal with some intelligent yet mellow clientele. When the concealed is revealed, one breakthrough leads to yet more breakthroughs. Daily looking more and more desirable, I upgraded my lingerie. In me was a haven, a hiding place and resting shade for those who wanted to lock the world out and relax.

It felt so great to come out and identify as an escort. Well, I didn't deliberately come out, more their smear brought me out… and so, out I burst with full force, it was liberating! All things worked together for good; their betrayal brought me to a marvellous place.

Life gave me lemons… I didn't make the usual lemonade. Absorbing the attacks, I went extravagant and made a speciality out of it. Oh fuck! I baked a carrot cake out of those lemons and still made more intriguing things, and proud of it too. Challenges breed more passion.

The horoscopes may say you are the problem in your own life. Don't look up your name to check what the naysayers and narcissists are saying about you. They will tell you it's impossible and unachievable, but their opinion doesn't matter. Life moves fast; I am not getting distracted by anything or anyone. I am just here, happening.

Don't waste your life altering your beliefs and striving to impress others. Be your own advocate, unapologetically. The heart of man is desperately wicked… even family can be the very poison of hell. Choose those who choose you and quit the desire to fit in where you are not wanted. STOP trying to appeal to an inhumane group of people for approval. Just be yourself, a free thinker, as you are, just as I learned to be myself, as I am. I lost myself trying to please everyone. Then I lost everyone in the process of finding myself. Believe me, it was not worth losing myself in the first place, but what choice did I have?

Too many dramas, too many chameleons, not enough time. Before you know it, life will pass you by while you're trying to please people, and spending your energy worrying about those *friends* cosying up with your enemies. Look inward; the enemy was always amongst you.

Good luck in finding yourself and remember, whoever you lose in the process was not meant to be in your life in the first place. Destiny decides who enters your life, but you decide who stays. Others are just in transit, passing through; not everyone is meant to stay. If you are not willing to risk anything, then you don't strongly believe in what you think. Be courageous to be disliked even. If it truly matters, you will dedicate your life.

Dare to be you, because what lies ahead to be discovered is limitless. Be the first one to accept and believe in yourself, and others will follow suit. If they don't accept you and believe in you, toughen up. Be the ultimate. If the microscopic minority still want to be in your life, they will adjust to your uniqueness.

No matter who approves or disapproves, live boldly, take risks, do not be afraid to step out into your dreams and make it happen. Be bold and live the plan that is written on your heart. You can be you, without snatching up a piece of everyone else. Some things aren't yours. As complex and interesting as you are, dare to live your own story. Well, that is why we differ! Establish dominance by being true to yourself every single day, and life will serve you better. The right people will always respect that. Everyone is a rare species and only you can reveal that scarcity within. Stop trying on new identities, because someone could be drawn to the very person you suppress! You have been around the crowd and lost yourself in there.

There will always be a void that comes from not being who you really are. Instead, fill that void, be open to discovering and revealing that thing that you have, that nobody else has. Keep moving forward and dare to leave behind what the world thinks you ought to be because after all, people will speculate unfairly, sometimes even… harshly. Perspectives are their liberty.

Real change happens when you are real, so be authentic unapologetically. Are people in love with the mask or the real you? Unleash the potential embedded in you and exhibit who you are, because there is no one else like you. When you are a counterfeit, there is no room to discover that talent… that gift within you, because you lose a little bit of yourself every time you are not your true self.

Whatever they orchestrated against me, I turned it to my favour, to enlarge my territory and multiply my opportunities. It worked for me and they regretted it but what's done can't be undone. They tried to diffuse the situation, but I had gone full-on and it was a case of 'It is what it is, so deal with it'.

How people harbour so much hate and think it's okay is inconceivable, but beware, they are in our midst, unless you have been living under a rock for the past decade. We share the same genes. They pose as friends. We work with them. We live around them and dine with them. They laugh with us and cry with us, with crocodile tears. When faced with these sour, deceitful and desperately wicked people, I choose not to come down to their level. I consider it a test of my faith and I choose to fight only one fight: the good fight of faith. Sooner or later, it will turn around in my favour.

Forget the concept of an eye for an eye. It's out-dated. The best way to silence your enemies is to thrive and flourish. Let your progress reduce them to silence. Forget what you can't do and get creative about what you can do, by leveraging your gift or talent. Embrace your uniqueness and let your light shine. Don't shine with somebody else's light.

They led me to the deepest of freedoms and in no time, I was getting better and maturing well, because everyone has value, and this is what I had to contribute to the world. This was my calling, and I decided I was going to be good at it. The more they reasoned it out to make me draw back and shrink in fear, the more I let my light shine brighter and brighter.

I pay tribute to all the escorts who committed suicide because their families and loved ones found out about this secret part of their life. May their souls rest in peace! Laura, an escort who dived to her death from a thirteenth-floor balcony in the Deansgate, Manchester. Distressed and upset hours after her evil client, Mr Jackson, told her parents about her secret life. Rest in peace!

Her final messages to her family members before her death were: "Please forgive me. I love you very much. For me it's too late. I lost my mind," and to her father: "I think you deserve another daughter."

Evidence was also heard that Mr Jackson had contacted the family of yet two other escorts some years earlier in similar circumstances and was convicted of harassment. The thing is, even miserable men love to enjoy the company of escorts. Clearly, he was a pathetic attention-seeker whose aim of disclosure was to destroy the escorts' lives when he couldn't have his own way. Sadly, he was never prosecuted for his part in Laura's tragic death and has since left the country.

I will not boast to be the brave one for not ending my life as some do. Even though alas! That was what my haters' end goal looked like. I quashed their expectation and proved that they don't have the final say on my life.

Fuck me, I'm a happy hooker. I rose to the level of justified, to which few others ascend. I not only reached that level; I continue to rest there comfortably…

Flooded with insults and curses, "I hope a car crash leaves you with broken legs so you stop working," said my sinister sister, who failed massively at being an escort, until one day, she shredded my saucy lingerie which sent the men's pulses racing. As though that would change anything. She did not shred my desires. "I hope you meet a client who stabs you to death and I pray that it happens soon," said another vicious Christian.

I am all for peace and unity, but the greatest discernment is to know that family can be the tumour and the very poison of hell that we need to steer away from. The anger, malice and jealousy imbedded within family are toxic. People are trying so hard for people who don't care, resulting in pain and depression. Blood is not thicker. Love is thicker. There comes a time when love is best fed from a long spoon. If all it brings you is pain, distance yourself, let go. A surprising concept I know, but it works.

Some people prefer to cut ties and never face you again because they feel that 'sorry' will somehow lower them. Others struggle with forgiveness because they know they will repeat the same mistake all over again. They have no intent to change, and others still because they just hate confrontation. But often, people will stop speaking to you when you are right, and they don't like realising they are wrong. Be wise and know if it's even worth putting the effort in or if it's better to say good riddance. Usually, it's the latter. Not everyone is meant to be in your life. Find love in places where it can be found and it's not always in the DNA.

Some days are such that we find ourselves surrounded by wicked people, days when you go forward two steps and they want to knock you back three more. When they are pulling you down, it means you are a step above them. Always remember that haters do not waste their energy on untalented, ungifted people. Count it all as joyful when there is opposition, as that means there must be something good about you. People can be so cruel and hurt you deeply. They can seek to gang up on you, to try to destroy you, but always remember: no matter the opposition, if you are destined to reign in this life, you will always be crowned with supernatural favour from on high. Won a new contract? Promoted at work? Some people will suddenly hate you because they can't stand to see you progressing. There is always that co-worker who tells you congratulations to your face, but in truth, they want for themselves that very position to which you have been promoted.

Despite my imperfections, they will miss me when I'm gone, and they will have something pure to say about that sister, daughter, friend, and aunty. With arms wrapped around each other, they may say, "Her warmth, love and interest in other people was astounding, a tremendous loss, an amazing lady who had good energy." Who knows! They may even admit, "A remarkable lady who was treated a little unfairly."

There is no greater pleasure than sharing life with appreciative people. Having lived deeply, and so many have drunk from my well, you can be certain that I will never leave a life unused. When a fuck ton of adventure is laid to rest, what will the plaque say on my place of rest? Leave it BLANK because a life with gravity lives on. You are not dead if you leave a great legacy. My fighters will continue to fight for an open and tolerant world. Until then, I will enjoy each day. If we lived each day as though it was the last, we would worry, fear and fret. Just live and spend each moment the best way possible.

Death is not the real tragedy, for we are all going to die. The biggest tragedy is the wrecked hearts and wrecked dreams that survive the death. I call them my clients, punters, admirers, sometimes my LOVERS. We have nested in each other's hearts and seasoned each other with understanding and acceptance. Happiness is a state of being surrounded and saturated in love. It doesn't matter from whom because remember, blood does not define family; love does. I see the world through the lens of love, and I continue to create the world I want to live in.

Love is never mutual; the efforts are never equal, and you can never find the same level of loyalty. Someone must sacrifice more than the other.

I have been hurt, betrayed and constantly tested.

Sincerely, tenderly, I loved and cared for people more than they have loved and cared for me. With sacrifice, I have crossed oceans for people who wouldn't cross the street for me. With forgiveness, I have fed mouths that have cursed and condemned me. With compassion, I have helped those who have betrayed me. I have been there for haters who turned their back on me at the most crucial hour, but I will not get distracted in hate. The concept is simple, yet I learned it the hard way… to choose people who choose me, and I am mindful who I give my attention and energy to. I truly believe that everyone should live their true authentic self with no fear of what people will think. I will leave the hateful wolves to their own destruction; their judgement and opinion do not define me. As I am WORTHY, I will not plead, beg or adjust to be loved and accepted. Being as I am, with no alterations, have been the surreal years of my life. I can merge with you, but I will not metamorphose until I collapse… and lose myself again.

Following blindly, I was once deeply seasoned in religion; until the vanity project exploited and betrayed my heart. I left once I found them to be corrupt, no more happy, trustworthy, kind and honest, than those who are atheist. It is the epitome of hypocrisy, thus creating pain and confusion. Many people are not even in harmony with themselves, so how can they be at peace with others, in their artificial world of deception? I stopped giving religion its undue credits. Is it really such a hard concept to grasp… that we do not need religion to be a decent person… that we do not have to agree on anything to be kind to one another?

People want to look 'good' by projecting an image that does not reflect their true selves. They are wearing masks, whilst imposing their judgements on those who are living kind and gentle lives. What if… hear-me-out, human beings of all genders and choices can live together in mutual respect?

Hotel managers testify that porn rates increase during conferences. That is normal, because they had more guests, but when Christian conferences came to town during a national conference for Church youth, youth pastors by the hundreds flooded into a certain hotel, taking nearly every room. The number of guests who tuned into the adult movie channel broke the record, far and away outdoing any other convention in the history of the hotel. Still, they preach, "god hates porn and masturbation is deadly… its symptoms include nausea, paralysis, loss of memory, weakening of organs…" Because, apparently, viewing pornography in hotel rooms is easy, confidential and inconsequential.

From my boudoir to the pulpits, my clients have included pastors and preachers from many religions who class themselves as saints or strong men of god. Some have disguised themselves upon entry, but it was a waste of time because I already had knowledge of them. There are those who love their jobs and live in fear of being discovered, and then there are others who have just been open and declared who they are. "I'm a man of god, a pastor, but I have needs."

Judging is the greatest intellectual weakness. Mine was a judgement-free zone and I had all the teasing techniques.

Be flexible to perspectives and refuse to be a slave to rigid ideologies. Depth is brilliant! Don't reclassify kinky sex as a satanic ritual, because after all, your spouse will only get kinky elsewhere. It's not complicated. You think he is dreadfully boring; I know he is secretly freaky. Be the fetish he wishes for; behind that mask is a kinky monster. Wake him up with your mouth. No act of kinkiness, no matter how small, is wasted. It's okay to have a savage hunger… Spontaneously spread your legs wide and say to your man, "Give it to me! I want you now… just do it." There is no such thing as dirty, unholy, gross or disgusting beneath the sheets. Every man has a hidden fantasy and it is up to a woman to unleash it. Men, please return the favour too. It's life. It's sex, so why not be open, wild and crazy? Get on with it and stop being tight and judgemental. Women! Be innocent – be filthy… men crave both. It's not demonic to have a kinky moment of pure beast and then snap right back to dainty when you are done.

Sex is a vital part of humanity for survival. "All we do is kneel down beside the bed, pray and sleep. We rarely have sex and she will never get fully naked," said one randy pastor about his killjoy wife. She was too spiritual for kinky sex. He came frequently, to pluck his fantasies from my fruited tree of life. Strangely, wives want to spice up their sex life even though they hardly have sex. Too prude to give a blowjob, why even have a partner when you have a phobia for willies? It sounds obvious, but a good start is to actually have sex. *sigh*.

If she was too uptight to have an orgasm, I would give him my full glory, legs spread to ninety degrees, for a truly magical experience… even more if he paid me well. You think he's dreadfully boring; I know he's secretly freaky. Sometimes I brought in my blonde friend because he loved a coffee-and-cream threesome. After all, a generous man deserves a delicious double. What's not to love? Whilst there was sexual repression and frustration at home, I was his favourite adventure.

As I am, I never rejected a man in need. I saw it all with my slogan of 'Come as You Are', even with your Jewish kippa, clerical collars, wearing rosaries, scapulars – some wearing both. These are supposed to be the sacramentals given to the faithful. Still, other saints would remove such items first, and of one man I asked, "Do you remove it because it is a sacred item or what?"

"No, I remove this and my watch too because I don't want any objects getting in the way when I am having an enjoyable time," he said.

I have had men forget these spiritual weapons or miraculous medals on my dressing table, but I always kept them safe until they returned.

There is no such thing as a strong man of god. Alas! By whose scales do they measure this 'purification'? They preach a message which they themselves have trouble living. They pretend to be transparent. They pretend to conduct themselves with grace and dignity throughout. They think of themselves more highly than they ought to. They pick out the impurities of others and remain blind to their own. Eventually, you will get tired of what's not real.

Whilst others are still struggling to come to terms with the appalling scandals still emerging from the pit of serpents… the church, the perversion, the moral depravity shows how deeply ingrained is the hypocrisy. What if the religious system is just a 'good' place for evil to hide? What if religion is a shackle masquerading as a key? What if it is an impediment to global peace?

Chapter 11
Be Wise, Condomise

Enduring the impacts of heightened stress and sleep deprivation whilst living in deplorable conditions. It had been a long, cold, snowy and bitter winter in a damp house. A gruelling season which increased the likelihood of disease. I did all to protect and comfort my child, but given the circumstances, he fell extremely sick and was hospitalised with a severe bacterial infection and pneumonia. We were discharged after a few days' treatment of intravenous antibiotics, but other than looking forward to going home, my biggest worry was how to get home with my now recovering child. We had come to the hospital in an ambulance; in a state of emergency… at midnight… we couldn't go back in an ambulance. I had no bus fare, let alone money for a taxi. His pram, which was given to me by a woman at the car boot sale was not with me. It was the last thing I could think of carrying with me in the ambulance. I held on to his hospital admission nametag on his wrist and took a leap of faith, to explain to the bus driver my dire situation.

The journey from Manchester Royal Children's Hospital required two buses, so I needed even bigger faith because that meant explaining to two drivers. I knew what a long journey that was going to be. As I explained to the first driver, he was too busy dealing with a flow of students boarding after school. He gestured me to board before I finished explaining my story. We got to the City Centre but that was only half the journey. We still had another bus to catch and I hoped that the same favour from the previous bus would follow us in the next one.

My son was weak. We were both tired and his legs were unstable, so we rested at the bus stop whilst I figured out which driver looked more understanding and sympathetic.

As if these struggles were not enough, as I sat there, someone who had been to Malawi spotted us. We talked, and he told me some news that caused me great concern, that Alfred's father had been diagnosed with HIV and was suffering many complications; it could be AIDS. Instantly, fear and paranoia hit me so hard. Bells started ringing in my head. Back then, he was the first and only man I had slept with. Even since he had returned to Africa, I still hadn't slept with anyone... but what if he had been positive for it back then, before we came to Britain? Worse still, what if this was the reason our son had complex health issues? Were we all infected?

Exasperated with worry, I used his phone to ring our doctor for the next available appointment. Doctors on the frontline in this part of Manchester have a lot of immigrant patients to look after and are always in high demand, but they tend to know which patients are sincere and not out to misuse and drain-dry the generous health care system.

Yes, I know how it sounds, but sometimes we need to be reminded where we come from, because if we stop the waste, the NHS will not deteriorate further. Here is where I come from: Malawi, the warm heart of Africa, one of the poorest places on the planet, where the enemy is tribalism and patriarchy... (its citizens blindly support and blindly oppose based on tribe). Its incurably selfish leaders put power before people, there is no transparency and rampant corruption are an integral feature in the system; they find scapegoats rather than solving problems. They stone the petty thieves to death and appoint the great ones to public office. Sad reality – steal big. If only they could dismantle and burn the tribalism and corruption to the ground, it's a beautiful country with limitless potential to thrive.

My mind goes back to the ward where I delivered my bundle of perfection. It was 8 March 2000 at Ekwendeni General Hospital in Mzimba, Malawi, which serves a community of over 75,000 people. It was a chaotic night of difficult labour. The untold agony of waiting my turn for an available midwife, as I watched other women giving birth because there were no concealed curtains for privacy, will never leave me. After his birth, we were in desperate need of chloramphenicol, an antibiotic to treat his bacterial eye infection, and there was none. He suffered. He may never fully comprehend how good he has it in Britain and the hardships and struggles he could have continued to have in Malawi. Nevertheless, it is up to me to educate him that we are partakers of an awesome privilege resulting from the arduous work of many.

So, when I called him and explained the circumstances, my doctor heard my cry and booked us in for blood tests at the earliest opportunity. He counselled me on what would happen in the case that we were HIV positive and very kindly assured me that we would be appropriately supported. It was Friday, and what could I do to spare myself the anguish and anxiety of waiting for the results? Having HIV is no longer a death sentence but still the anguish mode was activated for a few days… staring sorrowfully at my son. The following week, I got a call from my doctor and my heart started pounding immediately.

"Do you want me to come in, Doctor?"

"No, you don't have to; your results have come back negative. I am happy for you. Well done for testing."

Nothing else mattered. I was the gladdest thing under the sun.

It is important to remember that in Malawi, a huge fraction of the population is infected and so are many of its people in the diaspora. Its national anthem is a fervent prayer to god to put down the country's three biggest enemies, notably hunger, disease and envy.

In the long run, HIV positive or not, we are all affected, and we still carry in our hearts all those we loved. What threatens one of us threatens all of us. It took the best of us… lest we forget. If we all kept a book of names of dear friends and family who have been swept away like a flash flood, to this epidemic, there would be less arrogance and stigma. At the peak of the crisis, it was a decade of many deaths. I was there. I remember when AIDS took the best of us. Every day, people died a little bit more as their HIV nibbled them into full blown AIDS. It was over for them. I always remember… my cousins, vibrant aunties and uncles hoping to survive another year but transformed into wasted, skeletal dying shells of themselves. AIDS took my family.

It doesn't remove the heartbreak as it changes one's life drastically but more and more people are living with HIV because people rarely die of AIDS due to antiretroviral medication with incredible success rates, more especially in the civilised countries where the best help is at hand.

With correct and consistent use, I have remained a Condom Queen! To combat the toxic taboos and stigma I frequently remind people, how vital it is to know their HIV/AIDS status. Use a condom, and emphasise the obvious… It stays on during sex!

Stop assuming. The only sure way is to get tested and to ensure your willing participant is tested too. The obvious is restated but apparently too hard to follow. Be wise. Condomise.

Durex… built for purpose and my ultimate pleasure enhancer. Intense lust is mine and I have always enjoyed playing with you. You have served me well and kept me safe for many years.

Other than safeguard their health and reduce their infections to others, some who have tested HIV positive are bitter, careless and with ill intentions, they ensure that they are not the only casualties in this. There are measures and precautions we can take. Establish dominance by being wise… Condomise. Always have a condom in your purse or wallet for you never know what's on the menu.

If it needs saying, you don't have to be a prostitute or promiscuous to be infected… it is not limited to certain people. I remember… I was there… not all who have died of HIV/AIDS have been promiscuous; just like those living with HIV are not necessarily promiscuous. I have never contracted any sexually transmitted disease, but I have gone through many, many condoms, more than you all, in my aim to stay HIV negative if I can; Forever, even for a hooker, is possible. Safe sex is everyone's responsibility, we need one another so let us come together and fight HIV/AIDS.

No one ever regrets using a condom, yet also, the surprisingly sad and frustrated faces I witness when they see me unwrap one are surreal. I was constantly bombarded with calls requesting 'meaningful sex'. I ALWAYS ask them to elaborate. Perspectives. If I got paid, and I was protected, the sex was meaningful. According to many, it was the Girl Friend Experience (GFE) with the aim of having unprotected sex. I have been dangled extra money for unprotected sex. Others, upon arrival, tried to lure me into unprotected sex, bareback as they call it, often saying to me within a few minutes of meeting me, "but I trust you; I know I can trust you. I know you are clean. I'm clean too." Many men confessed that it was their first time to ever use protection. "I just want to pull your knickers to the side and slide it in without discomfort." Sometimes the best reply is just a deep sigh. It doesn't take days, weeks or months for one to be infected with the virus; it takes one moment, seconds for HIV to pass.

There are some who believe in having one partner. They get tested as a couple, and it transpires that one person they trusted, the only one they slept with, had brought it home and infected them. That is why it is advisable to always use condoms. Be wise; condomise. In this world full of lies and deceit, love and trust are scarce and far away. The cheater tells you that it was a mistake. No, it was not. Cheating is deliberate. Sleeping around is deliberate. Take responsibility and be wise; condomise.

What about the stunningly good-looking men or women who say, "Look at me; I'm clean?" They will tell you that raw and wild, skin-to-skin is beautiful. I know it's tempting but remember my words… Be wise; condomise. Don't chance it. If it helps, call a condom a necessary evil.

HIV Negative? Hang in there. Make healthy decisions.

HIV Positive? Live positively. Make healthy decisions.

HIV Positive does not automatically equal death.

We live in a better world; you can plan for your future.

Your private health information is your private health information. Nevertheless, in sex, at what point must one make the responsible disclosure of their HIV positive status? To my shock and awe, because he was the first and so far, the last, Arnold did; clearly loving of himself and others. As one conversation led to another and when I asked, he asked back, "Do you really want to know? I am positive, and I have known for fifteen years." It didn't make any difference to me because, after all, be wise; condomise.

Those living with HIV are often discriminated and stigmatised at some point in their life; then comes the issue of self-acceptance and then disclosure. Never let HIV define you; instead, use it to make a difference, to inspire, to encourage prevention and positive living. Although I am not living with HIV, I have taught people living with it to normalise it and stop stigmatising themselves, because the more they hide it and feel ashamed, the harder the self-acceptance and disclosure becomes. Don't be afraid of the unknown. There are always new infections, so it's up to all of us to encourage our families, friends, partners and everyone around us to take steps in fighting this epidemic, with the ultimate aim of decreasing new infections; with frequent testing, medication and condom use. We can't stop people shagging, but together, we can be wise; condomise.

What one does not know does not exist? Not with HIV. Lack of knowledge of your status is tantamount to perishing. In most cases, people contracted their HIV from someone who did not know their status or was not taking medication. Those who correctly adhere to treatment can suppress the viral load until it's undetectable. With certainty, if it cannot be detected, it cannot be transmitted. U = U.

We live in a better world. Be sure. Be wise, condomise.

With a heavy heart, I dedicate this poem to my precious friends and family whom I lost to the AIDS epidemic. Also, to those who died broken, alone and unloved, because the stigma was rife. It was the days of life of abandonment and contradiction.

I REMEMBER

Grave by grave, a deadly blade
Who can forget the dark dreadful days?
The peak of deaths of HIV/AIDS
I promise to never forget…
Hearts bled, the ground gave way
Death was never far away
Each day it took something
Each time we lost someone
Sadness and sorrow went on for years!
The whispers, the misery and dismay
A nation distorted with agony, no rest
Every family was put to the test
A pestilence of its own kind
Ridiculed, rejected the prejudice was rife

Isolated, forsaken, shamed and feared
Bigoted, the stigma never cleared
Treated as devils by the "divines"
A huge population gone in the ground
Until this day I recall the sound
I saw, I sobbed, I lost count
Merciless! It took so much
The pestilence! We had never seen such
Oh, what a grim era, I witnessed the terror
The damage it caused was horror
Faces, names, forever we honour

People we heard of, we knew, and we cherished
We all died a little inside when they perished
Bright talented stars, their lights extinguished
Day after day potential diminished
One after another AIDS slaughtered…
So gaunt, so frail, a precious life, unrecognisable
Unless you were there, it's unimaginable
They lived their own story
They now rest in glory
Trust me, I was there by their side when they died…
I felt that, and I died a little inside.

Chapter 12
Home Office

It's very crushing when your life has been held back, but the groundbreaking victory happened, and the world was so much brighter. We were granted citizenship! Others kiss awards, medals, belts, trophies. If you understand my journey, please understand why I will continually kiss, smell, and caress my British passport. Alfred only follows suit because he is a curious copycat but that's alright. After all the layers of fear and uncertainty, our fighting chance for liberty and freedom are wrapped up in it. That passport filters out all the vile and hopeless dreams. It fills me with positive dreams filled with hope and promises for our future. I was so relieved!

Waiting on an immigration decision for ten years is utterly exhausting. The crushing weight wrecks your life. You don't see the light of day because of it. That rubber-stamp in a passport has the power to tell you that your day, week, month or year has been cancelled because your application is awaiting a decision or further consideration. Beyond the complexity of the case, the files at the Home Office went missing during this course. When I got my indefinite leave to remain in Britain, the Immigration Officer called me to request that I go to the Dallas Court Immigration Centre to collect a big box of all the evidence I had been sending every week for a decade! He said, "You might want to keep these, because they seem sentimental. I have never seen so many documents and photographs in any one file."

It was unbelievable and unimaginable how many things were in it, because all I had were these letters to represent myself with the truth I had. It was like writing love letters to the Home Office; our whole life depended on this. Every doctor and school report, every appointment, every result, every medical and education assessment, everything that came to me, concerning Alfred, I sent to them so that they might consider our application.

30 September 2008
Border & Immigration Agency
The Prime Minister

"Understand that all the attacks, all that polls, all the headlines, all the criticism, it's all worth it, if in doing this job I make life better for <u>one child, one family</u>, one community.

"We're changing the world the only way it can ever really change – **<u>one life, one family, one hope at a time</u>**. That's the real power of labour to change lives."

Quoted from the Prime Minister, Gordon Brown's Labour Party Conference speech in My City of Manchester where he revealed his heart. (Tuesday 23 September 2008)

I was so touched by his statements. Above all, the story he mentioned of the young boy, David of Rwanda aged ten, who died as the world looked the other way.

Like David, my son too believes in Britain.

Britain is the rock of stability and fairness upon which he stands. If only you could give him the unconditional assurance he needs, the greatest gift and hope for his future.

If 'EVERY CHILD MATTERS', why is my cry left unheard? Is it too much to ask to give my child an ordinary childhood? Free from fear and torture and degrading inhumane treatment that he experienced?

For this cause, it will take me my last breath to beg for mercy and compassion on behalf of my son, that you should realise his hope for a better future.

Please don't look the other way.

I too believe in Britain.

Sandra Ntonya

Chapter 13
Paul – Sorry You Misdialled

A lady in the neighbourhood found love in a 'connect singles directory', and she ordered me a copy, in the hope that I too will find the one. My husband was the only man I had been with, and it was scary for me, but I scrolled through many profiles and I gave it a go. I even made a few calls. Most white men were in their forties, fifties and some in their sixties… a few in their seventies! I left a message on their landlines – they were probably at work, and it felt like a reassurance if they had a landline in the directory. I laughed with my friend about the prospect of us both ending up interested in the same man.

One day I received a call back.

"Hello, is this Sandra the black lassie from Manchester?"

"Yes." I paid attention nervously.

"My name is Paul from Yorkshire, not Keith. Thank you for the message you left, but I am here with my wife, Sue, and we both think you got the wrong number. We didn't want to keep you waiting in vain, so we thought it wise to ring you."

I checked the phone number that I had called expecting a man named Keith, and indeed I had misdialled. Perhaps I was too excited and was already building castles in the air at the prospect of love.

He laughed, saying he was thankful the guy's name was not the popular Paul, because hell would have broken loose. They wished me good luck with the advert and to check the numbers properly next time. They considered it a strange way to find love, but I told them I didn't go out much, so it's an option.

We went on to speak of all kinds of things. I told him where I was from, what I did. We spoke like we knew each. "I'm from Malawi", "I have one child", "I'm currently being deported", "My son is disabled" … I spoke on and on and on to these strangers.

They asked me if I have a lawyer or if there was anything they could do to help. Sylvia is a retired banker and Paul, in his prime, a Doctor of Science, always in the lab mixing chemicals.

They were moved by my story and assured me that they would make time the following week to discover how they could help in this desperate situation.

I got all my files ready.

Paul wrote to my MP who responded to him, through his own MP, because that was the protocol.

What if we all asked that one question, "How can I help?"

One good deed can reduce someone's suffering. Multiple good deeds can transform the world.

Chapter 14
Paul – Not Sorry I Misdialled

"It was an immense pleasure meeting you on Friday," I told Paul sometime later. Warm and gracious and larger than life, it didn't feel like meeting a stranger at all. I felt safe; like talking to him felt like a heavy load had already been lifted off my shoulders because he carried the weight as his problem too.

Everything was unfolding to my favour. Finally, a voice, a mind and a heart in my best interests. As he went through my immigration paperwork, he saw my date of birth and then asked me what I was doing for my birthday the following week. I told him, "Nothing at all." His wife suggested that they come and take me out for a meal, which was very kind of them.

We went for a three-course meal at the Fairfield Arms on Ashton Old Road, a few miles from my house, while my son was at school and they made sure to get in a packed meal. I felt safe and secure in their presence. Their potent combination of compassion and justice was a true reflection of humanity and civility in all its glory. This family stood together, to shield an immigrant like me. I felt that they would campaign with their last breath to ensure that we didn't get deported.

Sylvia was quite reserved, yet we had some remarkable times. I fascinated her. I noticed how she stared at my hands and I even caught her a few times. Finally, she asked if she could touch them, because she always wondered how inside my palms has a very different colour to my body. She touched them, and I told her that was fine and that my feet are the same, but I couldn't remove my shoes in the restaurant. We laughed and carried on eating. She admitted that she had worked with black people before but had never touched one.

They asked me about Christmas, just around the corner, and she suggested that we go and spend it with them. Oh, Christmas morning, we were ready on time – English time. African times are always late, a culture of never on time; that's the norm. Now I turn up at every appointment on time and I learnt it the hard way. When in Rome, do as the Romans do.

When we were on our way, Sylvia was at home, preparing Christmas dinner with her son as they awaited our arrival. Alfred took the passenger seat and I sat comfortably in the back thinking to myself, "What a fortunate wrong number I had dialled!" It was a very merry English Christmas.

Brave on many levels and brilliantly articulate, Paul was a chemical scientist who still had a personality. More intelligent than funny, he enjoyed sharing some rare jokes I didn't always understand, and his wife always had to explain them to me. They may have been important, with great safety tips but he often blinded us in his scientific world. Sometimes his wife gestured me to ignore him… That was the funny part. The collisions of an elderly British couple are simply amazing comedy. We all cleaned up together before we sat by the fire and watched TV, chatting away. I felt overwhelmed that he had to drive all the way back to Manchester to drop us off after such a big dinner and all that relaxation.

Such rare people to encounter, but when you are in the company of a truly authentic person, you know you can rely on them, no matter how tough things get. Love does not cave in, to the effortless way out. He sacrificed his time and much more. I was on the receiving end of this unmerited favour and I was not going to ponder or question, because good things happen in life and this was my time. As I am open to give, also I am open to receive.

I was once weary, burdened and felt like I had the weight of the world on my shoulders. This man alleviated my sufferings. I felt a peace that surpasses all understanding. He still remembers the voicemail I left on that day when I misdialled and always said to me, "When you do get married, if you do get married, look no further, I will walk you down the aisle."

Nothing occurs by accident or coincidence. Don't always wait for an invite. You are not interfering. It's just perfect timing. Wherever we are, we are all instruments, uniquely placed there to be the source… to give someone an expected end. If we do not benefit others, then basically we are shirking our call of duty.

Be it to the broken-hearted, the poor, the depressed, the 'destroyed and damaged', the anxious, the lonely, we are all set aside for a specific assignment. You may be a random unexpected source, but if not you, then who? Help unlock someone's jigsaw;

fulfil someone's dreams, desires, goals and aspirations. Discover your platform to dispense help and heal the world. It's a cold world out there. Be that perfect stranger that breathes life into someone. Be the restorer to that person who sees nothing but impossibilities, straighten someone's crooked place, be a light on their dark path.

Never assume that your time and resources are wasted when you have done something for someone who can never repay you. The day you plant the seed is not the day you eat the fruit. In due course, you will reap in abundance; somehow; elsewhere.

I immediately felt that I had an advocate, an emboldener, a helper and a standby in case I needed extra reinforcement. How could I be stranded? Occasionally, someone does something so beautiful without thinking, "what's in it for me?", that it restores my faith in humanity.

Paul was not fighting this battle on his own terms, nor with any selfish sense of entitlement due us, but as an old-aged citizen, a concerned citizen. In his plea to the politicians, he stated that helping Alfred to remain here would not cause serious disruption to the livelihood of the British people. Also, having read all medical documents, he told them it would be a waste to cut off what has already been invested in Alfred. Specialist education would stop for him, if he were to return to an uncertain fate in Malawi.

In his own words to the Home Office:

"I am writing to support Sandra's application to remain in the United Kingdom. This is a terribly sad case. I hope it can be understood and accepted that Sandra and her son are not just statistics, but fellow humans needing help and support, which we in this country, a nation of great wealth and resources, have the power to give. I ask it also to be considered that the welfare of a second person is at stake, that of Sandra's son, Alfred; a child who is even more in need of our help and support. Indeed, Sandra's application to stay in the UK is as much for her son as for herself.

"I have not known Sandra for very long, only a few weeks in fact. Our meeting came completely by chance. She dialled a wrong number and thus inadvertently left a message on my answering machine at home. I called her back to let her know that she had misdialled, and in the conversation that followed, I started to learn some of the circumstances of Sandra's life, an unfair burden that no one asks for. In the weeks that have followed, Sandra has become a family friend and Alfred is truly blessed to have an incredibly strong mother. To my wife and I, it is an absolute honour and privilege to know them both and assist.

"As I understand it, Sandra came to this country with her then-infant son at the behest of her husband.

"Unfortunately, her son was subsequently found to be autistic and to suffer severe learning difficulties. This tragic circumstance led to the breakdown of their marriage, her husband apparently blaming his wife for his son's difficulties and subjecting her to violence as a result. Mr Ntonya has failed to provide for his wife and child with any support, financial or otherwise, and has now returned to Malawi.

"There is a strong probability that if Sandra is forced to return to Malawi, she will again be subject to violence from her former husband, and, worse still, it will be exponentially harder for Alfred.

"Sandra is not asking for charity. She wishes to be able to work and pay her way. Her record demonstrates this, and it is to our collective shame that she is now left with little option but to provide for her son in the way that she does.

"Alfred attends a good school where he is happy and where he receives the sympathetic help that he needs, and it would be a great personal tragedy for him if this education were to be forcibly terminated. He also receives the medical support that he needs. Further details are given in the accompanying statement from Sandra. This is the statement, made under oath, that Sandra submitted at her appeal hearing, ref IM/14828/2006. It is a harrowing story.

"Sandra is an intelligent and capable woman who is asking merely to be like other UK citizens, to be allowed to become a responsible member of our society, to pay her taxes, to enjoy the freedoms that we take for granted.

"Just this week, a Home Office report (quoted on the *Yahoo* website) has stated that immigrants to this country are net contributors to our economy, and not a drain on our resources. As an example, I cite the National Health Service, where about half the employees are immigrants, without whom the service plainly would not function.

"As I have already mentioned, Alfred Ntonya is receiving help and support in very meaningful ways. It would seem to be very perverse now to deprive him of this, and it would be a waste of the resources already invested in him.

"Expressing a personal view, the UK has a duty to give this help and support. In the 19th and 20th Centuries, Great Britain, through its Empire, ruthlessly exploited its colonies in Africa and other parts of the world, making immense profits doing so. It left behind, on withdrawal, a legacy of poverty and corruption from which much of Africa is still suffering. Sandra and people like her are to a greater or lesser extent victims of this legacy.

"We are constantly lectured these days about globalisation and the benefits it brings. But surely globalisation is not new. Humanity is truly globalised. So why then should not the concept apply in human terms as well as in business? I am reminded of the poet John Donne's words, "No man is an island." The verse ends:

"… send not to know for whom the bell tolls; it tolls for thee."

"An appeal on behalf of Sandra is an appeal on behalf of our common humanity.

"Obviously, I am not able to say if Sandra has a legal right to stay in this country, but I feel very strongly, on compassionate and moral grounds, that she should be allowed to stay here, to bring up and provide for her son in secure surroundings, and I plead earnestly that Sandra and her son be granted UK citizenship.

Yours faithfully,
Dr Paul"

And another:
"Dear Mr Johnson,

"I would like to request your advice on how to deal with an immigration issue. I realise that this is a difficult topic for MPs, and as the people in question do not live in your constituency, I cannot ask you to operate on their behalf.

"However, if you could cast an eye over the notes below, I would be very grateful – the key question is have you any thoughts on what else, if anything, should we be doing to help in this case?

"I am writing on behalf of Sandra Ntonya and her son, Alfred, originally from Malawi.

"Sandra came to the UK with her husband and baby son – her husband had a student visa and was intending to study here.

"Alfred is the central figure. His development as a child was slow – he is now nine – and this led to hostility between husband and wife. Sandra was blamed by her husband for the problem and he became violent towards her. Her husband also insisted that Alfred should be treated by primitive methods from Malawi; for example, as his speech development was poor, part of his tongue was butchered, and any speech that he may develop is now permanently impaired.

"The marriage foundered and ended in divorce. Mr Ntonya completely failed to make provision for his son and deserted his family and went back to Malawi.

"This country has been very kind to Alfred. A small flat was provided for them by the local authority in Manchester and Alfred has the support of a social worker and attends a special school, where he is very happy and making progress.

"Sandra, on the other hand, has no visa, no NI number, and is not allowed to work legally. She would like to stay in the UK for the benefit of her son, and of course she would like to be able to earn a living, and pay her way, and her taxes and NI contributions would also help in some measure to pay for the help that Alfred receives.

"What makes the situation serious is that in Malawi, Alfred would have none of the help he receives here in the UK. Not only that, but his father would be legally entitled to take Alfred away from his mother, and there is a very real fear that this child would again be subjected to treatment that we can only see as cruel and inhumane.

"Sandra has been in contact with her local MP and has local legal representation. However, the situation has become urgent as she has very recently received a letter from the Home Secretary, telling her that she should leave the UK."

In response to this effort, on 16 November 2008 (a day before my birthday), I received a Notification of Temporary Admission to a person who is liable to be detained, under the Immigration Act 1971, IS.96 instructing me to go and sign in at the immigration centre. Refusals and notifications of being detained or deported, such scary letters always seemed to be timed on my birthdays, never a happy birthday for an immigrant. Paul was horrified, as was my MP. I was weeping from shattered hopes and sudden dark despair. Feeling my sadness, he postponed his schedule to Germany and reassured me that he would take me there to hold my hand. I was broken but not alone.

Although detention is used sparingly and as a last resort, I wasn't sure if it was an interview or just for me to report to them but seeing as many people have been detained and deported from there before, I decided that Alfred must still go to school. I said to Paul that, "Life continues to shock us. If I do get detained, please keep these contacts and get in touch with his social worker after my detention." I was going to leave my son behind. It was better for him to remain in Britain if I go. I told Paul to promise me that he would check on him every now and again and to always remind him that I had no choice but to abandon him.

It was on this day that a friend reminded me of the seven-year rule which stated that when a child has been in the country for seven years, they must not be sent back as they will have established their life in Britain. How much more a child with complex health needs? Our seven years in Britain was due in four months, but in my mind, I was seeking compassion more than entitlement, so I didn't go to that meeting with the intention of reminding the officials to check their calendar. Whichever way you look at it, one must obey that seven-year rule (which has now been extended to ten years), for it is simply Britain being a country of morals, a country that understands that every child matters and deserves to be in an environment that brings them joy; uprooting them from a country after over a decade is unfathomable.

I felt helpless, as did Paul. I told him what it would really be like if Alfred returned to Malawi. We both trusted that Britain would look after him in the best way possible.

He would be like the gaunt and lifeless twins I knew in the neighbourhood. Abused and neglected, they watched other children playing and having fun while they were chained to a tree all day long, their father asking people to stone them. He believed they were like that because they were a bad omen.

The memory of how they were locked up has remained with me for many years and I have often enquired about them. Just like them, Alfred would be branded a devil, a curse, and would suffer a horrific scale of discrimination and abuse due to his disabilities, were he to return to Malawi. The harmful practices rooted in traditional beliefs are beyond comprehension.

Paul agreed with my decision.

I approached the immigration centre with Paul standing by my side and handed over my letter. They looked at me, asked Paul who he was and told him he was not allowed in. They were not interested in answering further questions. I felt like a criminal.

Paul said to me, "I will go to the car and make a few calls." I hugged him as the officers watched on. I sensed how helpless he felt, but so was I.

They explained to me in more detail that what it meant was I am liable to be detained. The Secretary of State has deemed it appropriate that I am admitted in the United Kingdom temporarily and emphasised that it must be understood that this is not a grant for leave to remain in the United Kingdom. Although I am temporarily admitted, I remain liable to be detained. They asked where my son was, and I said: "at school". That letter served as temporary admission whilst my case was being looked at and a decision was being made. It required me to stay at my address and they then explained to me that basically, I was to periodically report to that UK Border Agency Office.

If there are people in your life to love and support your dream, you can get through anything. If you come across anyone that needs a hand or even just some kind words, do not hesitate. When I returned to the car, Paul hugged me like I hadn't seen him in years. In the shelter of his wings, I felt comforted.

Ultimately, Paul's fight for us was proven not to be in vain. In my grant for indefinite leave to remain, received in 2010, his noble efforts were greatly acknowledged by the Home Office. In excitement and tears, I called him the very minute I opened my special mail. I told him this was too beautiful to be read to him over the phone. "We need to meet for a group hug," I told him. The whole family was overwhelmed and that evening, his son sent me an email to say my immigration case had brought them closer together as a family because they always had something to update about. The race had come to the finishing line, and I looked forward to another chapter of a friendship, which did not revolve around immigration paperwork.

Many people may reach you in the dark but there is always one precious one, with true strength... who pulls you out, into the marvellous light. Paul was that gentle whisper after the fire. There are no words big enough, no hug strong enough, no smile wide enough. I am so grateful, if I had a thousand tongues, it still would not be enough to express it.

Chapter 15
Take the Wheel

When does struggle end? When does freedom start? Having lived a whole life of constraints… restricted and belittled, I waited day after day, for winds of change to blow. And so, it finally happened. Unshackled, I turned from being grounded to standing my ground no matter the situation. Finally, from having nothing to lose to discovering the fullness in me without measure. I controlled the process, including how much pleasure I gave and that was priceless. Being in control is a privilege that I took to a whole new level. Every day, I raise a glass to freedom.

One day, I woke up from the slumber and I heard the chains falling. Did my world change or was it these adventures from which I emerged as myself? Like a wild animal blazed out to wander astray and explore, I returned to my true nature. Fired up, I realised that no one has more power and authority over me, than me. Not only did I find true fulfilment through my strange new world of sex work, but most importantly, it opened the world to me, and I felt empowered. Every day was a new canvas with a chance to move smarter and better. Having grown up bound, in a horrifying and abusive culture where things were set in stone, and the tradition followed on to my marriage, this freedom was miraculous. It was a childhood of dictatorship… submit or be slaughtered and then a marriage of 'put up and shut up; your job is to do what I tell you to do'. As though I was a lump of clay, they tried to mould me to fit in a narrow box. My unwillingness to submit made me a rebel.

Look at me. I am the captain now and I don't need a licence to play. Every day, I get to fall asleep, knowing that tomorrow I shall wake up with a choice. Each day, I step into a life that makes me feel whole. The more I enjoy myself, the more I desire. When you get to a place where you desire without permission, you are ultimately free. Yes, a new Chapter dawns for me!

It may seem inconceivable, but many aspects of the culture were exploitative by design and focussed solely on objectifying women.

The tormenting theory that we came from a man's rib meant we were confined to one specific thing. To please him. If you didn't possess the required features such as submission and purity, you were not complete or valuable and certainly not 'good-wife' material. How can we be who we are in a world like that, bound by harsh commandments that clip your wings with fear? It is impossible to manifest your true character. Through the darkest hours, not all hope was lost. When you have hope, no matter how thin it may seem – you have the master key to counter the obstacles.

I attempted webcam adult work, but I failed massively because that was not my calling. Given my circumstances, you may say that being an escort was not a choice that I casually made. Let's just say it was a beautiful calling with staggering possibilities, and I defend my position with my last breath. Rather than sitting behind a computer, being instructed by taskmasters how to play with myself and commanded what to do next, as though I am battery powered, a lustful woman like me deserves to be touched, fucked, and explored. Hands are healing; I loved to touch and caress, so I listened to my heart and settled for what I enjoyed most. Timing and tenderness are art. Being an escort showed me so many sides of the performance artist that I am. Not even a million strokes of a paintbrush would paint that art. Character is a luxury I was denied for a so long.

Oh, the gruesome childhood flashbacks! The past is seemingly very near, and it never disappears. I look back in sadness and anger at the confinement. It is a massive awakening to the fact there is restoration for all the years that the destroying locusts had eaten.

When you have been historically denied the expression of anger and you harbour so many secret thoughts; life can be gruesome. Eventually, anger becomes empowering and you guard yourself with utmost vigilance. For the first time in my existence, I felt released. Finally, I was paving my own path, charting my own course and setting my own boundaries whilst creating balance. Indeed, this crushed people's expectations, but I don't mind; I am a lover and a fighter.

Finally, dear readers, I was at the wheel and didn't need to convince anyone that I exist. For once, why can't people be proud of how happy I am? Charting my days and deciding my own workload, I was mesmerised that the decision-making was in my hands. The boundaries were up to me and I was nobody's fool.

Unlike the girl up the street with the haunted ass; everyone fucks it and leaves her with chlamydia, at least I was having life-changing sex by charging for my milkshake. I put heart into everything I do, and I looked good doing it. Every missed call was potential for money calling. There was always someone craving a late fuck… and money is a real panty-dropper. It was a fair, healthy and meaningful trade, with new insights on humanity. Cultured men drove many miles to spend a moment with me, even if just to buy my used panties or take me to the nearest dogging site.

Built to be played with, it was entirely up to me, whether to give a man a quickie or an afternoon delight. Whether to send nudes, have sex, swallow cum, sixty-nine or have a gangbang, it was my choice, to add it all up and take only what I needed. Whether I wanted to spend my evenings having my insides wrecked or on my knees deep throating with some dipping sauce… whatever… and I didn't feel guilty about it. I did so much and still the sky did not fall. Astonishingly, it built me up and filled that void. Whenever I felt stunning and brave enough to withstand the thrilling heat of anal sex, I did it and got extra treats. So much use for a beautiful ass and mouth. I was enjoying my sexual freedoms safely.

I never rush my clients. I would rather do it right than do it quickly, unless of course… it's a quickie.

"If you fantasise it, say it and we will sort it…" From A to Z, there was a whole alphabet of fun to be found in me. Constantly bombarded with calls for sexual desires you cannot imagine, my days were filled with phenomenal adventures. I was mysteriously deep; always with new ideas to explore. We are what we fantasise, and a brilliant hooker is multifaceted. Delightfully chaotic and a beautiful mess; I love it when a kink comes together, into a splendid adventure. Forever craving what we should have had or longed to have had, deep within us is a burning desire… a sexual fantasy to fulfil. Roleplay… my clients' fulfilment hinges on it and I was happy to share myself with the world. It was a privilege to be a full circle of so many enchanting and meaningful characters deeply desired by them. Saying beautiful and harsh things in a teasing and tantalising fashion, they deserved all of me, in whatever role. Usually, I was the leading lady with the total say and that was exciting. Always playing the top, never the bottom. Above only, never beneath. Always the head, never the tail. An auntie. A dirty cousin. Dominant in-law. Horny headmistress. A sexy secretary. A naughty nurse and practising some *'Fifty Shades of Grey'*. The only games I play are in the bedroom.

Some sessions needed surgical gloves and I couldn't list the various things that nearly got stuck in their asses. I didn't always argue or question their ideologies, nor did I have to make sense of the short thrills and fetishes because that was their escape… A beautiful distraction from the real world. Accommodating a variety of these strong but short insights made a difference to my mindset on numerous levels and the passion keeps growing.

Sexually, if you unleash your dark side, there are literally thousands of ideas left to be explored, including many you would have never dreamed of.

Was this survival schedule degrading or damaging to my energy? Alas! Only I can answer this. It was conceived by pain, nonetheless, I never left it because it facilitated opportunities and was empowering and therapeutic. I found the critical aspect of my fight to be humanised. Ironically, mine was a sad and sorry world because of the hand that was dealt to me. I had to find a way, somehow… to survive in a challenging and ever-changing world. As a true performer and born survivor, I turned despair into hope and made a speciality of the challenge. I became an extraordinary escort.

Find your happy place, fight to stay there and keep rowing. Constantly reinvent yourself, without giving a fuck. I was not only giving so much; I was achieving so much. No one had more power and authority over me, than me. With so many moments of tenderness, I was unfolding myself and discovering who I was. I recreated my world, discovered my purpose and this empowered me to grow, learn and make a positive difference.

Discovery in any form is thrilling and echoes our life forever. I embraced the freedom to design my own birds with different adaptations – falcons, sparrows, eagles. On eagle's wings – strong, empowered, sharp and soaring high over mountaintops. Finally, my own life was exciting to watch. From a mess to a message, I became a gift, a choice, a voice to share with the world.

If you think you are in a mess, think again. I was in a jigsaw, pressed on every side. But because I had enthusiasm, I was not crushed. My life is no longer a mystery that was hidden for ages. Assuredly marked for greatness, not all ego is bad. After the storms, I can boldly say: "Things can only get better." There is not much to unpack because yesterday is gone. Learning from past failings can be infuriating, so just forget your last step and focus on your next, but this time use some wisdom so that you don't stumble and fall. It's a leap of faith, but why not! Faith meshed with strength and courage is the powerful way of connecting with your future and it gives you the lens to see great opportunities and act on them. Don't be a hostage; recreate something in you, that life serves you better and your future shines brighter.

I don't want anybody in my life who doesn't want to be there, because they are an unfolding calamity. Take it from me because I swear by it; just let yourself be. After all, every moment, people are judging you silently, sometimes loudly. Be fearlessly authentic. It's okay to live in your truth, whether people approve of it or not. Be courageous and unapologetic about who you are and how you live your life. Stop lusting for acceptance and focus on what you know to be true, not so much on how anyone perceives you. It's your life's journey. Don't proceed on a path that has been laid out for you. Chart it yourself and start living the life you love, with your own compass and you at the wheel. Now I have the wheel, I am on the right track and will never again bend out of shape to suit the masses.

You are in a great place when you are walking your own path, and there can be no regrets. Everything flows. When you are growing and healing, there is no room for regrets. I did my best and couldn't change anything because the only way was through. And I did it my way.

Other than be ignorant at the expense of others, why can't people shove the drama, cruelty, bullying and pettiness up their fucking asses? If only we could recognise the power of one's free choices, we would be more tolerant. Sultry hookers have become a staple in many lives. They have a plan you can trust and enjoy. The right one is engaging... enormously entertaining, convincing and keeps men balanced. With a track record of getting the job done without cutting corners, hookers prove time and time again, that they are forces to be reckoned with.

Chapter 16
Torture Chamber

Since childhood, my love and yearning for Britain intensified due to my love for Diana, Princess of Wales. The dazzling smile and sparkle in her eyes! She was everyone's princess, the princess of all nations, not a typical princess but a typical queen with royal love, a role model to all humans. Her wings and healing hands spanned across the world and grabbed onto millions. An essence of love, brave and beautiful inside and out, her death was a loss to the world and the monarchy. The precious seeds that she planted in her boys germinated into the gracious men that we see today. An icon who knew how to set an example. The strength and courage she had, to make the world a better place, was astounding. My favourite childhood memory... I spent many days in the library at the British Council, inhaling books and magazines of the princess, her tiaras, her grace, her beautiful gowns and in my own little naïve world of wonderland. I was completely swept up into her seemingly magical life and dreamt of the day I would go to that great land, Britain, where there dwells the most pure, gentle and sweet soul that has ever laid feet on this planet.

Terror within, terror without, when was the last time the world felt normal to you? Ever felt so right that you just know it's a temporary state of normality? Despite the obstacles that were put in her way – suffering from bulimia, depression and self-harming as she struggled to keep it together and live up to the expectations of the monarch – looking at her life, we can perhaps recognise our own somewhat desperate and terrifying situations. But amid all that suffering, a true humanist is still capable of feeling the pain and suffering of others. As you see the word 'suffering', what great attributes does your life display? Love? Inspiration? Sympathy? Compassion? Or are you just vaingloriously preoccupied with arrogance and slaying on social media, thirsty for fake praise and kisses online? That is a low life. The higher life considers others and affects the world in a positive way.

My father was obsessed with *BBC* radio and although all he could receive was a rattling channel, he still sat by his tiny radio for news on the day of that most horrific news, when the world cried for losing an utterly brilliant and enormously caring woman. Who can forget the heartbreak of that premature and catastrophic death? Alas, it was a valley of tears. Rest in glory, Diana! You left the world too soon, yet I hope you have found peace at last, from the hurt and turmoil. You are forever the Queen of Hearts and twenty-two years on, that is the reason you live on in the hearts of many around the globe.

Meanwhile, in Britain, due to having no work permit and no entitlement to state benefits, in my desperate need, I relied on the help of the British Red Cross food bank, East Manchester. This was where a shameless man in the storeroom bagged and handed over our food parcels, but fondled us first, and then if we declined, we would return home, from the food bank, with nothing. I have a lump in my throat writing this. He didn't care that we had children to feed, he was just a sexual predator, his priority was caressing big African bottoms and breasts, rather than giving us aid, and in this environment, he had access to plenty. The measure of the food parcel tallied with what part he fondled. I saw a bottle of olive oil on the shelf which I kindly asked for and he wanted to touch me under my skirt for that. Take it or leave it. He caused so much anguish to so many women in need. No wonder so little of the money raised reaches those disaster zones and the only recourse open to the vulnerable and needy is to just pretend it isn't happening.

After a lengthy chat with one of the sincerely dedicated staff at the organisation, it dawned on me that they were not aware of the sexual harassment that was going on in the storeroom. Whatever action was taken, that was the last I saw of the abuser. Due to having no access to public funds, they further considered my child's welfare and made a referral under section 17 of the Children's Act 1989, local authorities have a duty to safeguard and promote the welfare of children in exceptional circumstances... such as disabilities and other special needs... whilst awaiting a decision from the Home Office.

I was not the only victim at this house of horrors. Many immigrants who had no access to funds, have a harrowing story of irrevocable damage to tell. By the time you are granted leave to remain, they make sure you are worn down with long and deep emotional scars. At the core of this was the xenophobic, racial exclusion theory of 'go back to where you come from', which was cruel and torturous by nature. People would seriously 'build that wall' if given the chance. The invisible walls are in fact more damaging because they treat you like another ungrateful immigrant despite being the most grateful.

It is a reasonable expectation that power must be matched with compassion, but in this case, interacting with this obnoxious team was excruciatingly painful on every level. This team of arrogant bullies considered this brutality to be acceptable. Hence, they swept everything I brought to the surface under the carpet and covered up for each other's vile behaviour. They felt superior, indispensable and beyond reproach. They faced no consequences and they carried on working… with no moral compass. Their every action and interaction were aimed to abuse and disrespect.

It's a long road, if not impossible for an immigrant to challenge systemic failings and the abuse of power by those in higher ranks, at the very heart of the state. The distressing realities and harrowing experiences lay bare the urgency of change. Yes, I tried. I tried to voice out the appalling ordeals and today, still on the road to recovery, I seek to pass my strength on to anyone who suffered in silence at the hands of William, the chief tormenter and his enablers.

Bearing in mind that even in the most civilised of countries, the world can be a very unequal place when you are an immigrant. Despite having unbelievable strength, it was almost impossible to defend myself from these appalling injustices. How can we dismantle inequality, when others feel that certain people are not worthy of any kindness or respect? No matter what we do differently, we should be bound together in what makes us the same.

Thank you to those true humanists who reach out to engage in solidarity with the underprivileged and the oppressed. You work hard, to get people justice, against incredible odds. You continue to highlight the difficulties and keep the momentum of change going.

Dear William,

Perhaps a decade is a long time, but then again, maybe not. The wheels of time turn on, but it is still current, heartbreaking and unforgivable. The way you punished, humiliated and treated migrants cruelly forever pains me; we could not run away from the terror because we needed help. You made it painfully obvious that you felt inconvenienced by us. Evil is a strong word, but it's the right one. I and many others were at the receiving end of your abuse. It should never have happened. You made it your mission to pursue a hostile environment… and we were expected to accept it. You boasted how harshly you treated migrant service users and "keep them where they belong"? I would still want to know where that is! In the gutter? Please do tell. You and your team were revolting and downright repulsive. How could you endorse and facilitate such discrimination, and be so comfortable with it? We trust Britain to do what is right, but you didn't radiate anything that they stand for. You were feckless all the way. History will revile you for the waves of abuse that you put us through. Your unquenchable need to torment us led me to believe that cruel and calculative people like yourselves will always desire to work with those in vulnerable circumstances – the defenceless and the voiceless – so that you can manifest your abuse and conceal it in unison.

We are all freedom fighters in our own right; compromise is what drives us upward and forward. No matter the question, kindness is the answer. I sometimes wonder if what I did was enough. I dared to be powerful, I dared to defend myself and others, and you turned up your torture temperature so high, just to inflict more pain. You degraded us. You took so much. We may never completely heal from your blatant, cold discrimination. You got off scot-free and remained employed.

On behalf of those you treated inhumanely, just know that we were not sleepwalking through life; we were awake, and we were hurting. Shame on you!

Sandra Ntonya.

I wanted to highlight this injustice to my MP, of the torture chamber that existed in the local authority, but he already had enough on his plate, so I had to walk this adversity alone. My immigration case that he was dealing with was the core of my dream, my hopes and my son's future.

At my first appointment after the referral, I met Susan, who immediately said to me, "I see you are from Malawi."

"That's right," I said.

"I have been there," she said disgustingly. "Horrible place and people; the customs and excise charged me unfairly, so don't expect any smiles from me."

"I am sorry on their behalf and my heart goes out to you."

She said, "Don't bother. I hate anything to do with Malawi."

I tried to make conversation with her, to calm her down. "Had this occurred when you had been in Malawi on holiday or with work?"

"Oh, never mind," she said. "At least you know where I stand with Malawi and its people."

She was very angry, vile, harsh and brutal throughout the interview (or interrogation, depending on how you want to put it). She lacked humanity. I was desperate for help, so I stayed on. I was there for help. She wanted to get her own back on Malawi and sought to take it out on me. I didn't want any more trauma. The physical and mental scarring from my son's father was still fresh. I was humble to her. I submitted, but that only seemed to spur her on.

There was no avoiding this woman: I had to meet with her every fortnight to collect a food voucher to cash in at the Manchester Town Hall. That meant it was wave after wave of abuse from Susan and her team.

Even though Alfred was aged four at this time, he was still in nappies and frequently attended medical appointments because his challenging needs were extending deeper and deeper beyond what I could afford. For his wellbeing, we needed extra help, but William was deeply resentful that I even wasted his time discussing the wellbeing of a black child. Incredibly insensitive, the racism was beyond offensive, but deeply harmful. Susan told her line manager to assist her in making it loud and clear to me that, "It's not our fault that you have a disabled child. That's none of our business. You are not the only one with a disabled child. It's your child so get on with it." Salt rubbed into the wound! Did I need a constant reminder?

I wanted them to behave legally, within their powers. As an assimilated migrant, I feel I know what Britain stands for, and this was not it! Britain is a community that promises to treat everyone humanely and equally regardless of race, sex, ethnicity, disability, gender identity, religion or national origin. Surely it should be an absolute honour and privilege to truly reflect and represent this awesome country, but there is always that rotten apple who represents Britain in a very inhumane way and gives it an awful image. If not for the local authority, who will meet the humanitarian obligations and maintain values? It was co-ordinated bullying; they simply do not stand for or speak for this great country with its great constitution and great powers.

Nothing can improve without first accepting that improvements need to be made. Be a freedom fighter in your own right. I was reliant on their handouts for food but still, I saw so much and was ready to shout it from the rooftop. Evil thrives in darkness. Do the needful and shine light on any darkness. I raised the detailed profile of the brutality to the council bosses and the Principle Manager

Carlton, whom I met twice, so that he could potentially stop more abuse. My truth, my pain and on behalf of other service users… everything flayed out, and that wasn't easy. Crying for reason, my voice echoed and faded to nothing. Speaking the truth, no matter how difficult, … is necessary. I suggested to the Principle Manager that he conducts a survey to at least prove the gravity of the abuse because many who were suffering in silence pleaded with me to not name them. His response seemed promising. He accepted that the issues I raised were serious, but he failed me and many others. As with most things where inequality and injustices exist, his outrage died as soon as I turned my back. Everyone escaped accountability and the abuse continued. Dismissing my concerns, I took that to be Carlton's endorsement of the hostility towards immigrants. They want the power, but none of the responsibility that comes with it.

When I returned for my next review, unashamedly, they had allocated me a different caseworker, another one who believed that that immigrants deserve to suffer, and she took it upon herself to carry on where her colleague left off. I was pushed to the side and it was covered up. A catalogue of failure by civil servants who felt no need for universal standards to be upheld, let alone humanise immigrants.

One woman I met outside, was sobbing after her review. Confused after she had been bullied and stripped of her dignity. With a deep sigh of anger, I felt helpless too. Another woman with two kids, scared, balled up into a corner… crying, she told me how harshly she had been treated. Instead of supported, many were left feeling helpless and depressed.

Violators of the law and those who abuse their powers in office are quite good with whitewash… to cover up, but the truth prevails over the darkness, no matter how many coats they apply. Apart from devastating lives and silencing voices, they did as little as they could. For seven years, I witnessed so much and heard some tragic accounts. My aim was not to expose them, but to promote fairness and justice so that they tackle their despicable failings accordingly, but every door was slammed as they applied more layers of whitewash, to cover up for one another. This team exclusively dealt in evil.

Dogs bark when they sense danger, but these dogs were barking up the wrong trees because we did absolutely nothing wrong to deserve such resistance. We were not rebellious, domineering or posing a threat to anyone. I have always been one for defending the British culture and its values, with a willingness to assimilate and be absorbed into its traditions of the land, for the good of everyone. It is a privilege to live in a democracy that respects the rule of law and the principles that underpin it and is committed to its defence. Integration is what connects to greater acceptance and peace into our lives. It saddens me when certain immigrants don't want to integrate and despise everything that Britain stands for; hence why my most unpopular opinion is that people should either assimilate or go back whence you came from... because they are a distraction to the safety and wellbeing of a great country.

When I went back and updated the British Red Cross, I was urged to be strong and courageous because a lot of service users under that team do go through heartache and pain. They just chat to each other about it with no one daring to make a complaint against them, so this was supposed to be a breakthrough to cause change. I asked other victims if they wanted us to make a joint complaint, but they all feared it would add worsen things. They were right, because that is exactly what I got after my official complaint: torture. Anyone that got in their way or disagreed with them had a huge storm coming. It cannot properly be described to those who have never been in that situation, but when you are awaiting a decision on your immigration application, there is usually nothing else to discuss apart from immigration! The one thing that gets your attention in life during that time is the topic of immigration; because your life depends on it, it consumes you. This sounds kind of fatalistic and maybe it is, because there is no profound way of how to fix it.

After so many experiences, I observed that there are many gaps and failings in the implementation of local authority and company policies regarding sexual harassment, abuse of power, unethical behaviour and other behaviours that lead to violations of human rights – but who is responsible for putting mechanisms in place that ensure a professional assessment of all actions taken to date? In my experience, 'nobody', because people in positions of trust want only to cover their colleagues, and that leads to blind eyes in the establishment.

Talking of failings by people in positions of trust, to execute their duties properly, turning blind eyes and deaf ears, discrimination and prejudice, in my experience, the Rotherham scandal doesn't surprise me one bit! A court heard that a gang allegedly spent more than a decade targeting and sexualising teenage girls in Rotherham before subjecting them to horrific acts of a degrading and violent nature.

Why did it not shock me when the scandal emerged? I know the toxic mindset of those in power that led to this failing because I have been failed before. These victims from troubled homes or living in children's homes were 'not worthy' of being protected. My heart goes out to them.

On 14 June 2017, the Grenfell Tower fire broke out at the twenty-four-storey block of public housing flats in North Kensington, Royal Borough of Kensington and Chelsea, North London. It caused seventy-two deaths, including one stillbirth and over seventy injuries. An independent review of the building regulations and fire safety is in progress because the rapid growth of the fire is thought to have been due to the building's exterior cladding.

As a Housing Association tenant, the last time the electrics were checked, the contractors clearly said the electric is in a shambles, but it's a pain to do all over again, so you must just be careful. That is how heartless and inhumane people are willing to go in their pursuit to cut costs and corners at the cost of lives. I, for one, wonder if this was the mindset that killed the seventy-two – a pure act of terrorism. May their souls rest in peace! It was on this day that fear gripped me even more concerning my own 'shambles' accommodation, as the contractors put it. They sign it off as safe while they take off and never look behind them at the hazard they left, a hazard that could potentially cost lives. I carry on being careful even though I don't really know how, as they carry on as normal and sleep in their safe homes.

It takes one person with no regard for human life, especially the lives of immigrants, to ignore something that may potentially destroy lives, as if we are undeserving of life. It takes one person who does not give a damn what other people's futures hold, to sign off hazardous jobs as 'safe'. I have been there. I have been shocked, and now I hope to rewire it someday because I am a leaseholder. Eastland's Homes themselves dismissed my complaint.

Finally, I got my leave to remain on compassionate grounds, so I did not have to deal with William's vile team anymore. I still felt for those voiceless people that were still suffering the same grief.

In vengeance for all my complaints through the years, they got in touch with a man they knew at the Manchester City Council Town Hall demanding that I go and see him. I went to the meeting, which was personal, not official. This man Trevor yelled at me that he had noticed that I lived in a council house and he knows British people who are homeless. "Today, you will be homeless like most are!"

Then he told me to sign some forms to hand over my tenancy. I asked him where I was supposed to go with a child. "What have I done wrong? I am not in arrears. I am law-abiding and never a nuisance. I have never breached my tenancy. The house is adapted for my disabled son; why have you made this decision so suddenly?"

"There are hostels that will accommodate your child," he said dismissively. "Just sign here. I have things to do."

This happened under the roof of Manchester City Town Hall, corruption right before my eyes, hoping that immigrant is an imbecile who will sign any dotted line. Shocking. I interrupted his plan and his conversation made it clear that he had been instructed by William and his team, to make me homeless for standing up for justice. He wanted to evict me because I had made a complaint about his colleagues. There was no investigation and they will never know.

Trevor got away with it. However, our meeting didn't end well for him, as I refused to sign his form.

Fortunately, a housing association was taking over from the local authorities and I emailed the Chief Executive to explain the circumstances.

They were very helpful, the injustice corruption infuriated them because I was a secure tenant for over a decade and the local authorities tried to evict me because they wanted vengeance for my complaints about them. As soon as they realised that they would be caught out, Trevor called me back to the town hall and said, "Okay, you can stay in the house because I have taken pity on you." Too emotional to say anything, I just walked out with pain.

Being granted my leave to remain meant the end of this tormenting era, but I still felt that it was my responsibility to bring them to account. I contacted the local ombudsman office, not for self-interest or to spread the news far and wide but for them to investigate and stop further abuse. I thought it was a safe space to speak. I thought it was never too late for justice. Initially, they assured me that they would allocate an investigator, and then suddenly they said it was too late for an investigation.

In the end, you wondered how many people get away with severe injustices and never an acknowledgement of their brutality. Something had to change. The hideous network had to be broken. Behaviours had to be adjusted and new codes of conduct brought in. Otherwise, these people would continue to misrepresent Britain. When people talk of grave systematic failures that leave behind an awful impact, I can relate, but where does one go when everywhere is a dead end and doors are slammed in the face?

In April 2012, in the best interests of justice, I contacted the Local Government Ombudsman (LGO) in what would be designated Case ID 11023517. In fourteen emails to the LGO, attaching copies of all my complaints to the council bosses, I highlighted the alarming bullying, their cruelty and total disregard for immigrants' human rights, in the hope that they would hear my cry and investigate the undue pain and suffering we had to endure. These people, this office, had used their power in a way that was manifestly unfair, and I was one of those seriously oppressed by their conduct. All their ways were contrary to what you would expect from a local authority in Britain. So many things happened, including things that were unnecessarily intrusive and beyond ridiculous, a total breach of human rights. To these bullies, immigrants awaiting their residence permit are those whose human rights are least deserving of protection, and so the breach of privacy was a laughing matter to them.

The LGO was the furthest I could go. Are they lazy or uninterested? They need a real shake-up as they simply said the time had passed for an investigation. There will never be justice and most importantly, changes and closure. I wanted this to be the absolute last possible moment that these civil servants abuse again. Nobody should be subjected to them ever again. A few years too late for justice are not only shocking and pitiful. It is an approach so dangerous in a modern democracy.

From the other side, it's very easy to say, "don't look back in anger" but nothing is understood, until it is felt. Some trauma we carry for the rest of our lives… and yes… I do look back in sadness and anger.

Chapter 17
No Work Permit, Just Love

Back before I received my leave to remain, I worked hard to get a job in a care home for the elderly, after a few people had told me that it's the only place they do not strictly ask for a work permit; they consider what matters the most. "You are so caring and that is the utmost importance. If you work hard and look after the residents with kindness, you will be alright," I was told.

I made a few applications, sat a few interviews and was successful in all of them. The world needs people who demonstrate that they will deliver excellent care to the vulnerable. I was spoiled for choice for places to work, so I went for the one closer to home. I earned less than one hundred pounds a week. Nonetheless, it covered my rent, gas, electric and food, survival of the fittest.

The manager was great, and the residents were interesting. I was much loved, they simply loved to be around me. Be the charisma and enthusiasm that people want to be around. We talked, laughed a lot and they always asked when I would be back on shift. They felt safe around me, saying thank you unceasingly as the other staff eyed me badly because I went more than the extra mile. I worked nights, so I only saw the manager briefly.

One day I went to work for my night shift and was surprised to see my manager's car still there, because I usually only saw her in the mornings. She came to the door with a sad face and I wondered what had happened. It didn't look good.

"I'm sorry," she exclaimed nervously. "I can't let you in. Your husband was here this afternoon threatening to report us to the Home Office for employing you without a work permit… I can't afford the hefty fine… I am sorry I will have to let you go."

As I stood there, too limp to say anything, one of the residents, Evelyn who always lifted my spirit came to the door and said, "I told the others that you were working tonight."

I couldn't face her.

Facing my manager, I told her, "Thanks."

I heard Evelyn ask my manager, "Is she not coming in?"

That was a painful end to an all-too-brief era.

I had left Alfred with a lady who was expecting me to give her some money at the end of that week. My world was already in tatters. Struck by sudden lightning… fear, anger and helplessness, that's all I felt as I sat at the bus stop and watched the world go by.

Right in front of me, things were falling apart. I had a life to defend and protect. My little boy… This was our only safety net. This time he took our daily bread and tossed it to the wolves. And I was so sorry. Our livelihood snatched away from us by his own father. I have never felt more hurt in my life.

Oh, the painful reality of life! Feeling the bitter sting of poverty, whilst I was earning a living… grinding hard without assistance, I wanted nothing more than to feed his own son. He was finding a way to burn my job and increase my suffering. How much more was I supposed to endure?

***

I was moved out of that hazardous room we shared, into a small ground floor flat that was specially adapted for a disabled person. At last our little sanctuary, it was miraculous. It had just become available on a cul-de-sac and had two bedrooms and a communal garden. It was so vital to have this little space because topped up with weekly physio and hydrotherapy, Alfred made outstanding progress. Getting closer and closer to one day, he started to walk, until sitting him down became a challenge. Watching him walk creates belief in everything that got him up and reminds me just how incredibly privileged we are to be here and how we must not cease to be eternally grateful.

Once we had moved in, what we considered a blessing, someone thought was a curse. The elderly lady next door never responded at my greeting. She just stared in raw anger and disgust. One day as she spoke with another lady so obviously loud, "I can't believe how the bloody Council had me down. At least you don't have a coloured neighbour. If they don't move me, I'm getting private accommodation." I felt alienated and upset.

Lorna, in her seventies, whom I later became good friends with, assured, "They seem alright, at least she speaks good English. That will do me."

One day, I was cooking whilst Alfred played outside. With no speech, he couldn't tell me what was wrong, but he sounded distressed and made ambulance noises. I assumed he heard an ambulance, but he started pulling me to go outside, still making the noises. I expected to see an ambulance, but I saw it was the lady upstairs, with almost her last breath, underneath her voice shouting, "Help… help!" It was a harrowing sight. With a big cut on her head and blood everywhere, she was in her dressing gown, trapped and squashed in a gate which was locked. In such shock and pain, she just about managed to say, "I came out to get my post. I missed a step."

Alfred had already brought the phone before I went in and got it. Urgently, I rang the ambulance. The iron gate had to be cut before they could get to her and save her life. As she left in the ambulance on the stretcher, the medics thanked Alfred for a job well done. She was in hospital for a while. We didn't see much of her when she came back and not a word until she moved. Sadly, in her alternative universe, it was NOT the coloured boy she detested who saved her just in time.

Within the same year, another neighbour moved out because her two sons had become very friendly with Alfred. Innocently, they asked me why Alfred could not speak, and they insisted they would teach him. The three of them spent some time at the fence chatting and laughing with him and I would always hear their mother shout them back in, saying, "I have warned you. Don't go near that boy!"

They had a trampoline that was no fun on their own. They wanted Alfred's company, but their mother wouldn't allow it. Rejection is rough, and it has an impact on so many parts of your life. By this time, I was not just surviving; I was living. My tight budget could afford a trampoline for Alfred, but some things are not meant for sharing. It wouldn't be any fun on his own.

Alfred had problems with his jaw and was under the care of an orthodontist, awaiting an operation. There was also the permanent damage to the underside of his tongue, where he had been brutally cut as a baby. As mentioned previously, it was a traditional ritual that made no sense but was beyond my control and he drooled excessive saliva due to this.

Seeing her boys, Brook and Philip, playing with Alfred in the communal garden made their vicious mother angrier. One day, upon hearing her boys crying because she smacked them whilst screaming down their throats… reminding them of the restrictions of playing with Alfred, it made my blood boil that a mother was segregating our children and taking away their right to play. As someone with a history of abuse, and as someone still recovering…

other people screaming and raising their voice absolutely terrifies me. I knocked on her door and pleaded with her, "Please don't ever, ever smack your kids in my son's name. Put our colour aside and stop tormenting the kids. My son is sad. Your boys are even sadder. What is wrong with you?"

With pride and ego, she rang her brother, claimed that I had harassed her and asked him to beat me up. Within minutes, he pulled into the cul-de-sac in a black car at near 70 mph and was ultimately rather embarrassed to find no show of anger from me. All he said was for me to leave my sister and the kids alone. Then he drove off at normal speed. The housing association tried to resolve the matter via a mediation team, but it needed both parties to be willing to participate and she chose to move to a new house instead of being friendly. It was easier than to have her boys play with a black disabled boy.

It was lovely to have new neighbours in both these houses. I started to see the extraordinary human decency in the land.

Chapter 18
Twice Aborted, Twice Strong

I almost didn't exist!

I checked my schedule and realised I had work to do; to be fruitful and multiply. Yes, I was too important to lose.

It was not until my early twenties that I learned how I was thick-skinned even before I was born. After my mother conceived, not even an abortion could handle me. Still I am pro-abortion. If pro-choice means anything, I am just that, and I will not apologise for it, to those who believe that life begins at conception. I am pro-family, pro-parenting, pro-adoption and above all, pro-ownership of your own body. Pro-deciding your own destiny... and the abortion stigma no longer serves us! It is a vital medical procedure and a social good.

I am the living proof that using the withdrawal method is a sure-fire way to have an unplanned pregnancy. As well as the rhythm method. How could my mother be pregnant if my father was so careful not to ejaculate inside her? He insisted that he knew nothing about this conception and forced her to have an abortion.

The house was on anger fire as he screamed the place down and my mother was scrutinised. "It can't be mine. Go to the man who is responsible for this. It can't be me!" She had no choice but to go to her doctor for an abortion.

Her doctor, upon seeing my mother in dire stress and having heard the circumstances and threats, reassured her all would be well. He did what had to be done. He gave my mother an abortion pill with a guarantee. "I swear by this, by sunset, you will be bleeding heavily."

For two days, nothing came out. I hung in the uterus, going nowhere, and my father at this time was threatening to leave my mother. All she wanted to see was blood and it wasn't happening.

My father, nicknamed 'Idi Amin' in the community, was a vicious and dictatorial figure with extreme mood swings, we lived our entire life in crippling fear. A monstrous man who mercilessly tortured us, he exerted power and control over everyone, he was conceivably a god. We flinched and crumbled with terror when he entered the room. It was the ultimate home of pain and suffering. We were beaten at the tiniest infractions, until he inflicted painful wounds and we hand no choice. Tears down my face. He had a rifle and threatened us at any given opportunity. We always tried to obey in advance, but each day, the time bomb was set to blow any second. We lived under constant fear of the sudden beatings, he scared the life out of us. On our bodies, we are left with many scars of his violence, as well as the psychological trauma. When he stormed to his room in anger, he was either getting his rifle or the hosepipe which was cut to size for thrashing us. Those parents who admired his level of cruelty but were incapable, brought in their children for this abuse and discipline.

Shackled and abused, my spirit was yearning to be free, loved and hugged. In my innocent mind, I had an imaginary stable and happy family and in my darkest moments, I sat by the broken fence for many years, hoping that they would come and find me and take me away from the storm. Every person deserves a place they can feel safe. I didn't get that as a child.

Nothing more than a domestic servant, my restrained mother's life was solely reliant on my father's opinion and orders. It takes a lot of submitting to get to that entrapment. Dictators will "drug" you into a vulnerable state to comply. They ensure you become dependent on them as your main source of hydration and they make sure you die of thirst when you speak out.

The pestilence of torture was harrowing. There was no clinging to my mother because her duty was to appease her barbaric husband at any cost. To keep her dark marriage, she not only watched from the stands but contributed to the enhancement of the abuse. He went so far and stooped so low to maintain absolute dominance. When someone has physical, mental and emotional power over you, it's almost impossible to think logically. He did not believe that she had been to the doctors at all. It was a furious race against time, and he demanded she go back. The doctor was shocked to see her back in. The pill he had given was designed to destroy the embryo with one dose. He gave my mother a second dose and promising her once again that it would work.

There are many pains in life, but this was the most painful wait for my mother. As soon as my father came home from work, he just wanted to be to be told the *good news.*

Considering that I have been detested for having a disabled son by the very man who should have walked through this valley with me, I could relate to what a grim time this must have been for my mother. The atmosphere was awful. She must have felt alone and afraid. Her marriage was on the rocks.

My father's anger calmed by each day that passed, and one day he pardoned my mother… Yes, pardoned her for his own ejaculation! On 17 November 1980, they had me. One thing is certain, deep in their hearts, they agreed that a tide arose that lifted all the boats. I turned out to be the cornerstone in the family, the helper, the unselfish one, the generous one, forever faithful, loving and caring, the mediator, advocate, comforter and counsellor, to bring the family together in all disputes. When their exam results were terrifyingly bad, I was always assisting my siblings with their homework. I was the pick-me-up in times of trouble.

Realistically, I was not born. I was knitted. I was spared to spare others. Nonetheless, rather than receiving it with grace, my gentle heart was exploited. My siblings shot arrows of strife, wickedness and division, envy and bitterness. I was always watching their back while they stabbed mine.

Like a haunted house, my parents were all for division and felt more comfortable to see us jumping at each other's throats. If for a moment the tension and hostility calmed down, they didn't know how to react… They were suspicious of what we might be brewing up, so they triggered a fight immediately.

Childhood shapes us. My son and I share something painfully huge. Abandoned, unwanted and detested. Our traumatic early lives gave us the 'opportunity' to turn bitter and heartless, but the courageous are still willing to love. We never closed our hearts. We turned out to be such conciliatory humans, because anger and bitterness get you nothing – gets you nowhere. It is better to have loved, than not.

I was a foetus that proved to be resistant to the toxic pill that sought to terminate me. I must have been thick-skinned. I walked through a valley of the shadow of death and was not harmed. I walked through the fire and it did not burn me. I must have been clothed with more wonder working its power. I must have had an advocate within me, strengthening me and fighting on my behalf that I remain whole. The substance was lethal to a foetus by design, but I was shielded and preserved at my most delicate moment. Even the shredded survive.

It's not unreasonable to say this was unforgivable but suddenly I realised that what didn't kill me made me stronger, so I continue to walk on in victory, knowing I am a survivor and can endure all things. Where is the love? What mother does that? Would you abuse your children to impress your husband at all costs to stay married? Clearly, I wouldn't. A distinction without a difference? The circumstances revealed she was cruel too. Applauding evil makes you evil.

When I am faced with any challenge, I don't magnify the problem. The tests and trials become bearable because I magnify my ability to conquer it, and that works wonders for me. We have all encountered challenges in our lives which seemed unpleasant at that time, but everything yields an expansion of being. No experience is wasted, including the pain.

Struck down but not destroyed. When crushed, pain brought out the flavour and sweet perfume which was savoured by many. This chaotically beautiful fragrance was conceived from pain. This ocean of wisdom derived from a pain that made me stronger.

Whatever was meant to harm you – be it harsh words, rejection, cruelty or betrayal, draw strength from it. Only you can let your inner strength shine like a beacon in the darkness. They pushed me down, I went higher. They backstabbed me, I landed on my feet. They even tried to knock me down with a baseball bat and it simply passed through me.

I was brought to life by my haters. They hate it.

"The bubble would have eventually burst, one way or another!" some would say. Well, their malice accelerated the bubble popping.

Surviving two abortion attempts feels like I dodged two bullets. I am a survivor, and this is another of my incredible story behind my strength and courage. It's been a long road, but miraculously, here I am, providing action-packed unlimited play for adults, delivering a truly personal service in a truly personal way. Most importantly, I almost didn't exist, now my existence is not only known, but chronicled.

Chapter 19
The Brothels

The rubber stamp in my passport, its terms and conditions! Employment and recourse to public funds were strictly prohibited and my application, compassionately supported by my Member of Parliament was "currently awaiting further consideration" … for close to a decade. I was in dire need of money, with a mouth to feed beyond my own, let alone sustain a living. My MP asked the Home Office on my behalf if I could at least be given a work permit to get a job and support my child. A quick reply, "NO," came back from the Home Secretary.

Realistically, the skill to accumulate money is the most profitable. Seeing as I was destitute, and she often helped me out, including with sanitary towels, one day, a Good Samaritan in the community suggested that I get a job at a massage parlour. At this rate, I didn't want *easy*. I just needed *possible*, and I would work out my own formula. "They may not ask you for a work permit and usually they are short of black girls," she said. I told her that I had never given a massage in my life and wouldn't know what to do. Surely, I would need some sort of training? I went to an internet café down the road and took down the phone numbers of many massage parlours.

As it turned out, the first number I rang, the pleasant manager Trisha asked if I could start that night! They said, "I actually need a girl for tonight; I have been asked for a black girl all week and even a few times today. You will kill it here, girl!" To my shock, I was asked my bra size and then the weirdest yet crucial question: "Do you swallow? Do you do A-Levels? And most importantly, do you do ORAL WITHOUT?" I needed a translator in this foreign, kinky language.

Swallow… sperm. A for anal, because that is some level. Suck it raw… without… a rubber because some dicks go floppy at the sight of a condom, the only way to resurrect it is indeed without.

People apply for jobs, go through the interview process and wait a few weeks in anticipation… they either get denied or accepted. They follow up and still don't get a response, worse still, they see the same job post advertised again. It's disheartening and contributes to trust issues.

My job was just one phone call away! I aced the two-minute interview and was employed in a twinkle of an eye.

In her desperation for a NEW girl, because it was good for their business, she told me that it didn't matter. I was told to arrive at the parlour an hour early, to talk me through the process. I was excited that there was no mention of passport, visa, or work permit. Desperate meets desperate. It was time to resume my duties.

There I was, on a dark and damp evening, on my way to Chorlton to a place called Vanessa's. I had written the address down in my diary and when I couldn't spot the sightless door, I asked a lady at the bus stop nearby if she knew the place. She didn't. Next, a man said, "I think it's over there."

I gazed where he was pointing but must have thought I was blind because I still I couldn't see it. In a nearby chip shop, one of the staff members was more than happy to leave the counter to take me there. On the way, he asked me, "Are you working all night? I will book you when I finish work; I am one of their best regulars."

I remember thinking to myself he would rightly need a massage after a hectic long day of standing, cooking, frying. (I hope, dear reader, you are smiling at my innocence!) Eyeing me up and down, he pressed the buzzer for me and left as I was buzzed in. No wonder, I couldn't see the entrance… It was a backdoor!

A leap in the dark is a giant leap of faith.

I received a warm welcome from Trisha who told me that all the girls were busy in the rooms. All I could smell was cigarette smoke as she puffed away in my face.

"You will kill it here, girl!" she repeated her words from the phone conversation. "Especially if you do oral, even better if you swallow!"

I asked her if she will teach me how to give a massage and she looked puzzled. Before she could respond, another lady came down a set of stairs, wearing what I then learned to be holdups, fishnet stockings and a baby-doll dress.

My heart started racing. I had never seen this in my life.

Then another girl came in half-naked with towels in her hands, describing how difficult the man who had just left had been. *What in the world is going on here?* I thought. I was in a maze, wandering, scared yet intrigued – and that dreaded word 'passport' still hasn't been mentioned.

"What's your name, bebe?" Trisha asked.

"Sandra," I told her.

"Is that the name you want to go by, bebe? That's not a lovely sounding name. It doesn't make you sexy."

She asked the other girls to find me a name and I told them, "I may not realise that you're talking to me if you don't call me by my real name."

"We will call you Cassandra; that alright, bebe?"

Of course, I said yes. I was at entry level.

At least the name had Sandra in it. *That will be easy*, I thought to myself.

"You can get ready," she said. "The night girls should be coming in soon."

I followed one girl to the kitchen and asked her, "Is it difficult giving a massage? I have never done it."

"Have you never worked, bebe?" she asked.

"Only in a care home for the elderly," I told her.

She finally told the manager that I was clueless about what the job involved. Assuring me with a wink I still recall, she said, "You will be fine. You will nail it here. There are lots of clothes in there. The night girls will show you what to do. You will be fine."

The two girls started getting dressed as two others came in and immediately undressed. Trish said to her, "You've got a booking; he's on his way."

Amazingly, I was not treated as a rival. The girls made me feel welcome in an industry I was new to. With excitement, they picked some clothes from a messy, broken locker and from their bags and helped me wear a lovely Basque, fishnet stockings, French knickers and I tried on different high-heels until I found the right size and they brought out a stunningly sexy black beauty. A supreme sight to behold. Showing off, I couldn't stop looking in the mirror! That was it! From that moment on, it ignited my intense love for sexy lingerie which will NEVER fade away. A new world and stunning fetish were sparked. Always wrapped up in heavenly lace and body stockings, I became the sweet sin to savour.

No matter how huge their dicks were, the body knows just what to do when it's fired up. It's fascinating to see how the brain will try to find a way.

A gentleman came in, paid and went upstairs.

Trisha shouted, "Do you mind if Cassandra comes in on your booking? She's new and has never done this before."

They were both happy for me to do the work shadowing. No massage took place, she gave him a blowjob while I watched. Then the humorous, horny, heavily tattooed man asked if he could lick my pussy. So sexually naïve, I got nervous. I had never received oral sex. I had never enjoyed sex with myself. I had only ever slept with one man in my life… my husband, who had never performed oral sex on me. From zero to abundance... the joy that happens when you do "let it go". My hunger was quenched. My calling was found. My heart was racing because having another person in the room was bizarre too.

I was anxious but my first day in a brothel did not go as you would expect. Did you think I was going to be a dropout? There was no beginner's manual but that orgasm right there, I wanted that exact feeling again. Who knows if this beautiful night will ever come again in this lifetime? He licked my pussy like his life depended on it because it bloody well did. My orgasm was like a pot of boiling water whose lid was about to explode. If this isn't a sign, I don't know what is. Thrown above and beyond the horizon, I knew I had the potential to be something truly magical, and boy did I forever stretch my limits.

The girl was staring at me as I moaned and squirmed with pleasure. "You sound like you needed that darling." She was right. I was on the verge and have never stopped since. Now I land vagina-first on people's faces. The beautiful night led to some beautiful conversations about our challenging lives. She was a dental nurse who worked here, "on the side" as she put it.

Cocktails, cocaine, pills and potions. Don't people do things sober anymore? Do they hate it when they are aware of everything they do? To get them through the challenging shifts, most girls used intoxicants. They either required caffeine in copious amounts, drank alcohol or did various drugs. I did not partake, nor was I tempted; so, the other sex workers became wary of me. After many raised eyebrows and snorts of derision, I assured them to keep calm and kinky on. I was not an undercover working for the authorities. I was just an Inuit legend who had never seen the outside world.

Ten per cent of our earnings went on food, so we ordered takeaways throughout. "We need more energy. All that sucking makes us hungry," we justified when our curry was delivered, and it was deemed antisocial to decline. One must be profoundly strategic in the sex industry. Welcome aboard! Your daily mileage may vary.

Oh, how my eyes opened. Very seldom in life do things come together perfectly, I marvelled at what more awesome things this life-changing sex would bring. Whose bright idea was this again? I mean, there is so much laughter and less judging in this place, the future is shaping up to be so much fun. I'm selling my time and having a damn good time in the deal! It felt like for the first time I used that high-school maths in real life and the brothel experienced a drastic increase in customers because of me. The Madam explicitly boasted that I am a whole package... shockingly good, bound with dark chocolate, drizzled in honey... with a dollop of kinky and a hint of hoe. This is art.

My marriage made me mechanical and almost killed the creativity I never knew I had. With zero foreplay, the sex lasted forty-seven seconds, done and dusted, upon entry; his dick gave pleasure only to himself; it was sickening. Sex was not something he had with me, rather, something he did to me, and he was certain that he would do what he wanted with my body. He would ignore me until he required my holes again. No wonder I climaxed only once in my marriage and purely by accident. My husband just happened to do something right, accidentally. It wasn't his intention to pleasure me. To him, I was just an ashtray. I was loyal to the wrong person. That was not art.

As well as my good mood, there was enough foreplay in the brothel, I was properly aroused. *This is a good place. There is a lot of good sex. why was this hidden to me for so long, I mean, just look at me* I thought to myself. A man who was not even my man had the desire to make me feel good and he was paying to pleasure us. What planet is this again? Realistically, I had no life... someone told me to go to the brothel. There, the table was set, something creative and promising happened. Destiny my friends, one cannot escape destiny. The rest is history. What's not to love?

It was unbelievable that these men accepted my very wet pussy and thought it was great. For some fucked up reason, in my marriage and its culture, a wet pussy was gross, obscene and unacceptable. Shun natural pussies. We were given advice on how to stay dry, to keep a man. It was commendable for a man to leave a woman with a soaking wet pussy.

The man left, we went downstairs, and the other girl gave the manager feedback about how I was loving my new job. I certainly was, and that is why I never left it, and I am not packing my bags yet.

My new presence kept the red lights on, the phone was constantly ringing. "Yes, we have a new girl with us tonight, Cassandra. She is black, filled with caramel, five feet four, thirty-four DD. She specialises from A to Z across the board. Book now or forever hold your peace."

My first experience made me lethargic, but the intrigue and euphoria quickened me. That was a warm up! By the end of the night, I had a few of these experiences which, essentially, stirred up so many things in me, there was no need for further consideration. I liked it this way.

Time to get my rear in gear. Before long, being a butt slut was the norm, but it was my little secret to the world.

A photographer came in one day and took some pictures of all of us for their website. A rota meant I would go in work and find men waiting for me in the lounge as they chatted to one another, sipping tea or coffee.

"There are three gentlemen waiting here, Cassandra," the Madam would say. "Just make your way to the room, darling."

"Hi everybody, I'm Cassandra," I'd say. "I won't be long."

They'd all nod their heads to each other to agree I was worth the wait. Not having time to sip a drink because I proved popular was awesome. It felt great. What was this magnificent thing that I do so brilliantly, unlike anyone else? What was so unique that these men didn't want to miss?

There was a tiny CCTV screen where the Madam could see all the men before she buzzed them in. One day there, a man and a woman buzzed to be let in. She them on the intercom what the woman wanted, because women were not allowed in. "I have brought my husband," she answered before demanding, "Let us in."

"He can come in, but you can't."

"I said he's my husband," she insisted.

"Yes, but I'm not letting him in if you're coming in too."

"Okay, I will wait in the car then. Just make sure he does something. What girls have you got on?"

"Two are busy but I have a new black girl available."

"Can she make sure he uses condoms?"

As she pressed for entrance, the woman tried to come in as well and this annoyed the Madam. "I said you can't fucking come in!"

She turned away at this but was still heard to shout at her husband that she will be getting feedback, so he had better get his act together.

I was amazed.

The man came in, articulate and well-spoken. He made his payment and was told what room to go in. "Cassandra will follow you," he was informed.

When I entered the room, I found a scared, nervous man. Unlike most men we got there, he was still dressed and sat in the chair in the corner.

A man showing no signs of lust, it felt weird, as though we were sitting down to a game that neither of us knew how to play. With a sad face, he told me that he was forced to come here by his vicious wife. He was a senior in the NHS hospital. I told him I was just new and getting used to the whole thing. He gave me £20 and said if his wife does come in, I should say we did have sex…

A sneak peek into my first day was not what I expected; nevertheless, despite having no knowledge or experience, they saw my full potential and it remains a legendary moment in my work. Then again, there was no time to be bad at something. It's not perfection that ensures survival. Desperation causes you to dare, to break boundaries.... to be flexible and adapt.

I then progressed onto better and cleaner massage parlours. Or at least I thought I did. Several times, I pushed myself to the point of utter exhaustion where I just knew that I had burned my own fuse.

I thought that during menstruation I really ought not to go to work, but the manager wasn't having it. Severe period pains were not an excuse for a day off in a sex job! All they considered were their clients, so I had to learn step by step how to disguise a menstruation cycle. Some of the girls were losing their patience with me because this was way out of my comfort zone.

Due to my naivety, the girls had to teach me how to cope with working on your period. Some used a sponge that you inserted like a tampon, but how in the world do you take it out? Apparently, you pushed like having a baby and just pinched it out. That made me cringe and I felt like just packing the job in.

Step by step, one girl gave me a sponge, lubricated it and helped me insert it, promising to help me remove it before I went home. Towards the end of the day, I kept reminding her not to forget me.

A few of my colleagues dreaded home time because they were being picked up by their pimp and that was sad. One of the girls, Julia, constantly received calls from her boyfriend who was also her pimp, asking her how much money she had made so far and each time she looked on the verge of breaking down when she hadn't made what he expected because he became violent with her. She admired how incredibly lucky I was, that I had liberty, my money was mine, to pay my bills and provide for my child, to put food on the table. All in all, it was a great freshers' week for me, and yes, I felt lucky.

Having slept with only one man in my entire life, to working in a brothel was like throwing a kid in at the deep end of the waters. I started counting the men and asking the girls if they counted. In her Italian accent, Georgia said to me, "Soon the number of hair strands on your head will equal the dicks you have." That was a prophetic utterance; indeed, it came to pass as I lost count.

Then came a girl from Kenya, with her work name: Sonia. She was in Britain with her husband whom she had met a few months ago when he went there on a safari. An asset to the brothel for bringing them money in, Sonia was tiny and petite. Every man wanted her because they manipulated her image into 'child-like', it made my skin crawl. The other girls became hostile towards her and I even heard that on my day off, someone slapped her for "getting in their way and selling like hot cakes". The others were jealous. Obviously, the police were never called over this attack.

Eventually, I moved on to another brothel called *Connections* in East Manchester. A wonderfully odd place, among other things, it was an effective drive through sex centre. Sunrise until sunset, it boasted of meeting some of the most intense of fantasies and expectations and we sustained that reputation. Some sexual cravings are difficult to confess and categorise, but here, we had them covered across the board. I know the world is full of consumers, and the search for pleasure is perpetual, but still I was staggered at how many men, all kinds, frequented the brothels... which had the right to exist as massage parlours. Sex is a viable business. It is beyond pleasure as it engages our humanity and people are fascinated by it. Attempts to ban brothels would be the death of play and art for many.

Unlike other brothels, this one opened at the break of dawn, because, well, you know... it's never too early to give or to receive a morning glory. The men who needed something kinky to kickstart the day, came very early for a quickie with their favourite girl... and they were ready for the day. It takes longer to microwave an omelette in a mug, than it does some services. Pants down, most men would keep their shoes and shirt on because, literally, their mission was just to ejaculate; even better if their chosen girl swallowed. Some reckless and brave men waited outside to prey on the girls arriving for work and lure them into their cars for a raunchy blowjob. It was tempting because the cash was all ours to keep, but it became a sackable offence, so I didn't dare. Swapping numbers with clients was not allowed too, but where there is a will, there is a way.

Lunchtime was the happy hour and tremendously busy, because… well, why have a desk nap at work when you can have a lunchtime quickie and be quickened for the rest of the day! Some girls just randomly turned up to work at that hour, as *dinner ladies*, in case extra back-up was needed. As for the clients, we knew that they would either be late for work or unable to return, following the sex-related fatigue they sustained that hour.

This brothel has since been demolished in a regeneration programme that has seen Lime Square Shopping Centre built there. However, it will never completely erase my wealth of stories. Trading on it and even having a coffee stirs up some fantastic experiences of what was initially there and will linger in my mind a long time. *Connections* was a dark, decaying, filthy brothel with enormous demands beyond measure, where the cream of society indulged with the common girls. But that is a reality you are not ready for. Sometimes a living nightmare for those working in it, its blankets, the Madam confessed to me, had never been washed for the five years she had worked there yet it fully deserved five stars for being hugely entertaining for those who wanted to indulge in all things kinky.

I got in trouble a few times for putting used towels in the washer. Apparently, I was supposed to put them straight in the dryer unless they were beyond saving. The shock in me outraged the Madam. "Listen, the dryers kill more germs than water. Read up on what heat can do." There are no elegant solutions for kinky needs, and the men glorified this filthy place… expecting it to give the filthiest service. What you think is beyond tacky and distasteful is what flows perfectly in the sex market. Live the best life, have the best sex. No-holds-barred, specific requests, no limits and rightly so. There is no immaculate GOOD sex.

I left *Connections* after the Madam found another job in another brothel, in Salford, Greater Manchester… *Louisa's*. She took me with her because I was the sultry siren. Having pussy made my life easier and created some opportunities.

Here, I met Amanda, a blonde-haired, self-confessed schizophrenic with some rampant paranoias. She believed in the power of crystals. The desirable rota in every brothel is to have a variety of hookers on each day for a broader choice for the men, so I worked with her regularly. She was famous for providing every sexual service under the sun. What was the secret behind these back-to-back bookings? She didn't just do the basics. Amanda was so extra but so necessary; she certainly pulled in the crowds. "Why limit yourself to just one hole, when you can have both?" was our thought-provoking, willy-tormenting question to the men.

There is something arousing about the joy given by a woman in the sex industry. A wild angel in heavy syrup, Amanda would always get me in to have a threesome so that I could earn some extra cash. Just girls being supportive pals, she often reminded me "when you suck dick, never neglect the balls babe." It was daunting; my then innocent heart was mortified. The men didn't need much prompting because their top fantasy is having two, star whores putting an amazing show. One of us was a sweet nectar to nourish them, the other a bitter poison to finish them. What a pair!

Driven by passion, Amanda was a spectacularly kinky gift to behold. It dawned on me that hookers are a special kind of athlete. There was no pill to absorb her filthy offerings, but the best teachers change lives forever. She instilled in me some blazing, timely wisdom and coached me to greatness. I marvel at how survival dragged me into the unknown, I explored and evolved into an all-out multifunctioning jezebel, with redeeming qualities. Clearly eloquent and filthy, I pushed myself onward and upward like a skyscraper, and sculpted my own ideas to earn myself some extra money. The uniqueness I brought enriched lives.

… Indeed, everyone is kinky when pushed far enough. So much supply meeting huge demands, we were just like every sensible person using our creativity and courage. Every second, there is someone acting on an attraction or arousal to someone other than their partner. We have all missed someone that wasn't ours to miss. Perhaps the best sex is usually with the person you shouldn't be fucking!

Amanda was in love with my persona and she understood that I was at the base level. Exploring my curiosity, she laid everything bare and taught me the strokes of a genius; how to specialise across-the-board, if I were to be the popular girl to dive for.

The place was tangled with rage and bitterness, there were always some boring little dramas. Admired by many, understood by no one, the working girls hated Amanda to the core, but our hearts aligned because a part of her wilderness touched mine. I was patient and had the acceptance and willingness to understand her. The rest were alarmed at how she was so gracious and nurturing to me. Gents forming an orderly queue, her busy schedule inspired me to work hard. I became her fountain of living water and she became mine.

Bound by her own chains, she held on to a horoscope that read "Die… die, my darling. Find an ocean. Find yourself an ocean to drown in." And a clairvoyant told her, "I have seen your future, and there is nothing but death. So, stop bothering about the future."

Your mind will always believe everything you tell it. Feed it hope, truth and love. Only you can discover your own truths. But still, I loved her enough and made every effort to weaken such chains. I told her, "No, Amanda! LIVE!" I was like a sensory light; her darkness disappeared when I appeared. Each day, I left her better than I found her, and that hope was locked in her heart. Not for brownie points, it's much deeper than that, but the right words can resurrect someone and bring them tranquillity. My words are always a true expression of my heart. It was a pure communication between the two of us. What is rooted and grounded in my heart is what my mouth speaks.

Amanda was semi-literate and struggled with basic things, but her passion was like artistic talent and gave her value. I was struck by her energy and she proved yet again that there is power in the mundane and that we are all skilled at something. We had what men wanted, including those from the upper drawer. If they share the same sky, under the spell of a woman in stockings and suspenders, men will say similar things under the influence of sex. How dare they be aroused by common people…" The world comes together in sex. As well as a pierced clitoris with a ring on it, she had dentures which she removed when the session got fiery, but men barely noticed. If they did, there was minimal fuss because she did it all. Her performance was a little bit dramatic when she was in that seXXXtravaganza mood. I got quite embarrassed. Nonetheless, that was her uniqueness and I want to emulate her. Between the sex intervals, she hardly had time to have a drink or lunch because there was always someone waiting for her. *Goals!* I thought to myself, *When I grow up, I want to be EXTRA like Amanda, without it being a challenge! I want to have several clients queuing up for me, waiting their turn as they chat away in the waiting room.* It's good to dream, because years later, I was accustomed to this kinkiness. When you are so good… you do some stunts during sex, clients sit down and wait their turn… better still, just join in because the more, the merrier.

There were consequences for poor performance… Some girls were instantly, unfairly dismissed, upon a client's complaint to the Madam. "She was a bloody waste of time." That was it! No excuses because you were only seen from their angle.

As the next client waited, she always sacrificed time and made them wait a little bit longer, just to have a few minutes' chat with me. Burned out with regrets and desperate for answers, she thought hope was beyond her reach. A life full of fear, she pressured me into reading her palms and was rather disappointed when I told her that I was not a clairvoyant, nor did I believe in black magic. "If you are reading horoscopes and palms, you are reading deception. Stop it now."

I was still on baby steps, feeding on milk, but the more I did threesomes with kinky Amanda, the more I could do. They were essentially seminars. I evolved, I learned from the best in the industry and was soaring high in no time. Surely, I had it and this path had been just waiting for my inner fire to arise.

Her menopause was just kicking in when I first met her. Nonetheless, not even the hot flushes could stop her…

Timing is art. So real, raw and mature, her days were intense with back-to-back bookings. Evolve, or life will be miserable like a slow antagonising death. She enjoyed gulping down several mouthfuls of sperm and she showed them first before she gargled and swallowed, because that turned her on. That art performance excited the men too. As I would cringe, she would say, "It was yummy for my tummy and good for my bank account," but I wasn't convinced. I told her that if I wanted to get dirty, I would rather go out in the garden, cover myself in dirt and pretend I'm a carrot. We can't be in elementary forever! I knew that I needed to up my game, grow and start chewing meat if I was to capture the attention of men. They wanted what they didn't get at home, and even if they did get it at home, bread eaten in secret is more delicious.

Like hungry lions, it puzzled me how Amanda's two sons always waited impatiently at the door after work, to grab her earnings from her. Several times, I asked her if it was even worth coming to work; she broke down in my arms and said it was safer spending the day in the brothel because it was more disastrous quarrelling with her sons at home. Now that she had me, she said it was therapeutic, she wished we never went home.

It was merciful that I didn't have tigers waiting at the door to grab my earnings from me. However, I had a stage ten clinger who became a stalker, it was dreadful. He happened to be my friend's husband who knew our rota. Each time after I finished work, on the poorly lit street to catch the bus, Mr Fletcher made it look like he had just bumped into me by accident...and asked me if I wanted a lift home.

Things took a darker turn when his mask slipped even further. Shaken to the core, I had to quit the brothel.

This time, I became an independent escort, confident that I was hot like fire, the masses desire. I took with me all the in-depth tricks of the trade, most importantly, Amanda's teasing and toying voice still echoes to me: "Look in their eyes when you suck their dick and always leave them wanting more."

My mind was exposed to something extraordinarily different. I met two sex workers who had abandoned their life of privilege and chose to work in the brothels, but it was packed with some "vulnerables" and most of us got into the industry because we were in a pickle. The lack of money being the root of it all. We were not all excessively lustful sperm-diggers, craving sex with dozens of men a day. We were everyday people with complex stories... who had simply fallen foul of awful circumstances and mine was immigration, the lack of a work permit. Well, that was how it was for me to begin with, at least. With a child to look after and not two pennies to rub together, it was survival.

To my astonishment, what a delight! I marinated in it and became a seasoned escort.

When I was a wife I was forbidden to say "no" to sex, no matter the circumstances. I was merely just existing for my husband's sexual gratification. I owed him sex and affection! It was everything about him, nothing about me. I still have the horrendous memory of the forceful sex, whilst I was in a fragile state with life-threatening malaria. Almost unresponsive, he insisted that my extremely elevated temperature would make him feel phenomenal!

Oh yes, I still remember the sad moment when Alfred was hospitalised with extremely serious dysentery; we were told to prepare for the worst... but my mean-spirited husband forced it upon me to go home because he wanted sex. The body is easy to give, but at this point, I wished my vagina had blades on demand! Terrified and with infinite sadness, I gave him sex. My mind, as you would expect, was with our son, on that hospital bed. Every heartbeat could have been his last.

Finally, in England, I savoured the freedom of sex and consent. Even with a sex worker, consent remains the rule, and can be withdrawn if the need exists. There are some seriously predator-like men on the loose, who think pussy is an entitlement. Don't you just love it when they respect your rate, get consent and pay-up? I like the feeling of being respected. This is what we call a healthy relationship. They recognise their wants but also respect my limits and we talk about it in a light way that doesn't get uncomfortable. They ask if I'm okay. No wonder I developed into a powerful sex tool. Stretch your mind to deep dimensions, for to be closed-minded is death but to be open-minded is life. Allow yourself to flow and overflow. Everything stems from abundance. Daily, I discovered something. There is a euphoria that only my job can deliver. My fears and insecurities vanquished. My ambitions still fresh, daily I compulsively sought new ways of seeing reality… I pressed forward into new experiences and a shipload of sex. Time to play, every day was leg-over-bend-over-face-down-ass-up day. This is what my life got to, the higher life, of discovering and creating. A vigorous woman with many ideas? You will be surprised where an open mind takes you.

Was I taking too much too fast? The talent just oozed out of me, I brought out the greatness in full force. By the time I parted with Amanda, even though I still could not swallow, I had developed the key specialisms. I mastered things quicker than a hot knife through butter. A compliment from Amanda was the ultimate accolade. The kinkiest in the northwest of England had trained me. I evolved into something new, with a seal of approval in the marketplace and registered on the website Adult Work. I was more professional, strategic, forward-thinking and in high demand because I exceeded expectations.

When kind and generous people get older, the more they love to help others, and teaching brings them joy, because they are helping others who are starting a new journey.

We don't all have to be accredited and approved life coaches. It's called being tolerant and supportive. I was pleasantly surprised at how Amanda donated a lot of her time to help me. Like stock trading, every new trader needs a mentor. People will say this is unsafe and it won't work, but something is only impossible until someone does it. We are all searching for true fulfilment. Take a chance; don't be timid in moving forward. Whatever path you choose in life, it should be something you enjoy and want to be good at.

I found true fulfilment in being an escort. Who would have predicted that the path I took to survive would decode my life and bring me so much joy and freedom?

How you get to the track is different from how you stay in the race. I did not keep in touch with Amanda, but she made an indelible impression on me. Wisdom is knowing what associations to take with you after work. Not every cloak is to be taken home. She infused me with a deep sense of kinkiness. I mastered the basics, to becoming exquisitely filthy and having deserving men queue up for more. The way was paved, I never despair about my future. I learned the tricks of the trade from the best in the trade… I felt ordained.

Twerking gracefully is an art not everyone can master, and that was something stunning I brought to Amanda. She was mesmerised how I did it smoothly. I attribute that superpower to my roots. With deeply ingrained misogynistic traditions in Malawi, anything and everything to please a man… we were taught to twerk, from a young age. "Your waist is not your own… it is for his pleasure."

You can never be too creative. "When he's inside you, squeeze him in and spell 'SANDRA' with your waist. Make spelling mistakes and try again. Whine clockwise, anticlockwise, in-out-shake-it-all-about and start again".

She giggled each time she tried it and asked me, "are we there yet?" Iron sharpens iron. Technique first. Speed second. She got there in the end. Teach a woman to twerk and she will turn around and try to teach it back to you like she invented it. It was hilarious. Meet the twerking tasteful blonde.

What do you know? I know seduction. I love to strip-tease. I know how to drive a man crazy and wild in the bedroom, but also, I understand that taking time to seduce our minds is crucial for play. Beyond that, I was an escort who wore many hats and provided for a full range of emotions, because there was harmony between my mind and heart.

Kinkiness is not something you choose to have one day and then put on the shelf the next. You either have it or you don't; there is nothing in between. When you know that every part of your body is a beautiful accessory, you give a no-holds-barred service.

My life would have been miserable if I had painted them with the same brush and jumped on the trash wagon of 'all men are trash', predatory, arrogant, exploitative, manipulative and violent.

A man hurt me. Men hugged and healed me to restoration!

Chapter 20
My Calling – Justified

We are all creators, but so far, many have not shown any creation because they are so blinded by being, and they forget to live. Having revealed my inner world to him, my regular client, MJ, a Barrister at Law, said, "Sandra, you are an unusual, possibly unique woman. Stay different."

Indeed, I wasn't just any hooker. The most interesting of us contain a multitude and I was the perfect blend of order and chaos, unusual and with character. MJ was one of the lucky ones to devour me and he truly appreciated that I had thought up some alternatives, way better and more honest than a miserable marriage. There were no twisted vows, but I was surely a crutch to lean on, a goddess in the sheets and a path to a vibrant future of fun and frolics.

When you find your calling, you hold on to it. Who can shame me, when I am not ashamed? There is no shame in my game, just sauce. Plenty of sauce. Despite all the judgement and stigma thrown at me, my deeds are justified, and with bravery, I weave it all in, exposing the truth, scars and pain. I hereby share my existence with you all; the battles and passions that changed my life tremendously. My chronicles are not a narrative widely accepted by multitudes, but still, it is my life story. The undying love for my son, the ultimate compassion from Great Britain, a passionate plea to remain in a country that lifted me out of the slimy pit of misery and set my feet on solid ground.

Others will sneer at those us with fewer opportunities. Alas, when you don't understand artificial impediments and how the system of oppression works, it's easy to do that from a place of privilege. With very few rights and dignity afforded to new immigrants, 'no recourse to public funds' meant Alfred and I were barred from accessing all statutory welfare benefits. 'Employment prohibited' meant just that.

These are my experiences. Feel free to have your own. Write them up or write them off. I wrote because, frankly, the only storytellers we can trust are ourselves. Only I can share my most deep and buried truths and pain. As you read my life and its impact, a part of my wilderness touches a little bit of yours.

To even assume that the world has equality of opportunity is absurd as it is fatal. Alas, the horrors of discrimination and the barriers we face! Hold your peace, I have had my fair share of being disregarded. Who can toss away the tears? At times I was treated extremely unfairly and had to fight to be humanised, but sometimes even that was too much to ask. Others will still find room to only condemn me. How could they understand when they have lived a different life, unchallenged? How could they fathom it when they clearly have no concept of life outside their ivory tower? Others, without being unpleasant, this will resonate in their hearts so perfectly due to their own experience of social disadvantage. Others will have frequent pauses, look deeper and find beauty in this, because my life is more than a story; it is an exhibition, a gift of hope and possibility to the world.

Despite everything, this is my testimony, entirely true and I am thrilled to share with you the tales that led me into sex work and why I chose to carry on. Who can silence my harrowing experiences of cruelty and injustice? Confessions are truths. When your eyes have been opened to the truth, nothing anyone does or say will cause them to shut again. Life is not only what you make because we don't live in isolation. It is a diversity of experiences; including those of others, that overlap and affect us the most.

Behind my feisty character is humility and an ocean of tears. Sharing not only what is comfortable, sometimes I wrote in a puddle of tears whilst recalling the heart-wrenching memories of pain and the passage of time. Happy tears. Sad tears. I cried many tears.

In my agonising journey, as I endured the stigma and rejection of having a severely disabled child. Others around me have not valued my strength as a mother, but I have. Others have not appreciated my hustle and growth, but I didn't expect them to. No one gave me a pat on the back, so I did it myself because raising a disabled child single-handedly, with a complicated diagnosis, in a foreign land, journeyed me through immense sacrifices and hardship, as I strived to create a possible life for myself and Alfred. I did my best. I did myself proud and I will keep being great.

If you want to flourish, break the waves and harness the wind. I may have looked perfectly poised in the storm, but it was impossible to survive with dignity. In vast darkness, in a tunnel with no end in sight, it was time to get creative and ignite my own light. Courage and effort will light the dark. In the process of mending myself after brokenness, there was something unfolding within me and I got to know who I really was, a symbol and a source of blessing. I get hurt, sad and angry too. I get remorseful and I get shy. But most of all, I am the essence of love.

Love is what gets you to the mountain. Faith is what makes you stay. I love deeply and that is my superpower. I invited the world to love me and then dared it to still love me. Strength and courage are at the centre of all this and the answer lies in my stunning wisdom. Wisdom is the principal thing. Without it, I would never have fulfilled my calling. You can never be too careful, but to trade smartly as a hooker, one needs to be vigilant, resilient and discerning. You interact with a range of perspectives, including the lonely, disillusioned, unstable, and bitter. I was able to seamlessly interact with flamboyant gang members, drug dealers and their rivals; we know better than to turn our backs on them. My milkshake seemed to be their first choice. Always feeling generous, they love to pamper a hooker!

It was not about striving to be perfect and consistent in all my attributes, nor was it about discovering the genius in me. Some of the things that I did didn't have to float my boat, but still I did my best.

For survival, I ventured an unknown path in what seemed like the most ghastly and terrifying place to end up, but there I discovered my unique self. What started as a nightmare turned into a passion, with exquisite moments I had never experienced before. In a twinkle of an eye, my legion of clients became the support group I never knew I needed. Usually concerned and respectful, from them I found solace and exhilaration as there was always a little love and comfort baked in. Each day brought creativity out the creativity in me, and most importantly, healing.

'Greatness' is in the eyes of the beholder. What one calls a filthy and ugly world is another's breakthrough. I went through the dark to see the light. To others, it was a mark of sin and disgrace, but trust me, my job did not have dominion over me, nor defile me, except it awakened my many desires. Also, from it, I found love, peace, tranquillity and became the perennial source of life to those who sought an escape from the shackles and chains, in this entangled web. In life, you just never know what story you are walking into. It was more than a journey I embarked upon, or simply a job I commenced.

No one is living a tried and tested path in this unscripted journey of self-discovery. With disappointed and betrayed hearts, we are all in the process of being educated to educate others. Our stories are filled with consequences of bad choices, guilt, blame, anger, expectation, broken pieces and immense pain. The world is built on stories, so we can all take some leaves from other people's books.

There is nothing beautiful and meaningful about life. We are all seeking fulfilment in a world whose systems are designed to work against us. Every moment is a tough, ugly battle for survival. We can never prepare for the worst, but we can do what is necessary at that moment, to tilt the odds. We can make life beautiful with our intellect, bravery and creativity. Individually, we are forced to create our own meaning… and find our own beauty of life.

We have been unsure, insecure and wounded at some point but whatever state you find yourself in today, surf through the waves. It's okay to have a moment of lamenting. Just don't let it drag into days. If you are walking through the valley of the shadow of death, don't give up. Ride the waves and don't cave in. This too shall pass. I have been in the ground before and thought I was buried, but I was planted for greatness. I have been in the fire, but it didn't burn me. I came out refined. I have been in deep waters, but even they did not submerge me. Be strong and courageous and know that not every challenge is meant to pull you down. Healing is a journey. You cannot rush it. It takes time, patience and you must dig deep… go to the depths, to find the courage. Don't despair. Only you know how far you have come. Only I know how far I have come. There is an extraordinary beauty in the ashes, and when we look back or look within, there is always room to be thankful.

As you read my journey, draw some strength, and tap into the faith that saw me through!

Others have commented that despite my bravery, I am going to need a lifetime of therapy because, apparently, my work *sells my soul*. Hello! My work is everything I need it to be. Creative. Promising. Therapy. Empowering. Unlike some, I don't contemplate quitting my job on my way to work, every single day.

From a young age, I was always an oasis, with some incredible virtues, many found me to be kinder than necessary, but also, before you know it, raising a child with a mental disability naturally brings out some additional patience, the need for compassion, tolerance and most certainly some strangeness.

Never underestimate the power of a single parent.

Let's unpack this for a minute, because folks still don't seem to understand that there is a burning social injustice and that we are not all holding silver spoons in our mouths! You don't have to come down from your tower of privilege to understand that life can be unbearable for so many. You may not understand the devastation that goes together with hardships but be still and take a moment to see the world through my eyes and experience the harshness in the tunnel that I was trapped within.

Ever think you have problems with no end in sight? I have been there; lived through that... my lane was paved by abuse, heartache and tears, until I gathered the broken pieces and learned to fly. You may wait forever for that light at the end of the tunnel. You are the change in the tunnel. Be bold. Be the light.

Whilst multitudes experience the joy and celebration of bringing a life into this world, I was mocked and ridiculed. My love for my child was held against me, I spent my life grappling with the stigma of parenting a child with special needs. As though he was something to be ashamed of, the nasty people almost crushed me in disgust... for the beautiful soul I brought into this world.

He is disabled, but he is my precious son. His existence brings me so much joy, nothing but love is reflected in his eyes.

There are degrees of despair. To be destitute, navigating the most difficult circumstances, parenting through pain, coping with a unique child whose brain works differently is a demanding role both physically and emotionally because you must enter their world with tact. The pain and struggles reminded me that I was alive and that I had an extremely difficult situation to conquer. Whilst his autism and chromosome abnormality has challenged my life, every day Alfred taught me more about myself and about life than anything or anyone in the world could. Hilarious and creative as ever, his brain is so amazing and smart. I live and think differently because he turned me into a super mum. Always in high-alert mode because I couldn't afford not to be, this unusual portfolio factored into my work ethics.

Compromise being the greatest skill in business and what moves us forward, I listen (listening is a super-power), and I am a great negotiator, I have come too far to learn that you don't get what you deserve. You get what you negotiate. Managing chaos, tantrums, able to work under pressure, sacrificial love, multi-tasking, able to calm the storms and make the sun shine again, knowing the cues when I am irritating, slow to anger, an extraordinary strategist, merciful, compassionate, gracious, discernment and always calculated. All these attributes were good for business and set me apart. Whilst understanding different mental styles, I spend my energy accepting reality than trying to deny it.

Hiring an escort? There is more to it than just convenience. Also, there is a real dark and magical side. If it's not a terrifying gamble, it's a leap of faith in the dark but fascinatingly, that perfect phone call can transcend and be the road to happiness.

With most men, it starts with being lonely and horny… in sexless, passionless partnerships. Long term frustration with no satisfying outlet. Some are in open relationships where they both take on others sex partners throughout their lives.

The world resists provoking such deep topics, but escorts are totally fearless, kind, strong and diverse people who respect your time and appreciate effort. Not only if they deliver that desire or the fantasy you crave, but most importantly, if there is a rapport, an escort is an oasis beyond your expectation, for they pay attention and genuinely care that even small needs are met.

Easily flattered. Easily fooled. Any man who has hired an escort knows that they take a gamble as they feast their eyes and filter through numerous advertisements floating around, whilst weeding out what doesn't appeal to them. The theory is that most men drink, to build up their courage, nevertheless, as with all things, it's a devastating blow if they don't get exactly what they ordered. They also can 'shop' for an escort based on multiple options at multiple prices, specialities, colour or reputation… and even by those who meet some certain criteria such as deep-throat, swallow, face-sitting, fisting, water-sports, hard-sports. By whichever method they search, it's overwhelming to decide, and some men continue to dither over who they should pick.

One man, disappointed upon arrival, stared at me and said, "You are not Chinese," because he mistakenly rang the person he did not select. Charming. In my lingerie, I just stood there… and smiled as indecisive man abruptly made a U-turn.

Mice die in mousetraps because they do not understand why the cheese is free. Those who have encountered disheartening situations take comfort in the online feedback and reviews left for the escort. Beyond an assurance, they were a flavour of what to expect. Nevertheless, it is for both the punter and escort to have the best experience possible. Many times, I have had to hang up the phone or block them instantly because their attitude is problematic before even conducting business.

The phenomenal ones take their time to show how generous they can be, whilst others are so abrupt... they hate women but love vagina. I have been undressed by all sorts. Depending entirely on their needs and their budgets, some stories told by my clients, as they have visited escorts, have been cringe-worthy and some funny, yet so have mine been. It's a risk both ways, but so is driving and many other things in life. Some have made a poor choice of escort and they must confront the choices they made.

Many platforms attract thousands of escorts to advertise with varying levels of talents and experience. It is a fast-growing segment and advertising means entering a fiercely fought marketplace with indulgent offers for the outrageous requests. Being the oldest profession, there will never be an end in sight, because the market continues to strengthen. With a stellar reputation, years of experience and specialising in a wide array of services, I offered men beyond the quality adult entertainment they required, and I was popular. I was staggeringly talented by just being who I am, and this improved my chances of being the chosen one. Whilst some surprises must remain a secret to all but those who have tasted... Men appreciate that it's not an easy task to find a brilliant escort, and it's even harder to replace her, so they look out for each other with some safe words.

Remember. You are a legend and a constant inspiration in someone's mind; thrive to always do better. Hence, why my intriguing feedback expanded and continued to stimulate other punters.

Sometimes you think you are striving for perfection and setting the bar too high but that is plain toxic. Even the solvent, good looking and intelligent, after doing the dating game, with a dozen failed relationships to their name... some men have decided that they are not good at traditional relationships. They are emotionally incapable of a long period of commitment. They do, however, have a strong desire for human intimacy, so they devote themselves to escorts. Whatever the arrangement, everyone deserves something beautiful to think about.

Non-consensual sex work is a societal evil and disgustingly problematic. I, for one, am against trafficking and exploitation in any form. Gross is when people think the same for consensual sex. Consent and non-consent do not overlap or intertwine; sad it would be if they did. It is hard to decide which is more arrogant, the bigotry or the pettiness. It seriously makes a mockery of what is criminal and what is not, whilst demeaning those with freedom and choice. I loathe men who feel entitled to women's bodies; apart from my work, I have been a sexual victim myself. Nevertheless, I was not sold out to the plain insanity #MeToo movement. Whilst many thought it was a feminist uprising and long overdue, the "always believe women" rhetoric is a dangerous sham, harms men severely and has no equality. These women were rising to strangle men, well after they had accomplished whatever they had set out to accomplish. Timing is art! Most accusations were nothing more than disastrous love affairs gone wrong. This was the height of cruelty to men, to trap them into false cases. At this rate of such generalising and injustice, when some women feel less important if they don't jump on the bandwagon, we will wake up one day and realise that the cosmetic fire and fury was life-damaging. The revolution is humanism. Others choose to be lonely; they are so happy and get addicted to loneliness. Some love to be alone and hate being lonely. Many are acutely lonely, it's paralysing. An escort is there when punters suddenly have a crushing feeling of loneliness. Many people are living life through a variety of apps to help avoid collisions and alert them of approaching turmoil. Apps that help keep you balanced; but do they work? The lucky ones finally find an escort with genuine interaction. Men told themselves, "don't get attached", but before they knew it, we had a tremendous bond.

Beyond sex, I was practising… first and foremost, emotional first aid. After each booking, I felt a little poorer for it because I gave so much of myself. Nevertheless, crucially, I felt empowered and enriched by my giving. My candle was searching for their candle and lighting it. I was sharing a light and planting a seed of greatness in others. This feeling replenished me to greatness again. Be a gift that keeps on giving. It was a stunning cycle. You don't have to be famous or lead a revolution to make an impact in the lives of others. Just be as good as you can to those around you every day. Exude love always.

My ability to seamlessly integrate passion with hard-core kinky fun attracted some of the brightest and most passionate clients across all professions. People connected at my Sunday Swingers' Parties. Keep Calm and Kinky On; the sex party is on. They were a whole mess of fun, a congregation for the bold and the dare devils. Beyond a gangbang, these parties were an exploration of pleasures with a diversity of thoughts and perspectives. Loving thy neighbour meant some kinky offerings, embracing each other's freakiness, unveiling our magical side… What a sweet, perfect communion.

Some… cold and distant, just came to stare, masturbate and whisper away. More outercourse - less intercourse. Others networked, recognised the loneliness in each other's eyes and fell in love. In a heart-warming gesture, a few came back to thank me when the party had its desired effect and they found the perfect match.

Things that make you say "mmmm". Each time I use a drinking straw, I think of this loving gay couple. After Jamie fucked his boyfriend's ass and ejaculated deep inside him, he took a straw, put it right in the ass and passionately sucked it all out… to completion. He said that act was monumental in sealing infinite love. I cringed a little, but hey-ho, to each their own. Is the ass known to contain treasures? All genders seem to be so much happier when butt-stuff comes into play.

It is I, the hooker. Always on standby to ride, bounce and deep throat that dick. People fail miserably to commit to a job if they have not yet found their calling. I immersed myself in mine because this is what I was destined to do. I impressed men even more because I had a level of sacrifice in me that was peculiar. Who said hookers are unworthy of love and cannot love deeply? I had so much love stored up. I was aching to love and tantalise. That companionable love, the love that is meant for a soulmate, went to my clients. I cared deeply about them and they opened their hearts.

Everyone has their own paradise. If you're loving what you are doing and enjoying it, you're on the right track.

Others still visit me at Christmas, my birthday and Valentine's Day. Some angry men stormed in late at night, feeling 'used' after some rendezvous at a nightclub. It made them bitter that they had bought some girl drinks in a bar or nightclub all night, with the expectation of mingling with them in private. Suddenly she leaves with someone else or doesn't even say goodbye! Like an Agony Aunt, an hour of more talking and less action suited me just fine. It was a win for them too after all, because it's better out than in and to listen to their steam before they paid me, but I always told them, "You have my sincere condolences but pay up first, then I'm all yours, all ears, after all, here, you are guaranteed to get… satisfaction."

Living from hand to mouth and catching up with bills, I had no safety net. When I was hired, that was all the money, the only money I was waiting for. After being swindled a few times… giving my all, my amazing skills, talents and having gone extra; "I will just go to the car to get your money," and they disappeared... Some men always have some disgusting tricks up their sleeves; I lived, and I learned, I always took payment upfront and this was not a money-back guarantee. Alas! Imagine the disgusting disasters if the payment was released to me upon completion of the job? Who gets to decide when sex is amiss or complete! Where there are no terms written down... what assurance have I that funds have been kept securely for me as I ride that dick?

In a climate of the raging war with mental-health, life can be dull, mysterious and bleak. We can't afford to be ignorant. Always be conscious of the social climate and cater to it. Sex is a top factor, but men are looking for the right balance of focus and enthusiasm. Being an escort is beyond the image. Be more – so much more. Besides sex, have other redeemable qualities that will leave that man wanting more. Be one with innovation. Be vivid, kind, healing and sexually plugged. That is the hallmark of a 'woke' escort.

Lonely nights no more. Who doesn't want to make an already good day even better? They say you can't buy happiness, but an erotic time with me is pretty close... Others can only dream of having such joy. I have walked through many hotel corridors, into presidential suits. Amazingly, when a wife goes away, rather than calling it a day and going to bed early, a husband will text one of us: "Come on over, I have the house to myself."

Men will take a moment to stare at you. They know you are desperately seeking validation, acceptance and compliments but that work of art is not always what devours their heart. Beauty is beyond how you feel. How you make others feel is beautiful too. More than my body, I am my soul... It's okay to be kinder than necessary. In a culture obsessed with looks, to be beautiful is lovely but to have men not only compliment your looks but appreciate your intelligence, tender heart, laugh and smile is awesome.

Sex is great, and I am pleased with my life choices. It was through this enlightening route, that I was able to feel and capture a huge spectrum of emotions. It was an honour knowing that they wanted more of me; to enjoy my body like there is no tomorrow but also, beyond youth and looks, I had a way of nesting into their hearts. Stimulation, entertainment and comfort. I had them covered.

I seduced punters with my tenderness of heart, not charms and spells, as my African people thought... because I was usually the chosen one. Viciously and in awe, they whispered beneath their breath... "It's a voodoo pussy."

No one can destroy you, unless you allow it. I embraced that phrase in my whole new world and often teased my regulars, "You are hooked to the voodoo pussy. It will never let you go."

They said I was the unlikely one to get lucky, yet also they feared I would thrive because I had wisdom and a sweet temperament. Whilst they were overlooked, I was overbooked. They held a lot of anger and envy when they were 'passed over', but that was because we stoked our confidence in different things. There was more to love. They found the love sought. I didn't need a small heart tattoo to remind me to love. Love leaves its own mark when it oozes from within. They put so much stock and faith only in outward beauty, so they called me the undeserving one. If you are so self-absorbed, you use only your looks to benefit you. You will be appreciated only for your beauty. What won my clients' hearts was unknown to them. Compassion and communication work wonders, but there is a whole universe within me.

Men will always desire beauty and sex, so yes, appearances do open doors, but there is more to it than what meets the eyes. In this oldest trade called prostitution, there will always be new, young and attractive offers. The shell is vital, but inner beauty truly matters. Seduction is beyond beauty. It is magnificent when they love your intelligent and mysteriously deep mind. With so much stock in appearance, when the spell of your outer looks starts its inevitable decline, what is left of you? You don't have to be the most articulate communicator, but, as you polish up your eyebrows, remember also to polish up on your communication and interpersonal skills. Beyond emanating lust and delight and a thrill to allure, my soul was shining. I was more than a potty for men to piss on or piss in. I was not a menu. I was a glory hole and human all through. Most importantly, I am the adventure that created magic.

Apart from being entertaining, I was genuinely engaging and understanding. A haven, a hiding place and resting shade. Men were humbled by my grace and humanity. With my lived experiences, I was able to offer hope, vulnerability and most importantly, strength. We can all agree that in much trauma and hurt, we want a warm heart that will understand. Drawing from one's brain is consultancy. When you glean wisdom from someone and exhaust their mental energy reserves, learn to embrace and acknowledge them in every way humanly possible. When someone has been the oracle of the hour giving you that small but potentially lifesaving gesture or word at the right time, always kindly remember that an understanding heart gets exhausted too.

They came in all shapes and sizes. Catering for all emotions including some extreme behaviours is what an escort does. Having the techniques to manage anxiety in demented extroverts and arrogant introverts, encouraging those on their road to healing, whilst tolerating men with weird horny-angry humour.

Me to him: "You smell really nice, what have you got on?"

Him, arrogantly: "Success."

I guess it's their choice also to wear unmatching socks, no belt... who am I to disapprove?

A man once came in shaking and shivering; I knew it was more than just the weather, even though it was bitingly cold. He looked dismayed and I asked him what the matter was. "Sorry, but I have just had an accident and am still in shock. I know I am going to lose my job because I will lose my driving licence."

I take things like drink driving very personally and discourage my clients from doing so. We've all heard the same jokes: "Just a reminder to everyone, not to drink and drive this festive season. It would be tragic if you were to hit a pothole and spill your drink." It's easy to joke about it when you haven't suffered the severe consequences of a drunk driver. Just remember, a huge part of a whole family has often been wrecked by the recklessness of just one individual. I tried to keep it fun with my clients, but I always ensured that no one was harmed during the session and safe as they departed.

Because nineteen-year-olds couldn't be bothered to call a cab after a party one night, my cousin was left on life support fighting for their life and ended up with brain damage. I cannot stress it enough: DO NOT DRINK AND DRIVE. Drive safely on the roads wherever you are and look out for your friends and clients. Be thy brother's keeper. If I was to let my clients drink and drive, I would feel responsible upon their departure. Who are they potentially going to kill? Even if they don't take drinking and driving seriously, I DO! Accordingly, I have always offered to pay for their taxi myself and advised them to collect their car another time, to avoid driving under the influence. Don't drink and drive. Don't text and drive. Don't snap and drive. Don't tweet and drive. Don't Insta and drive. JUST DRIVE! Nothing is more important than your own life and the lives of those around you. The life you save could be your own.

Please be safe.

Chapter 21
Feedback – Professional Testimonies

It's rather attractive when we know what people want and it shows in our response to them. Before long, I became a popular lady of the night, simply powerful in what I did. An enchanting treat with a sweet filling... with a promise to give something different than what they had known. I was always on someone's bucket list. Each time revealing more luscious layers of myself. I gathered a lot of feedback with a slogan of: "Keep Calm and Kinky On." A vibrant cocoa delight of Manchester, punters were assured that I was the girl to dive for. When you are touted for bringing fulfilment and transformation, you delight existing clients and bring in more at the same time. Every man wants to boast of his conquests, so this is what some had to say:

"Intelligent, articulate and exceptionally kinky. She surpassed my expectations. What more could one look for?"

"Fabulous woman in a class of her own, with a fabulous oiled up ass and intelligent too."

"A delicious lady drizzled in caramel, with a radiant smile. Very welcoming and professional, will certainly see her again."

"This incredible woman brought in her wonderful white friend. I had the best ebony-ivory threesome ever."

"Just when you think you know her, she surprises you. Top Christmas present for myself. She is absolutely amazing."

"Everything is as per her profile and I already look forward to visiting her again soon. No one does it better than Sandra."

"A lovely welcome on arrival and a meeting I will never forget. She is a fucking magnet."

"Lovely girl, the way she moves is mesmerising. Please treat her nice, boys. We found a tantalising thrill!"

"It doesn't get better than this... It can't. She is the Ultimate Ride."

"Guys, this woman can rock your world. She is one in a million and I will go back for more."

"Absolutely stunning woman who fulfilled my needs. I oiled that big ass and had lots of fun. I have more fantasies to pursue with this woman."

"Yet again, a wonderful time with a wonderful lady. The coffee treats and laughter stories are great for the soul too."

"She gets better and better and better. Mmm… those alluring curves; don't take her for granted guys, she is too important to lose."

"I must have found a new religion, I suppose. I see her to drown my sorrows with incredible sex every Sunday."

"Do you want great sex or a relaxed stimulating conversation? Get both with this beautiful lady. I will be back."

"Guys, this is some sexy chick with a round black ass, very nice in all departments. You're missing out on something special."

"It was a Sunday morning. There, between those thunderous thighs, I worshipped her between her sheets. What a goddess! Her beckoning hips can tease and twerk with a promise of endless bliss."

"Had a delightful bump and grind with this glorious honeypot. Bursting with passion, her curves drive me wild."

My feedback for them, my final and most essential words to my clients… the great guys with excellent taste:

"Thank you for seeing me. It was a *business* doing *pleasure* with you."

***

At the end of the day, sex is a skill which is acquired and mastered through practice. It takes time to understand your body. Over time, with myself and my legion of clients, I was present to explore it and it taught me everything I needed to know about my anus, nipples, pussy, clitoris… everything. I became an ocean of knowledge in my game. I beam with pride and wear every feedback as a badge of honour because I earned every one of them. Sex work is not degrading, and it takes a lot of strength to be so good at it that it looks easy.

In time, I moved on from the brothels and parlours, and seeing the passion I had inspired me to become fiercely independent, enjoying the flexibility and freedom. Taking the internet by storm, I was a rarity because unlike most African of taboos, I was a tremendously kinky and modest fountain of fun who enjoyed illicit encounters. Now that was a uniqueness they surely didn't want to miss out on. You're either kinky or you're not. There's nothing in the middle

Having lived under a rock, in a society of taboos and traditions and then became the ultimate pacesetter in adult entertainment. I was too metal for a Malawian. A beast in bed, an active listener, most certainly the girl to dive for, dipped in chocolate, bronzed with elegance, toasted with beauty and infused with love; what's not to love? An impressive escort by all accounts, they came to find out what made me a popular fountain of fun, with a desire to be served yet also excelled in giving pleasure. I didn't live up to their expectations. I went far beyond, for those men who demanded unforgettable erotic encounters.

Because I am a hooker. Next question.

The prejudice against the disabled was rife. In no time at all, I had updated my profile to show that those with disabilities were welcome, and this was a rarity amongst most escorts who ridiculed me and thought it was a desperate measure. Hookers are for everyone, but not every hooker is for you. Others are kind and thoughtful. Others are selfish and egocentric.

What made me stand out in the increasingly competitive world of escorts was not the usual shine. It was not the longest nails or eyelashes. I didn't need the sun or the moon or the expensive jewellery to make me shine; my acceptance of many, broadened accessibility and illuminated me. Immediately, I was contacted by many disabled people, the first being a man who had both legs amputated due to a car crash that tragically killed his wife and twin daughters. His life had changed in the blink of an eye and even now he questions why he was kept alive and lost everything. I was impressed by how he was cleaner than a man on his two feet, and even more impressed that he left a very happy man.

With a thick layer of imagination, I explored, I discovered and each time a client left, I felt incredibly proud and I was reminded that we are all skilled at something. I was the epitome of diversity, but I did not see my clients as a diverse group of people. I took them as individuals. Come as you are; I come as I am. Britain is a great country and one of the foremost reasons is the courageous people who wear uniforms. I serviced servicemen and veterans, some with amputations and other ailments. There is no prosperity without security; they put their lives on the line to keep us safe. Serving is selfless, please thank them whenever you have the opportunity. In my case, who said a missing limb is the end of erotic encounters that they were willing to pay for? It was rewarding to contribute to serve my booty, whilst many 'high and mighty' escorts, created unnecessary difficulties and rejected them due to their prejudice against the disabled. Well, that is why we differ.

Despite serving the country honourably, there are those who feel they have been abandoned by combat stress. With a focus on inclusivity and accessibility, I cherished and respected them, and that combination brought them regular. That is the hallmark of a good escort. I was serving as per usual and squatting where the money was. But this time, it brought a different euphoria.

I enjoyed visiting a young man in Cheshire who was severely disabled. His wonderful carers arranged that I go every fortnight to cater to his erotic needs because they did not want him to be deprived. They were present in the house to guard him whilst I was in his specially adapted bedroom. However, they always paid me by cheque, and I couldn't understand why. Since the bible days, cash is king for prostitutes and still quite fashionable, I bet you that will never go out of style. Fucking hell, why must I be the first hooker to be paid by cheque and wait five days for clearance whilst their son has enjoyed his cake? It felt like a vain attempt to avoid paying so I swore not to go back there… sad it was, because I was just starting to really figure out their son, getting to know what works for him and I was able to hear him before he even spoke. I loved that broadmindedness of the British culture even more. Not only did they combat the loneliness and isolation of their disabled person, most importantly, but they also did not shy away from nor deny the aspect of his sexual needs.

When I have a client, I see that man from an entirely unique perspective and notice things that other people don't, hence my insight into enhancing client experience was awesome. When much is given to you, much is required from you. Apart from bringing erotic energy, my vital role and chief delight as an escort was that people should not perish, but instead have everlasting, abundant joy by prescribing to the men what level of fun they need and how much, striking a balance with what they want.

Their needs versus their wants always flabbergasted me, sometimes to the point of laughter, other times to anger. There were always some men with annoyingly unrealistic expectations as though I was a miracle worker with black magic. There were some men with a two-inch dick who thought every position they watch in porn movies would be at their disposal. They just had to be told that it is as impossible as pigs flying. Pornography is the root cause of more pornography and unrealistic expectations. Whatever you watch there, please don't slap my vagina, unless it's with your balls.

Also, spitting on it is overrated but please take note; give my ass some smacks and you will leave me wanting more.

Others have popped the pills and drugs and still found no hope, but there is magic in the mundane. The rope to save you can be thrown by the least expected. Upon talking to someone caring, they suddenly became hopeful and kept their head together. I so loved the world. I was happy to go to supported accommodation for the elderly. This time it was a man in his seventies in Chorlton, South Manchester. I wondered why he always complained that I was not loud enough, as if there was anything to scream about, but then on my third visit, I suddenly heard his old-fashioned radio cassette player click because the tape had reached the end and he wanted to turn it over. He was recording the session for his personal use, but he kept denying it so that angered me. When I asked him to rewind the cassette, he felt embarrassed when caught red-handed, even though I told him that I forgave him. There was no keeping it discreet with this old man. He wanted everyone in the residential setting to know of his escapade. Last time I left my bra, he came rushing to my car in his bare feet, shouting, "You have left your bra!" I didn't mind him showing off with a bit of evidence. A life well remembered lives on.

People want to put on a show and pretend they do not hire escorts and that sex with hookers is revolting. Hypocritically, they do what they are condemning behind closed doors. Realistically, lots of men are in favour of nightwalkers. Others used me as a fetish, others for sexual therapy and many for companionship. That lonely man who wears leather pants may not have any friends, but he hires escorts to keep him balanced. I met disabled and older people. I met terminally ill men with catheters, who still had a need, and that need is there until the undertaker puts soil on top of them. A hooker can fix that. Just a simple lap dance in my lingerie cheered them up.

I was a realistic and fair escort with bespoke programmes, which was a different approach to the usual escorts. I was providing some comprehensive care which felt clinical in its nature at times, but my motto was always: "Bring it all in." Like a clinician, I had the right tools in my case to deliver a dynamic service more effectively.

At the sight of my travel case, most men often joked and asked, "Are you moving in?" I told them to keep calm; it's just my toolbox. For the good of my services and feedback, I had invested in modern capabilities so that I didn't fall behind other escorts.

Mighty results for me! The football match days of Manchester City and Manchester United saw me flourish and blossom, as the horny supporters with a lot of nerve endings filled the city to the brim. Win or lose, every game must end with a fuck, so at any rate, a hooker is part of their itinerary.

The peak time in my work was the Brexit period, the withdrawal of the United Kingdom from the European Union and the political process associated with it. The referendum and the uncertainty up until the triggering of Article 50 put ants in the pants of many men and it raised their anxiety even more when the Prime Minister declared that "Brexit meant Brexit". The effects of uncertainty... no matter the side of the debate, they all wanted to offload a frustration.

What better privilege than to buy underwear straight off my gorgeous body? Men called round to buy and collect a dirty pair of my knickers, for a decent price, because it's a fetish or even because they couldn't afford the session until payday. Sniffing that aroma of pussy keeps the demons away. That's an actual privilege.

I will admit I was starting to get addicted to all things kinky. Perhaps I wasn't good at being a wife, but I was certainly good at this. I could do it with my eyes shut.

Days of Heaven! Being an African... Malawian who had broken taboos, I went against what I was taught, to shut up and put up and be afraid and that the world was too big for me. Look at me now? A pacesetter. Neck-deep with clients from all over the world and I don't play the victim. It was a stimulating dimension for me. Each encounter was an experiment, revealing ourselves in all our warped glory. Who needs rescuing from absolute pleasures? What would you do if the one thing you love was taken away from you in an instant? This was such a splendid calling. I have never tried to work out how all this beautiful chaos would have been avoided because I would have missed out on some truly heavenly experiences... I really needed an outlet to release all the creative energy that I had been holding in. I was struck by my own energy, spontaneity and depth. Discovering how little sleep I can survive on, how important punctuality is, because I have knocked on hotel doors ten minutes late and disrupted people's schedules, so they told me to leave and that was a wasted journey.

Previously, I always operated on 'African time' which meant chaos and derailments. Late for weddings, late for interviews, late for court, literally late for everything because everyone will be late, until I learned things the hard way and punctuality became my greatest attribute. Time is money. Time is disruption. No wonder a rail company in Japan issued a sincere apology for the severe inconvenience imposed upon its customers after one of its trains departed twenty seconds early. It was not just twenty seconds; it was time.

My calling involved so many deeply unglamorous activities, a shiver would go down your spine at the mention of some of them, but it was not a burden to carry, because I had a passion for what I did, and I was perfect at it. Like every job, we do some things we did not sign up for. I was massively into voyeurism, swinging and group sex, more especially, harnessing and narrating, depending on my mood. With charisma and enthusiasm, I was simply powerful in what I did, and they followed. It's fascinating how they hand you over their power to destroy them. Not because they are weak, but they trust you will never use it. A hooker of skill and craft believes that submission is given, thereby exceeds their clients hopes. This is the luxury and depth of honour that should not be broken.

Also, I was the spice jar in people's relationships and that too was amazing. Become the glorious star that you think is missing in the world.

I was an escort for those who were hungry to connect with genuine interaction on a deeper level. From the comfort and privacy of their own rooms, meeting in cars and visiting couples, I catered for various fantasies in different scenarios, others, I accompanied on their honeymoon to fulfil their fantasies in ways only the most expressive minds could envision. It was great fun because the framework of the relationships was clear.

I gauge each day as a paragraph – a client as a punctuation. A day without a client felt like a paragraph with no punctuation, boring, useless, wasted and confusing.

In a life of survival and hope, each day as I waited for that predictably unpredictable phone call from a client, I hoped for a signal and a possible window of change – but what change? Each call I answered encouraged my imagination; my desire runs deep… give me this day our daily sex. The tables had turned remarkably. My days, my paragraphs, had now been enhanced with the most idyllic punctuations, bursting with flavour, seasoned with sex. Life is made of moments. I was making the most of mine.

Each appointment was crucial as it confirmed that I was pushing boundaries and breaking new ground. Sex became my route to vent off from the whirlwinds of life. My clients… my support group, I instantly found a strange peace within them… they were the key to my survival. Each day was living art, loaded with goodness and exhilarating benefits beyond pennies in my pocket.

I found not only comfort, but delight in recognising my weaknesses, because it was balanced by the sense that these clients were in my life by design. The relaxed, light-hearted, friendly and insightful chat that happens during that time is great for emotional health. Sometimes it was a mixture of funny and heartbreaking. Where I was weak, I was strong because we complemented each other. It was a force of raw creativity and passion. There is no shame in admitting that my days of pure awesomeness involved my clients. Whatever gives you Heaven on this Earth, cherish it. If someone is there to give you a hug, comfort and solace, let them. They are your beacon of hope.

Life is an ongoing exploration and there is no speeding up the process. No amount of profound wisdom saves us years of learning things the hard way. It may increase our understanding of the world, but things must be experienced… on this wonderful and exciting journey… including pain and discomfort.

How wonderful. How strange. In search of fun, somewhere along the line, pain brought us together, in want of hope. There is a seamless correlation between pain, love, loss, hope and laughter that heals the pain. With my legion of clients, we helped each other heal and kept our smiles. We talked about dreams and nightmares, desires, aspirations and goals and I reminded them that "we are alive because we have to go and get our expected end, those dreams have to be fulfilled". Have a hunger, a craving and an expectation. Some of you don't have dreams because you have given up. A living dog is better than a dead dog. He that is joined to the living has hope, and you don't have to go to hell first before you get to Heaven. Until the undertaker puts soil on top of you, there is hope. There is hope for you to restore and rebuild your life. Whatever has been destroyed and damaged with an addiction or words or hurt, you are not damaged beyond repair. When you are rooted and grounded in faith, you have an absolute assurance that there is hope. Faith and fear cannot room together.

Play synchronises with work, and I found out what made me happy. You cannot give what you do not have. If you do not have joy, what sort of parent, boss or teacher would you be?

Chapter 22
The Manager

I graced the football manager's day with laughter. It was the most mundane and inconsequential celebrity encounter I have had… It was a morning after an overnight booking at a prominent hotel in Manchester. My client had left early but gave me the privilege of using whatever I wanted, all in his name and room number, because some men are just generous; everything about them is a blessing.

I decided to use the facilities and make the most of the magnificent place.

I spotted the football manager many times either having his haircut or having his breakfast and he always smiled pleasantly and said hello but, on this day, he was in his sportswear, doing his body stretches. I signalled to him that I wanted a picture and he shouted me over. I don't remember who was more honoured between the two of us, but after a few selfies, I handed him over my business card and walked away without looking back. I left him looking at the details. Due to its creativity and imagination, at first glance, you can't figure out what the sketch is on the card but when you stare at it without blinking, you realise it's a porn card.

Well, after a few minutes, the manager obviously thought, *Oh shit! I can't have this card and she has my selfies!* He came charging down the stairs as if I had stolen from his cookie jar. He asked me to delete the now-controversial selfies. The security wondered what in the world was going on, as he asked for my phone, but he was too embarrassed to explain to them what had just happened. After all, nothing had really happened that needed security. "Everything is fine. I will handle this. I just need her phone for one minute."

I had this alarmed look on my face, as you do, as I asked him, "Have you not got your own phone?" The security wondered why he was panicking if everything was perfectly fine, so they stood close by to supervise the bizarre situation as I kept asking, "Why are you being so childish?"

All eyes on me, he kept saying, "Please."

I eventually surrendered and handed over my phone, but I put it on private gallery and told him he can find the selfies there. He is a man with like passions, easily distracted by an XXX gallery, so he took his time as he shook his head in awe. He must have forgotten what he was looking for. Finally, he found our selfies and deleted them, but it takes a real genius to know an album called 'recently deleted'. I had my fingers crossed that he wouldn't go to it, and he didn't. Relieved, we shook hands and he apologised sincerely for the unnecessary drama caused. I won a selfie, stolen from my 'recently deleted' album.

Chapter 23
Dirty Diaries

"Save me some sperm please, Sandra. I'm coming up your way later today." That was all he ever wanted. Although he was my regular client for many years, I have never had sex with Carl, but all he required from me was the used condoms, to drink the contents from inside them and use some of the sperm to rub on his dick and masturbate. This vampire in him would literally root through my bin to unwrap any tissue papers that he thought would contain a used condom. There is really no limit to how disgusting some people can be. If there were none, he asked to buy my bowel movements.

What we have is a failure to accept, tolerate and understand that what is gross to one person is delicious to another. Some things should never be assumed pleasurable to all, unless requested. Carl was a man from the upper class, who went skiing a few times a year when not working. In his role at work, he was making big decisions, and in his personal life, this was another big decision he made.

Looking at his family album on his phone, Carl always enjoyed talking about his family and I always admired his rich lifestyle and the state-of-the-art wedding he gave his daughter. He said he had a great sex life at home, but this was his dark little secret because we all have a dark little secret.

And then there are other little snippets from my life…

Client: "Please choke me during sex. I want to almost die."

Me: "Does your insurance company know that you like being choked?"

Some men's ambition in life is to go around blowing an escort's mind with some sizzling hot sex because they have the time, the money and the stamina. Is it sad?

When a man gives you oral sex and instantly, he stops and says, "It's your turn now," as if he had to. I'm on duty, so it's all about you; don't worry. It's my turn to pleasure you all the time! Why ask that?

Sex with strangers: so raunchy, synchronised and passionate. When he leaves, I think to myself, *Did that just happen or was it a sweet dream?*

Don't feel obliged. Sex is not compulsory. There are many other things we can do. I can shave you, give you a passionate bath and give you the hour of your life.

Some men are an absolute circus in bed. Do I have to keep lecturing men on sex etiquette and the essential techniques? I have been lecturing all day. I will leave it to the other escorts to tell the others how hopeless they are.

Men are wearing out all their energy in the gym, so by the time they get between my legs, they are already shattered. They blame it on muscle cramp. Save some energy if you want to enjoy the best of both!

When I was still working at the first brothel, I met a businessman called Richard. He asked me to accompany him to a swingers' club on the outskirts of Manchester for four hours. He briefed me on what was what, but at this time I had developed a 'don't-knock-it-'til-you've-tried-it' approach. He picked me up and assured me he would drop me back after.

We got in, stripped off at the door, put our clothes in the locker and towels were handed to us. Everyone knew Richard. He was a regular there and the staff were used to seeing him with different women, never with his wife though, because he had kept this a secret for many years. She had always thought he had gone to play tennis and was having social time with his friends after. He always made sure to wet his tennis kit before he left so that it appeared to be sweaty.

The swinger club scene was another new one for me. We went into the Jacuzzi and he whispered to me that he doesn't speak to the couple that was in there with us, and I shouldn't greet them. I followed the instructions.

Then we went to another room, my legs spread wide and as far back as I could keep them. He took care of business with his tongue; I just couldn't get enough of my newly found love for oral sex. Boy oh boy, a performance is a performance and you never know if it's going to be a masterpiece. I could still have been in a marriage and would never have experienced this feeling! All things work together for good.

I was screaming, maybe a little bit too loudly, because it wasn't until after my orgasm that I heard some cheering and clapping. I looked up and noticed it was a glass ceiling, with about a dozen people watching; masturbating and stroking each other. For a moment, I felt dreadfully embarrassed. I could have sunk into the ground.

I asked Richard why he hadn't told me about the voyeurs and the glass ceiling. He said, "Darling, it's not called a swingers' club for nothing! It's a group activity, so there will be an audience and you were stunning." Hats off! That truly awful feeling of embarrassment only lasted a little while. Once I processed it, it genuinely turned me on. I found a fascination in being watched whilst I get fucked. The more eyes on me the better. I feel sexy, confident and desired to be devoured by the envious crowd.

The following week, Richard asked me to accompany him again. It meant more money for me, and as it was great the previous time, I said yes.

The second time, there were fewer people there. We went into a room and another couple followed us. The man said something to Richard that I didn't quite understand. Again, I had my legs open at ninety degrees, oral time, my favourite time, and as I started to enjoy it, the woman came and took over from Richard. I was just about to say, "No, I'm not bi…"

Before I could say anything, I realised that I was having the best oral sex of my life from this woman and it was great. My thighs wrapped around her head, she was about to stop, and I pulled her head back on my pussy because I was just about to climax. I noticed her husband was watching us, masturbating, yelling out noises of pleasure, until he had an orgasm at the same time as me. Richard was sucking my nipples. It was a mesmerising scene.

The noises some men make when they orgasm! You would think something was stuck in the wheel.

Spent but so content, I said to Richard, "Sex is a different kind of magic." And I thanked her endlessly for blessing me.

Seeing the immeasurable fun that I was having in this partners paradise, he decided that the enjoyment would suffice as payment, instead of actual cash. Horrified, I decided that was goodbye. It gave me an ambition to create my own sex parties.

Discreetly, I had swapped numbers with the couple involved in that second visit, called Cindy and Mathew. Richard was not aware. They were engaged and due to be married. We maintained the friendship for some time until I accompanied them on their honeymoon in Dubai. It was there that Mathew's obsession with me began to grow stronger; he decided he wanted to start seeing me behind Cindy's back. Why do men always want to spoil it? Because bread eaten in secret is more delicious, but that was against the swinging rules and I felt uncomfortable. Also, he didn't want to put anything in the honesty box, which put me off totally.

The last time I went to a swingers' party with another client was a Valentine's party packed with couples. There was hardly any room to manoeuvre; what was the point? My client suggested we go upstairs, as he thought it would more spacious. It wasn't. We went into a room where everyone was fucking. Apart from it being steamy and smelly, as though some had not showered in weeks, it was exasperating. The man started to touch me, and I said to him, "No, I can't. I can't do this."

I could tell he was about to say, "But I have paid you."

So, before he did, I said, "Look, I will give you your money back, so I can breathe!" Nauseated, I made my way to the lockers, got ready and rang a taxi.

It was a cold winter night. I went outside and embraced every breath in that beautiful air, I will never take fresh air for granted.

United we stand, divided we fall. My neighbours knew that my milkshake brought all the boys to the yard and always looked out for me because I did likewise in a million ways. My panic button went straight to them, so did the champagnes from my upscale clients. When you are a thoughtful hooker with some elegance, you are celebrated. One day, some landscape gardeners tried to bully me as they mowed the lawn, one guy shouted, "She's a whore," the other sang, "cause she's easy like Sunday morning." They were shocked when a fierce woman from across the road commanded them to shut up: "You can't afford her... cut the crap and just cut the grass!"

Unexpected hooker in Gracious area. No one dared to distress me on their watch. They protected me with dragon fire... because I made the place a little better. My presence graced the community in ways you cannot imagine. They have their own stories, of a symbol of goodness swathed in a hooker.

As times have changed, expectations have changed. Many people want to engage in sexual activity, especially of an unconventional or uninhibited nature, but I loved what I did and did it well. The best part of the day was when clients chatted away and shared some wine as they waited for me to finish with a client, because sharing is caring. Like a bread slicer machine is not washed after each loaf of bread is sliced, did I have to have a bath after each client? I increased the rate for the one who found the engine ready to go so hot. That was the peak of the kink of fetish. Some like a woman well used. What's gross for one is magnificent for another.

I was a happy hooker. Like an artist, the more I did, the more I could do. But what was it that made me the girl to dive for? I met bankers, gurus, consultants, lawyers, architects, barristers, lawmakers/enforcers… those whose only company is their own deep-dark thoughts, freelancers working long unrelenting hours and salesmen working in the city by day. I got used to playing dead when their partners rang them during our play time. Even with numerous commitments and obligations, men know that all work and no play is toxic. Some men fucked during company time. Many disappeared from their colleagues for some passion during their business trips.

In every trade, we are expected to be expert at our game, but some people have no personality, they just conform to who is around them. Others almost lifeless and robotic, at times I had to coax a smile because some men are so shy and reverent, others a jittery ball of anxiety and nerves. That raw vulnerability was sexy too. I had to decide for them what they needed and walked them through the process. Forgive their inexcusable sloppiness... They are not coordinated enough for sex. We all need our own form of artistic expression and my creativity emerged through the art of sex. Most men need a real shake up, but if you are a traditionalist who tends to play it safe and avoid anything surprising, there was a place for you too. I was earning my living.

Working in brothels offered some degree of safety but becoming an independent sex-worker gave me freedom, the right to refuse service to the arrogant, rude and vile bigots. I love to be in control and the dominance involved in other cultures, faiths and backgrounds doesn't usually afford me that privilege. They believe that women must be abused, so I tend to avoid them at all costs even though they don't normally take 'no' for an answer. They can go and commission somebody else – we just don't sync!

Then there is a group of annoying savages who revel in being devils. You just cannot trust them with the cherished parts of your body. Love yourself and give up the money to save yourself. Be humble and respectful, because the world is a small place. It's nice to be important, but it's more important to be nice. One of my most horrible vainglorious clients learnt this the hard way when he accidentally added me to his family group on *WhatsApp*, and the vengeance was all mine with no mercy! It was my turn to grind him into powder. The family left the group one by one as I showed them what I was made of and revealed what this man had done. In the end, his whole family knew that this man – their dad, uncle, brother, husband – was horrible and racist to his escort.

Some say that sarcasm is the most subtle form of human expression, others say it's the physiological response to fear. I'm sure we can figure out jokes that don't demean or belittle others. Unless it physically pains you, hold back those sarcastic words because you can't take them back. Charming yet nasty, it always felt like injustice to me, so that was the most difficult part. It created unnecessary drama and I would throw their cash back at them as they explained that they were just being sarcastic.

What about those arrogant men… exploiters… who dive onto my bed, naked and say, "Surprise me… give me your filthiest fuck!" They think they are the best thing since sliced bread. Erm, no. I would rather not. Keep calm, I would love to just throw you out… Surprise! I'm a happy hooker, just living life. I don't like people expecting me to 'perform' while I'm just being me.

At times my romping shop was like an academy, teaching men how to conduct, so as not present themselves as idiots.

You are safer when you see no evil, hear no evil. I need another brain just for secrets. Sometimes, in their phone calls, I overheard some discussions of possible crime but, hey-ho, I heard nothing. My life is already complex enough as it is. It's not only in films that people trigger their own tragedy because they showed signs of paying attention.

The desire for supremacy is social poison! I hate to play victim. I do not play the race card. But the power dynamic is rarely, if ever, in our favour. They even decide what is affordable to you! It's toxic when a dominant race regards themselves as more human than the other… As though black people spoil their cosy view of the world, some folks are so racist to a degree I never thought likely. Money talks, and even a racist rodent knows that they can use that privilege to buy amusement by hurting one's feelings. Imagine a white supremacist, with a misplaced sense of entitlement, hating on blacks so much that they will pay extra money in order to carry out that hatred, and freely use racist remarks! They have nothing to lose but an ego to boost.

Are escorts actively perpetuating the sick racial theory by agreeing to these grotesque roles? These offensive bookings certainly reproduce and entrench racist thoughts which sustain racist acts. It was tough. Some choices we make from desperation and we still feel embarrassed by them. Slaving away for the rich, exploited for my grief and poverty. In a desperate strange world, £20 was an offer I just could not refuse. It pained me then, it haunts me now and I am sorry. Whoever said slavery was a choice, knows not the disease of a racist mind the calamities it brings...

Did I feed the racist by letting myself suffer for their enjoyment? Did I promote racism by letting a bigot pay to racially abuse me? It is disturbing to think that some people feel alive when they feel superior. It was not for the love of money but for the lack of it and that crushed my soul. In the brothels, they wield power over the sex-workers, their interest meant I had no freedom to eject clients or choose whom to provide a sexual service. If a walking - talking corpse convinced them it could afford the going rate, it was getting some pussy for sure.

That was the day I quit, and I have never worked in a brothel nor for an agency. I went my own way, to do only my wilful desires and it was certainly not to be paid extra to be abused and called a *Negro*. In a world of hate and divide, whilst I am at work; playing and engaging... I committed myself to a vision of bridge building and racial reconciliation because we are one race – humanity.

Putting my hand up to the wrist and stirring it inside someone's anus? Why has fisting suddenly become so popular? I'm not a surgeon, so count me out. Our lips can touch, but kissing has never been my strong point. In fact, I can count with one hand the number of deep-dive kisses; I became an expert in dodging attempted kisses. Hold on, I will suck your dick... Don't suck my tongue. But suck my pussy. That is my sustenance.

I keep the kisses to a bare minimum, but there is always that man who thinks if he hasn't shoved a good measure of his tongue deep in my throat, then he hasn't had the full experience.

Love changes everything. One day I will kiss someone. I will taste the passionate hunger in each kiss, no matter how soft. Someone who will kiss my scars and love my pain away. I know what to look for. I can discern a fool's motive from miles away. When you have seen and felt pain in love, look for a love that feels unfamiliar. One day I will open my heart to a man who loves me so deeply it pains his spirit if he hurts me. The opposite of my abusive father. The opposite of my abusive ex-husband.

The money is good, but overnight bookings are tricky. Spooning with clients and falling asleep on their chest is not idyllic as I may need to evacuate. The heart yearns for more. If you are fortunate to fall asleep and feel safe, knowing that you are loved, cherish that reassurance and never take it for granted. It's a cold world out there.

They don't all just want my body. They want my time, smile, honesty and effort. When cross-dressers book me overnight, they spend most of the night modelling everything in my wardrobe. The biggest chore is to put my entire wardrobe back in order the next morning. Still, that is better than giving a slow blow job for ninety-six minutes.

"What have you got planned for the rest of the day/evening?" Always moist and ready to be fucked, I was always in the mood to get someone up against the wall and do dirty things to them. I must have had dragon-energy because I have entertained many stag-nights and left the men mind-blown because that's what those parties are all about; they know exactly the escorts they are going to get here. It was an honour to be the chosen one.

When I was feeling sad and blue or in doubt, I wanted a client. When I was happy, I wanted a client. Delight blooms when I have a client. I love a man who will eat my pussy like his whole life depends on it. Not lick it cowardly with contemplation. Eat it with conviction and have a finger up my bum, because I suspect my G-spot is in that compartment. The dick, for me, is just the finisher. The grand finale, if you must, because penetration only summarises what you have just enjoyed doing to me.

Nipples are underrated. Even men should explore their nipples.

Whilst you are so busy at work down there, I am playing with my own nipples, because multitasking is not a skill most men have but if you can… Please squeeze my nipples harder and harder and the angels will be rejoicing, but do me a favour: Whatever you do, just don't twist my nipples as though you are tuning in the radio. And while I'm at it, don't scratch my delicate clitoris as though it's a lottery scratch card! That seriously rattles my cage.

Often, some men ejaculate whilst eating my pussy and that is a gloriously mind-blowing moment for me. You came as I was coming? Oh, my heaven! It makes me feel super that you ate it because you loved it, and, in the process, you were so turned on beyond control, nature took its course. You orgasmed as I did because when the clouds are full of rain, they can't help but empty themselves.

I prefer if all men spat their gum out before meeting me, but when they do come in chewing gum, I impatiently wait for them to ask me for the bin to spit their gum out. Some do! Well done. The stupid ones want to start licking my pussy as they chew gum. I still haven't worked out how best to express my anger when they do that. Like seriously, if your gum is that nice that you can't even spit it out, why not just enjoy it? If you want to dilute the taste and the smell of pussy with that gum, what's the point of even licking it? I don't have pet insurance yet. If you chew my pussy lips away and destroy it as you chew your gum, what chance have I got for compensation? It seriously rattles my cage.

All in all, some men are just so crap in bed… I have seen some disgraceful performances more than you all.

Looks and image aside, the handsome, genetically blessed men with vanity are not necessarily the ones who are best in bed. I have confirmation that some big dicks and good looks are just for show. They deliver nothing. They may be lovely to behold, but not hold. Most don't even have the sex rhythm or the thrusting techniques; I feel sorry for them. You're not handsome but that will do me. Again, I have met some 'ugly of the ugliest' under the sun, who have given me the most mind-blowing orgasms ever. It makes them handsome behind closed doors, so I have come to realise that nobody is ugly. We all have a uniqueness that needs to be discovered. Sequence is everything and they know the thrusting secrets of deeper, slower, faster and harder. They are so good. I'm sure they can dance too. They may not turn heads, but they undoubtedly go to the trouble of going the extra mile and they have mastered how to arouse a woman. Excellence doesn't come by itself. You have got to decide on it and work for it.

"Hello, are you busy today? Scan results show that I have a blood clot on my right lung. I want to come over at 2 pm, if you are not busy." This is not the typical text message a hooker expects from a client, but it was what it was. Clients have often shared many problems with me, but I have never had to remind them that I was not a medical doctor, because their problem shared with me was half solved. When they had their scan results, they elaborated to me what operation they will be having in due course, because I care; it was crazy!

"I have so much to tell you."

"You will never guess what happened." I heard these words often because my clients felt comfortable and in harmony with me. When an escort is your only hope to quicken your spirit, count it all as joy; at least you are not hopeless. I was the professional girlfriend who always received the breaking news, good or bad. Life is peppered with hate, but gracious people respond with graciousness, hence why they got emotionally attached. You don't have to be spiritually or politically aligned with someone to be gentle, kind and pitiful to them. They didn't just see all things bright and beautiful in me. My little darkness was beautiful and magnetic too.

Although I want to be someone's favourite person to talk to, different clients brought out different results in me. Our adventures included conversations, wild sex, and silence. Silence is often a powerful, yet misunderstood and underused tool which can be so heavenly and exotic. Indeed, actions speak louder than words, but I offered the gift of silence too because there is something eerily beautiful about it which must be savoured. Fresh ideas emerge and deeper truths come to surface… in silence around the right person.

To be silent or to speak? Comfortably share the silence. What did they want of me? Some people find love in silence. A quiet moment with the right person is never an awkward moment. They heard every word I didn't say. You can reassure someone living through dark days that they are not alone, without saying a word. Sometimes it's the only way that one can derive strength and positivity.

Weirdly lacking in hope, it's too easy for some to fall into despair. There are times when people just need to get away from themselves, to find their way back to themselves. Constantly recalling pain and grief, all they hear is whatever made them sad, whatever made them cry, whatever hurt them the most, the harsh words that were spoken to them. Your mind is the trigger, because those thoughts will determine how you feel and speak.

Peace on the outside comes from what is on the inside. When you go through a disappointment, don't stop on that page. Against any odds, keep the faith, no matter how frustrated you may feel. I was with a severely disabled toddler, in a foreign land, homeless and scarred from a violent and abusive marriage…with no work permit and no access to public funds. I was socially murdered… vilified by those who I thought would stand by me. I was disadvantaged and fragile. Come what may, as I travelled through the darkness, I never stopped seeing the world with hopeful eyes. No matter the pain you experienced, no matter the damage from the emotional wound, a better world is possible for you… only with hopeful eyes. Even as little as a mustard seed, hope can see you through the storms. What was broken can be repaired. What was stolen can be replaced with another of a better kind. It may not make sense right now, but those challenges are all working together for your good. Don't focus on who or what is the architect of your brokenness. They don't deserve your focus. Move on and enjoy the journey of this one life.

The struggle is real, and I sensed the despair that some of my clients go through daily. Needing the will to live before it's too late, sometimes being understood is restoring. No wonder they came regularly, not to be monitored or checked but simply for the want of perpetual joy, an on-going washing away of stress as though they are walking under a waterfall. Most destruction was in their mind, like they were having a civil war within themselves and they needed preserving from further destruction. My intervention was desired. Some people, you must look at them with the eyes of mercy, comfort them with a sense of whatever goodness you have and preserve them. It's upsetting to love someone with self-destructive tendencies. I have seen the fall, yet I have never judged the struggles. Isn't something slowly killing everyone though? There is no shame in admitting that we are all in some way broken and recovering in one way or another. Who among us has never looked up from the bottom of a pit and realised that they dug it themselves?

Every day is a raging war. If they are not running from something, they are running from themselves; their own life is like a war zone. Others just wanted to be around me, to know they are safe and to feel safe. We didn't have to say much because my presence meant so much. It was a realm which turned tears to laughter and fears were vanquished. By savouring my presence in the loudest silence, their chaotic world changed because they take a visit into their soul and tap into the joyful love that blooms in my heart.

"No rushing, no pushing. We are taking everything slow." People want to meet each other with the only aim of having sex as fast as possible and an escort is that fast track route to having sex. Life is already hard as it is and it's increasingly frustrating to sit on five consecutive dates, asking about favourite foods and hobbies, when they know their aim is simply sex. Take it slow, sweetheart. Meanwhile… he's here.

Whatever helps to restore imbalance, everyone needs a crutch because we are all battling something. I have done my part to tackle depression, stress and anxiety, the crippling illnesses that are taking away many lives. Loneliness can become a habit that leads to a dangerous addiction, because once you embrace the peace and tranquillity that comes with it, dealing with people becomes a challenge. But not everyone wants to be lonely. So many people are struggling and feeling alone so much that the world is collapsing under their feet.

In some parts of the world such as Malawi, people are hardly ever lonely. In fact, the elderly and ill are overwhelmed, if not 'suffocated', by friends and family who fail to give them the space they desperately need.

I sympathise with people on their own and coming to Britain made me realise that people go weeks without human interaction. Loneliness is toxic and as confirmed by the Royal College of General Practitioners, loneliness and social isolation is just as bad for our health and wellbeing as long-term illnesses such as diabetes or high blood pressure. Loneliness (like poverty) is a growing problem in Britain, with devastating impacts, and it cannot be treated with pharmaceuticals or referred for hospital treatment. This emphasises that we are social animals. I have done my part to combat this by being a listening escort, offering company, joy and comfort before people suffer more serious health problems; I have been a preventative measure and people have been transformed. Lonely people are known to consult the frontline doctors more than others because the only time they hear from people is nuisance phone calls, which disrupt their life. With loneliness forecasted to soar even higher, it's scary. An escort's impact is undeniable… they interrupt those periods of deep-dark isolation. Maybe even ease unnecessary pressure on the National Health Service.

The importance of escorts is often, unfortunately, undeniably huge, hence why they are ridiculed and issues affecting them often go unheard. They are real first responders! Trust me, if men don't see a doctor, a psychologist or a spiritual advisor for emotional support, they fearlessly share their turmoil with an escort. An escort will harness the wind, the tide, and make it just in time, to save them from that sunken place... because it is a more creative partnership. The oldest profession, with no end in sight, should have much more attention given than fate has allotted it. It is beyond a commercial interaction. We rise to the occasion with an open mind and an earnest desire to understand whilst caressing the necessities.

For some clout and attention, people use a tragedy to promote themselves online. They come out of the woodwork to 'tackle' the catastrophic issue of mental health and how it wrecks lives, only when a celebrity dies by suicide – five minutes later, they forget about supporting people around them. So many faceless farmers end their lives, but they do not react equally and vehemently. It's a cold world out there. Like a 'time bomb', we are all an evil away from breaking down; lest we boast. The biggest killer of men is themselves! I was on the frontline because men feel so comfortable to pour to an escort their private and personal issues. Rather than use misery to make some noise, give someone the will to live.

Never underestimate the power of escorts, conversation and your salvation. Always looking through the window adjacent to my flat, I thought he was the creepy old man, but he was just a lovely, lonely man watching the world go by. Tony was my charming and nosey neighbour in his eighties. He minded my business every day and it never offended me once. I brightened up the rest of his entire life. He lost his wife six years before. He cried in his coffee and listened to sad songs all day… "I would have been very lonely and probably dead by now, but you are so scandalous and filthy that I always want to know what you will do next." Sometimes he asked me if I had any outcalls because he wanted to drive me to them. The thrill of waiting for me an hour or two, whilst he read his papers in the coffee shops entertained him with a happy, healthy life. His face always lit up when he saw me coming out of my appointment and asked me if I wanted a hot or cold drink. It feels great to sustain and enhance people's lives through the power and art of sex.

I was in a social turmoil myself, but my job was a newfound responsibility. We are all on earth for a reason and if we did what we have been assigned to do, the world would be a better place with less regrets. Sometimes you must solve another person's mess and in the process of giving, you find a solution to your own mess.

Communicating and responding to the emotions of others, I felt a duty to work. Like an emergency service for some men. Some were burning up or broken, but we didn't have to take our clothes off to have an enjoyable time. The damaged ones tell the best stories, when you take time to see past their damage. They just wanted a cuddle. Tenderness. Completeness. Gentleness. Someone understanding them and really meaning it. Others were suicidal and just needed someone to tell them, "Don't be stupid; life is surely not that bad!" They were so down and wanted me to lift them up – mind, body and soul.

There is no standard template from which we are produced. Unlike most escorts, I don't like to be all about the numbers. It's not a race, and other sex workers are not a competition. We are not cut the same. I was in a league of my own, listening to problems, life journeys, and absorbing people's emotions upon meeting them. It was rewarding to be a precautionary measure to help men avoid toxic coping mechanisms for their mental health issues. Some habits destroy you; others help you to flourish. I was troubleshooting all things: mind, body and soul. Naturally, I reserved some qualities for those who reached certain regions of my heart; those who went the extra mile.

When certain clients entered my world, I always wished I had shouted: "Leave your demons at the door." It's impossible to please everyone all the time when some people are born to be unfulfilled. Even if you part the Red Sea, some people will never be satisfied. Erectile dysfunction is real, but they will still blame their limp dick on me and lie that the last one they hired did an excellent job. Some frustrated humans are taking it out on whatever is nearby, and they are out to put an escort in an unusually bad mood, because that is all they are programmed to do. They are emotionally unstable, highly erratic and irrationally argumentative termites who speak ill of other hookers. They work you to the bone, then spit you out to chew the next hooker. With a complete disregard for others, they fuck you vigorously until all the hinges fall off… that is when they know they have had their money's worth. They want to squeeze everything out that you have got to give, so that the next client comes and finds nothing. I mean, some people are just outrageously nasty.

There were some bittersweet moments, sometimes I felt like mine was a rehabilitation centre for badly raised men. I breathe a sigh of relief when I shut the door behind them.

My most frequently asked question is: "How many times am I allowed to cum in the hour?" Should I be aroused or terrified? Slow down your thoughts! Life is too short for serious consideration. For the most part, my experiences have been amazing soul-to-soul connections with the considerate, genuine, accepting and enlightening guys who found me gratifying. There are no words rich enough to convey the depth of some wonderful experiences. My good clients were appreciated and dare I say… loved.

What about the men who are complex and constantly seek the attention of women, only to be unpleasant and force them to assign a numerical value to praise them or rate them? Every escort refers to them as 'hard-work'.

The gross sense of entitlement is: "I have paid. I can do what the hell I want." Some men just don't get it. It's your money but my rules, and I don't care what the last escort let you do. No wonder people get thrown out of bars, planes and events… Sociopaths didn't deserve my time or personal and intimate skills.

Some men are just selfish babies and all they needed was a dummy. "Why do I exist rather than not?" is the only conversation they make because they are so full of hate and negativity; they have an existential crisis. They let their hurt and pain cause them to condescend to others. They decide they are always going to be the difficult punter to every escort. They cope with life only by trivialising others and I cannot stand them. Because they have been oppressed in life, they think they have the right to oppress others. It doesn't help me or them. Beware of such people for they are time burglars. Don't give them three extra minutes of your time. Annoyed, I always shut up and nod along as I watch the clock advancing and then heave a deep sigh of relief as the eleventh hour tells them I have had enough.

Brilliantly funny – brilliantly sad. It's great to celebrate fantasy but other gullible men, with an immature brain that is susceptible to believing fantasy as fact, basically cherry pick the most photoshopped and filtered escort who will not live up to their expectations; then they come running to an actual, factual person who portrays realness and indeed looks as advertised – an ideal mix of beauty, sass, ass and humour.

My subtleness and maturity were more reason for my popularity; I was impressive on many counts. I had many virtues that made me the chosen one. The most obvious manifestation of this difference was my ability to keep calm and kinky on. Admittedly, sometimes I was hard pressed on every side and did that which did not align with who I am and what I believe, but I'm sure we have all found ourselves in predicaments on the job. Nevertheless, those exceptionally rare occurrences did not corrupt my good morals.

To me, anything is all about art and discernment, so I love to get creative. I have discussed men's diagnosis and prognosis more than you all – with some clients going as far as brilliantly drawing diagrams, eager to make me fully absorb what exactly they are going through. I lose track of who is in which stage of what illness. They just need a therapist! I urge you readers to get checked for early detection of ailments. Also, I have seen more mashed testicles than you all, often resulting from childhood fights and pub brawls. Ouch! Refrain from fighting.

Is there anything too difficult for me? When men have been in intensive care and had their surgery, upon recovery, once able to enjoy life again, their libido returns with vengeance and they hold nothing back. They want an escort and my boudoir was the remedy and recovery 'functional-again' room. A secret hideout and fetish place. Others used their inhalers during sex… That was fine too, I guess I was twerking excessively. This place located in a neighbourhood of survival and hope had everything. I tried to be cautious and careful with those who were increasingly fragile, but they still liked it ruthless, so I went with the flow. With me, everything flows. X, Y and Z don't have to occur in that order... I adjust them on my terms. The one kidney brigade, pacemaker brigade, transplants brigade. I needed their next of kin. Imagine being told that you are beyond saving, and that you have less than a year to live! Some will be greedy, mean and self-serving. Others will be tenderly brilliant. I met them all. I took my talents to new heights. Meeting unknown people with complex social needs, without a discernment, I could never have lasted a day in my job.

This was far beyond personality and connection. Go on. Underestimate me! You seriously believe that blacks... hookers... have no decorum? I often judged my clients by how gullible they thought I was. It was easy enough to gauge the mood, attitude and atmosphere, but that wasn't safe enough, so I got to a level where, upon meeting my clients, I was quick to penetrate the thoughts and intentions of their heart. When you know, you know that the client is angry, stressed, happy, troubled, rude, self-seeking... and sometimes bizarre. Seriously, the list could go on.

Warning! Possible spoiler: Idiot narcissist ahead. So horrible, you start to wonder who hurt them in the past. So cold and calculative, they are usually the ones who instruct, "let's cuddle up tight." So tight I must tell them, "I can't breathe." Their hearts are closed, they can't love themselves and others. Why did it take me so long to realise that no matter how tender I am, I can't warm the fridge!

Note: to the timid men with so much sense and civility, they seem to get it all wrong. Don't be too smooth and gradual between the sheets. Leg-over requires some roughness, speed and a rough ride. Life moves fast. You can't afford to live it on slow motion. We are not fragile goods. Thank you very much.

Chapter 24
Rose Petals

Imagine the cruelty of taking away the sexual pleasure senses of women! Also, imagine the cruelty of taking away the sexual pleasure senses of men! Boy or girl, it is treasonable to enter an innocent child's legs and perform a barbaric act. All genital mutilation of minors must stop! Female genital mutilation is a heinous, horrendous, barbaric practice. Most of the black escorts I knew were very bitter towards me because unlike them, I did not undergo that brutality. With bitterness, they presumed that their crippled genitalia and lack of stimulation would be the biggest comparison amongst us. Possibly. As though it was my fault that their clitoris and labia was chopped off and the vaginal opening sewn up! They were bitter, upset and envious that I could literally enjoy sex and even craved for it. It has left them in sexual purgatory for life, but I have never thought them less of a woman because of this damaging, grossly demeaning and unconsented act. Tough. Trauma is rough, but you are still valuable and visible.

Nine out of ten women undergo FGM in some African countries and many cultures still curl protectively to this pernicious barbarianism. They could argue with their last breath, but it is one of the worst forms of abuse, and in my line of work, I have met some incredible survivors, with whom I have had heart-to-heart talks of how the knife, razor or hot objects used have deeply scarred them.

A beautiful rose trampled on the ground, FGM is a cringe-worthy, grievous bodily harm described by some as 'female circumcision', claimed by others as part of their culture and/or religion. It is a global emergency. Life scarring, yet preventable!

According to a leading Irish Muslim scholar who received backlash, he said:

"I am not an advocate of female genital mutilation, but I am an advocate of female circumcision which we see in the same way as male circumcision." How can we progress with this mindset?

Much to do with dominance, there is no medically advised female circumcision… no necessity under any circumstances and it cannot be remedied. The serious physical and psychological effects of genital cutting on a woman, by any terms, cannot be obscured. Not only does it take away pleasure. It induces anxiety, depression, pain, health complications… damaging self-worth… It is an excuse for cruelty and nothing but a sadistic, barbaric cut to control women's sexual appetite.

Hundreds of people have been convicted of FGM offences in France. In 1985 FGM became illegal in the United Kingdom and in 2019, the FIRST CONVICTION in Britain… a landmark case, a mother was jailed for eleven years, for cutting her three-year-old daughter.

Unless there is reform in these toxic cultures and traditions, there will never be restoration for the victims.

In Malawi, we were spared this cruel and barbaric practice. Nonetheless, the ritual was to do the exact opposite of FGM which was also a senseless torture all in the name of culture. Alas, the torment of traditions! Targeted when we are young and vulnerable, for up to five years, we had to extend our rose petals, our labia, to an inch or two and were inspected monthly to ensure we were doing accordingly. This 'shun natural pussies' stone-age practice still exists and parents who continue in it are regarded as switched on, compassionate and loving. The rule was "natural pussy or no husband". They sincerely believed it was a health and wellness issue that their daughters… who cannot be an aspiring wife without the enhanced labia. It was painful too and time-consuming. As objects used to give pleasure to a man, "They clamp his dick to enhance his pleasure," said one. "A penis cannot penetrate without them," claimed another.

It is often done out of love and respect for the men and is meant to be valuable. Baffling as it may seem to outsiders, cultures have their own interior logics which are often beyond comprehension and that logic is resistant to change, unfortunately. Once a cultural or traditional ritual is there, it is difficult to get rid of the thing no matter how demonstrably harmful it is. This was uniquely bad because we were children with no choice. In the end, the oddness and uniqueness of long labia added an exotic flavour and brought the guys to the yard.

It changes us, nevertheless, our life is still ours to live.

Chapter 25
The Cheshire Boys' Quarters

Once acknowledged as the richest village in England and officially the best place to live, Cheshire makes it in the top ten most affluent villages in the United Kingdom with mansions that cause a stir. From my poor area, who would have thought that I would frequent this prosperous place where those with high social status and fame, the filthy rich… celebrities, live? My sex-work took me there, with rich men demanding me to make my way 'now, now'.

Boys will be boys, or is it the damned sense of privilege? It was in this desirable place where about six or seven guys, all successful, sophisticated entrepreneurs displayed wealth and luxury… property developers, etc. They work hard, adventure always in mind, so they have a secret abode where they play hard, with booze, copious amounts of cocaine and hookers. They know the phrase that grabs a woman by the pussy… "how dirty can you get; your money is here waiting."

They are padded with money, but the idea that they are kind, thoughtful and classy is a myth. An escort knows the character they conceal and 'allows' them to manifest their true dirty colours. If only they were much nicer.

I was fortunate to be one of their hookers because once upon a time, they were all selfish, but they learned to be generous and kind after I told them they can't have "Buy one get five free! What part don't you understand when I say each man pays for his own dick? You are not all boarding this flight with only one ticket." They grasped it eventually but, in every group, there is always one with a hardened heart, a shameless sociopathic narcissist who still doesn't want to open his wallet but wants to have the biggest helping. It not only frustrates me, but it now annoys all his friends. He pretends he is so disinterested, yet he is hornier than all of them as he tries to be strategic to get away with not paying. Being a user is a mindset and eventually, a habit. College degrees do not guarantee social mobility.

All of them were with their wedding bands... Because they can't be seen around their area, their family probably thinks they are working away. They have often sent me to the cash machine to get more money to extend the booking and I have seen some mouth-watering figures as I draw out the allowed maximum.

Cocaine fuelled nights are a symbol that they have money and connections. Most of my client's tables would not pass a drug-test. If they are not snorting it off there, it was off a hooker's ass. Messy and with condom wraps everywhere, I love the sight of protection; clearly love for themselves and others... that they don't want to take anything home with them. Wise guys condomise. I have a soft spot for one of them and the feeling is mutual. I earned his trust and enjoyed his submission. He suddenly started to want me in a private room so he can kiss my neck and whisper some sweet things and I love the cuddles too. When I'm leaving, he tells me, "Please don't go. Don't leave me alone."

The others noticed his emotions and warned him, "Don't get too close." I told them to keep calm and kinky on. Don't be afraid to submerge in an escort. Some things look dangerous but are worth doing. Those who follow their heart, find themselves in the right place.

Chapter 26
Man-up-Man

Without twisting things and starting a war, I am all for stamping out sexism, because each gender or non-binary should not have their own individual issues and privileges. Gender equality goes for all sexes but it's pathetic too to obsessively spend all day attacking or discriminating against men and calling it feminism. We all need to stop the denial and the bigotry; faux feminism is a popular temporal trend, and it dilutes humanism in a way that harms others badly. What is the point of winning by tearing others down? Even that win is temporal. Social change begins with everyone. Where there is no isolation, everyone wins.

I am all for equality, but present-day feminism is a dislocated movement, headed in the wrong direction, with an ideology that's too toxic to survive. There are many other ways to attract attention without constantly screaming "men are trash". That's weak. Get stronger. This current approach has nothing to be with being pro-female and everything to do with being anti-men and wishing they didn't exist at all. Now that the men know we have clocked them out and we don't miss a trick, we will be just fine. Men are screaming to be humanised. Women are crying that they are oppressed. Rather than tearing each other down and hating on men, we can talk about humanism and empowerment and be great allies. Without ever naming it, because actions speak louder. I am all for whatever is right, empowerment and justice, rather than assertiveness.

There is a major clash between two superheroes. Man and woman. Feminism is only good when it aims for equality and the empowerment of women, but now it's just another way to segregate and vilify people. Let's just be human for a change. Humanism is even better, because it means I can just do accordingly as my spirit leads, without sticking my chest out and bragging about how important and great I am for doing a man a favour.

The last time I disagreed with a woman, I was told that, "It's so sad and disgusting that a woman is being pulled down by another woman." If men disagree with other men and don't like their behaviour or attitude, will they say men are pulling down other men? Such stereotypes and double standards are just flawed and low. Don't believe based on gender. Believe on evidence, experience, qualification and credibility. Let's get this clear. You will not be entitled just because you are female and the same applies to men. We need more than just feminism. The point is to see you as just a person. Humanism means I can be fair and hold a door open for a man who has his hands full, as indeed I do. I can give up a seat for a man carrying a heavy load, as indeed I do, without getting it twisted with the 'purity' test of 'real women' and 'real men'. Real people behave humanely and that's the world we should aim to create for our children, to stand up against inhumane or degrading treatment on another person – any other person!

An act to be humane is what will bring us close to the expected end – equality. Often men are ridiculed and mocked and told to man-up, and now they are burning out; it's drained the energy out of their soul. I, for one, found it interesting when actual science finally emerged that this often-misunderstood issue of man-flu could be real. That fact that it was confirmed by the British Medical Journal shows how real it is, and sheds light on my experience of men and their circumstances when they visited me. Men have weaker immune systems.

Dismissed and locked down as weak or sensitive, most men are swimming in darkness and currently hiding it from loved ones. Stereotypes perpetuate myths that men are expected to be hard as rock and fine about everything. Society's idea of a 'real man' is a hard-boiled husk who doesn't feel any emotions except anger, so much so that they are not a man if they show even a semblance of fear or compassion.

Now the anti-men discrimination is rife due to underrepresentation of women. We all live with contradictory thoughts at some point, which can be draining and painful, but men's mental health and depression is still so taboo, and the stigma is damaging. Where there is stigma, reason and love cannot exist. I don't add to it by telling them to man-up. They are simply being ignored because of their gender. The responses and reactions are damaging them – mind, body and soul. When I say come as you are, with your feebleness and weakness, they come running.

Although, our meetings are brief, and they didn't have to pull out their wedding rings... I imparted more into their lives than I took out and they had my attention through and through. That raw vulnerability and transparency is so necessary and healing. I don't treat men as disposable and shame them for being men. They are emotionally silenced in their masculinity and when one considers the staggering male suicide rate, it brings home how they can be treated unfairly and completely ignored. They are just dying for someone to talk to, a safe space, and an escort is their salvation.

That man with ugly scars on his body caused with a knife by his vicious spouse during a fight was only able to speak to me. He had just had a promotion at work, but his life was miserable. It was starting to affect his job. There is such a thing as a female abuser. It only takes a mind willing to see it and a brain willing to accept it.

Okay, let this sink in. I don't hate men, not even a crying man... This was a haven and a shoulder for them to cry on! It doesn't make them less of a man. I was hurt by a man and I was healed by so many wonderful men. I want the men that come around me to have compassion. If that includes crying, I will comfort. For me, that makes him stronger. With me, men could be their true selves and felt safe to share emotions without being mocked.

Men are victims of domestic abuse too, but astonishing modern double standards leave them with few dedicated support services, and so they may find it easier to talk to an escort because they expect to be blamed and shamed by society. I educate them about how they can survive through the lies and manipulation and safeguard themselves against fake cases and violent and aggressive women. There are a few disgruntled women making men's lives miserable with the toxic theory that 'Men Are Bad All Day, Every Day'. We must watch out if society is to be dominated by radical, venomous feminists who feel the need to be outraged by everything just to feel relevant. The generalisations and overreactions are bewildering, and I personally know of a woman who boasts how she broke all the handles of the cooking pans through beating her man, and she gets away with it! She makes out that she is a victim! There is such a thing as a female abuser.

I didn't always buy their stories or give into their demands, but I gained a lot just by listening, and I can say the struggle is real. I learn more about them than they do me. Reading their heart cover to cover, most people's goals are based on survival at this point. They try to be better, only to find something else they are not good enough at. Say no to merely just existing. Forget why you are angry with the world... even if only for a moment. Let's love, laugh and fuck with everything we have.

Find that thing you are good at, that talent, that gift and forget about being a master of all trades. When you don't know what you have been called to do, life will pass you by in a twinkle of an eye. Find your calling!

Many men feel isolated and excluded because their difficulties are used against them and most men can't put this hurt and alienation into words, but I knew they wanted a source of enlightenment and comfort. Without putting women down, please remember that I have been a victim of domestic violence myself. No person – man or woman – should be subjected to such horrendous ordeals. Women are heard. Men will be grateful to be heard too. It's hugely courageous for men to be emotionally open. In the intense pressure lies a stream of unshed tears. Women feel it. Men feel it. I advocate for both, saving the world, one soul at a time. I just call for a stop to brutality towards one another. Others have died at the hands of their 'loved ones'.

Another day, another story; I have heard it all including the tantrums. The repeated mistakes they have done and their regrets. I spare my sympathy but tap into their rage in tiny doses... There are some men out there who literally blame everyone but themselves. I wanted to scream. Unstable and reckless men. Hearing how the world is against them and of course it is not their fault that everything is fucked up; their decisions had nothing to do with it. They are stuck where they are and as always, their own failures are completely someone else's fault – sad story... it takes a real man to accept accountability.

***

Who said an escort is a dirty little secret just catching residuals? A fiery dragon yet overwhelmingly hypnotic, I had my own gravitational pull and got many people through challenging times... To drown their sorrows and it feels great to have been part of a solution, just with a different delivery style ... personal and intimate. An escort can be that surgeon who cuts out the hurt and turmoil.

Nothing concealed, everything revealed, they pour out their tragic tales. In turmoil, when men are afraid to let someone go, they contact an escort. When they have finally let go, they contact an escort. The combination of being earnest and kind had earned me a place in most hearts, because I have undoubtedly been better than the last escort they met, due to being approachable, down-to earth and compassionate about their mental health. I started spending less time fucking and more time talking, because people are under pressure, stressed, in hostile environments; I was graced to give them strength and hope. That's the future. That is what men will be looking for. Brains will trump beauty, but I was lucky to have both. One round was often enough because an intelligent conversation was more beneficial than round two.

We all have our own philosophies but, in the end, only solid ground can hold us. Above sea level, there is a shark, tearing humans to shreds... I heard the screams of constant streams of depression, stress and anxiety. These are not emotions or trends. It's like drowning, except you can see everyone around you breathing; you are both the prisoner and the jailer.

If an escort performs the greatest fix-it, go for it. Men feel like they must deal with it in silence because mental health is not acknowledged in their 'man-up' community where they are told depression is 'for losers'. They resort to an escort for hugs, erotic fun, cuddles and the chat after.

Their feelings mattered, and I realised men wanted an escort who is caring and engaging. My room felt like a confession box, but it's always better out than in. Don't bottle it all up; it's toxic. If you are battling depression, anxiety and fear, don't let anybody tell you to man-up, because men are not exempt from it. I am here to tell you that no matter how hard and tight a grip it has on you, you have the power to overcome it. Once the client detected that certain authenticity and sincerity in me, they held onto it and the friendship became stronger, and they became regular clients, which is wonderful when the feeling is mutual. "If you need anything, don't hesitate; I am here for you." There was more to my statement than just rampant sex, even though I was expert at that, but nothing beats telling someone that your arms are open wide, that you are there to listen and your door is open if they need you. I realised many are perishing mentally. I was in my own emotional turmoil, but still, I helped many others also in turmoil. Sometimes, your own healing and recovery comes during the process of healing others first.

Not all family is supportive, understanding and loving enough to stick by you during dark times. Others have been in the deepest depression, stuck in the cycle of paralysis by analysis, contemplating suicide every day, while dropping hints to family and friends, yet no one cared. They feel like only death will relieve them of that burden. But I grabbed them before it finished them! It's never too late to get things off your chest; talking and sharing can save lives. I exceeded their hopes and expectations because to whom much is given, much is expected. I was trusted with the bigger task of saving and serving; that was what I was called to do. We can only bless others with what we have, and much has been given to me that money cannot buy. When you are marinated in love, you look at people through the eyes of love. You see their need to be loved and accepted. When love is shed abroad in your heart, what oozes out of you is love. The fruits of love; patience, kindness and understanding, did not go unnoticed by my clients. That is what enriches our life. They cherished the gracious hour which transformed their life on a day that they were having trials and tribulations. Confessing their secrets to an escort… they justified coming to me because it was beyond sex. Justification takes away the guilt and so makes way for peace in our life. They were already planning another meeting before they left!

Guard your heart with all diligence. Don't keep letting them in. After heartfelt apologies, we all like to think that the greatest gift you can give someone is trust but usually, some people come back into your life just to hurt you again; to ruin you completely so that you never recover. You think it's romantic when you keep letting them in when truly, you are being awful to yourself. It's a total nightmare.

People have separated from their wives because their internet browsing history revealed they had been watching porn. Seriously. Others because they were caught masturbating. Seriously. Women need to modify their rigid mind and download the new kinky version to be sexually plugged.

Sex unites different generations and backgrounds. I met men of different social and economic classes, including those with electronic monitoring tags on their ankle, home detention curfews and many in the twilight of their life and the crème de la crème. I learned in so many ways never to evaluate people. If they respected my rates, mine was a level playing field. Come as you are. Some even homeless, because nobody forgave them and there was clearly not a second chance. In our heart-to-heart conversations, where I gave some harsh criticisms, some were only sorry they got caught; in others I sensed sincere regret – all they want is another chance, but their partner was thinking 'once bitten, twice shy'. In every separation, there is always deep reflection but what will one do with a second chance if staying faithful seems such a challenge and stolen bread seems to be more delicious? Most people don't value what they have until they lose it. We don't miss something until it's gone. I heard about some wonderful relationships that were destroyed permanently because of a lack of forgiveness.

***

Men! If they were not choking me with their dick, they were choking me with their cologne or body odour. A handful of times, all they needed was a shower and a toothbrush. By this time, I went past cringing and beyond but still with some uneasiness, I tolerated and didn't tell them, "Boy, you stink." In a luring and enticing tone, mixed with a little striptease as I led them to the bathroom, I told them that "the cleaner you are, the dirtier I get". That was almost hypnotic... like telling a kid to clean up before their favourite dessert.

I love to watch synchronised swimmers, combining acrobatics, swimming and dance in a discipline that requires and demands. I love just how synchronised they are, the teamwork, periodically holding their breath, the challenging manoeuvres, precise timing; it gets interesting and scary. No wonder it is described by some as hard and weird. They have figured out the strokes to be in one accord, nonetheless, even they get it totally wrong sometimes, despite the script and hours of intense practise...

I met many men in moments of uncertainty, in an emotional rollercoaster best known as a relationship. The mental gymnastics! People are dangling on their own nerves because everyone seems to be playing detective and trying to decode the opposite sex. Men say women are complicated. Women say men are complicated, but that shouldn't complicate your life. Stop exploiting and irritating yourself. In any partnership, how can two people walk together or exist side by side in harmony, unless they agree that they are an endangered species?

How do people stay married, happy and still counting? They seek to praise the other's strengths rather than tolerate their faults. Appreciate effort. People don't appreciate effort anymore. Be kind. Kindness makes staying married much easier. What is it that everyone needs to know to make it work? Mutual respect. The good old-fashioned respect is essential in any relationship. Self-awareness seems to be the biggest obstacle. How can you talk through dreams to find a balance together, if you are not even aware of yourself? How can you tie the separate interests into common goals if you have no self-awareness? Self-awareness makes issues almost more manageable to conquer. Even if tomorrow was guaranteed to us, never take the people you love for granted.

Focus on compromise. That's the art of a good deal. Don't focus on meeting halfway, because your significant other may be lacking. Love sacrifices and goes the extra mile. Love doesn't lust for power in the relationship. Let your strength be made perfect in your partner's weakness and their strength perfected in your weakness, because love compliments each other. Runners competing against each other can help each other after falling during a race. Two injured athletes helped each other finish a race during the Olympics. A high-school runner received overwhelming praise after she helped a struggling competitor finish a race. A London marathon runner gave up his own race to help an exhausted athlete across the finish line. Strength shows its maturity when the other is weak. Winning always makes you more of an athlete. They go out there to win, but if athletes are helping their rivals, why then, in marriage, does one aim to sell the other off to the enemy?

I will describe exactly what many are going through. It is unfortunate that most relationships and friendships are surviving solely because of emotional blackmail. The other knows what they don't want the world to know, so it's safer to stay in the relationship to preserve their dignity. That's the new low; it's not about love and joy anymore but fighting every day to survive mentally whilst keeping up appearances. There is usually one who loves freely and the other who gets loved back with conditions, limits, abuse and deadlines.

'The Rock' suffering from depression sounds rather depressing but is one of the biggest action heroes in showbiz. If he can be open about hitting rock bottom with depression, you know there is no shame in admitting that inner struggles are real, so don't think you are alone. Even those who are fit, with worldly fame and fortune, are so overcome by grief. They sweat blood. It was very generous of 'The Rock' to let us into his world by revealing his struggles, because toxic masculinity does exist. Men who are in touch with their emotions are those who embrace true masculinity by expressing themselves. Wanting a hug is not unbecoming of a man. Opening and embracing your humanity and vulnerability is humanity.

I was always considered different, if not peculiar. Some just wanted that touch, kiss, voice, that presence of a woman. Even a homeless man who begs outside a supermarket has needs. I have had an awesome privilege to meet two in my time and had some intelligent conversations, unlike with most clients. They all have a story, as do we all. We all have some stuff we regret. Some impacts far more severe than others. Either way, when you look closely, we all need saving from something. Many are there because the woman they loved and hurt will never forgive them.

People don't get into a marriage with the intention of getting out. No wonder a divorce drains all the energy out of both parties. It's truly devastating when things we thought had potential don't work out. I met a lot of men going through separation and they are not sure if the divorce can come quick enough; it's daunting. Others party until the break of dawn, to stay young and relevant, but why use an escort? To some, it's about getting the quick self-esteem boost. To others, it's about getting as much pussy as they can, because their dick needs comforting, but overall, they need help with recovery from the divorce as they move through the phases of grief. In the end, having done all to stand, none can escape the inevitability of hitting the bottom of the barrel, especially when they find out the grass is not greener on the other side.

For primary care, wellbeing and the need to calm the nerves of some men, one simply cannot imagine the tremendous impact I had on my clients. I catered for the overlooked issue of men's emotional and mental health needs such as depression, loneliness and suicidal thoughts. It was an enjoyable experience for them to get to know a strong, courageous and interesting person, but the best element of my work was touching lives and knowing that I am making a difference. Talking about the small steps and relevant changes for better health, seeking to improve mental and physical health, was rewarding to me. Healing one life at a time because I was created for good work.

A festive time for one can be a dreadful time for the another. For a reasonable price, at Christmas time, my website was always updated: "If you are set to be lonely this Christmas, you need not be. I am here to cheer you up, and no doubt we will inspire and entertain one another. Christmas, after all, is a time of good cheer; the more the merrier." No one is meant to be sad and lonely.

The hypocrisy and double standards of this illness of suggesting that men are weak; it answers my questions. They would rather show their weak side to an escort who will not judge and condemn them, than to their wife or lover who will only conclude they are weak and that they bruise easily.

'Be a man' is the vapid or brutal soundbite that sums up this stigma. An escort rarely tells a man to man-up. What's not to love? The concept that it's unmanly to be ill has seen my doors open to men who just want to be embraced, cuddled and understood in an oasis of love. I understand their weaknesses and fragility without making fun of them. Many people are so lonely yet unable to do anything about it because of social anxiety. Painfully shy, they are unable to express what they truly think or feel, they admit that being a man can be a grey and lonely road, it gets even worse at the top. They are afraid of embarrassment, fear of asking questions and interacting. They feel like they are trapped in something that will not let them speak or communicate with people, and when they do speak, they either feel ignored, or for no rational reason, when they are noticed, they feel insulted, judged, criticised and take everything so literally seriously.

Naturally, I had husbands confess the filthy secret desires they kept hidden from their spouses, but for me, it was beyond a popularity game to stay relevant. I was crucial beyond the sexual magnetism. My wisdom was fundamentally important. Men have discussed their health issues with an escort. We make it easier for them to talk about issues, pain and emotions they would normally bottle up. Physical or mental, I don't suffocate or belittle them like some of their wives do. This attitude of thinking that men are exaggerating their issues is costing lives. When they have little to no sympathy elsewhere, they get it from escorts. They could feel ill without someone making them feel like they are abnormal. I encouraged them to get help. Some I have told to ring their doctor in my presence, some have promised me that they will do it as soon as they get home, and many have thanked me later for saving a life.

Home is where the heart is? Not if it is a hostile environment. They left their meticulous homes, came to me just for a sofa, a blanket and a TV because they just wanted a warm heart; we enjoyed understanding each other. Monday was always the busiest day; after a 'quality' weekend with that nagging wife, they just wanted some respite, a safe space to recover and fall asleep… because here was a tender heart. They had one of those naps where they woke up exhausted and puzzled about their surroundings because they felt a rare serenity.

People long for affection and healing, they reach for an escort in the dark. They reach for a hand through the glory-hole. A life tied in knots; due to distress, pain, agitation and sleep deprivation… after taking *heroic* amounts of drugs, until they burn the fuse, they walk into an unknown call-girl and never sure if they need a leash, entertainment or supervision. At that point, only a genuinely kind heart can decide for them and lead them to the safe road.

The spectrum of possibilities of a touch, a smile, a kind word, a sincere compliment, a listening ear... because attentive listening is rescuing. You are either listening or you are not. My superpower is listening to someone ranting, and not give advice. There are times when people don't need advice. They just want to be listened to. I felt a responsibility to listen. I want to be someone's favourite person to talk to, but an understanding heart gets exhausted too.

It doesn't take away the heaviness or pain, but it loosens its terrifying grip to know that someone with attention to detail, is listening... not to judge right from wrong in what you are saying, nor give unsolicited *advice*, but to feel you. That alone, has the potential to turn a life around. We had some good laughs, without arguing which gender has it worse in life or attempting to make a really shit joke, simply because I cared. They are worthy of my attention. Others after feeling rejected on a normal date they just had, usually via internet dating, they visit an escort before they get home... to drown their sorrows.

It's little wonder that men don't like discussing their health.

When their cry was finally heard by this engaging escort, that's it; I got myself a regular.

To some men, home just doesn't work anymore. They avoid it at all costs. They hide their sickness at home, and even from their doctor. I can handle a sticky, sweaty mess and screwed up duvet without telling him to take 'the man-up pill'. Their pain is real. No one wants to be belittled when they appear weak.

Sex unites us. Sex with me is an experience. This was a job in all its dimensions. Clients come from all walks of life; different generations and backgrounds, passionate, articulate, charismatic, brutes and savages. I am still meeting the different kinds of men. Some, I can only describe as funny and kind. My room was a diverse melting pot and well-being boutique. Sometimes the potter's house, moulding and shaping ourselves into a work of art. Some days I was flooded with pompous undesirables, blinded by their superiority complex. Disconnected and detached. Before arrival, to grab attention, they gave a health-alert, warning me how massive their dick is and asked if I can certainly handle it. There was nothing beyond my call of duty. Only to find it was tiny!

The proof is in the pudding. Please don't tell me how awesome you are. Just be... awesome.

At the same time, we must survive the opportunists (users). Those charming clients who befriend us solely to get free sex, we see through you, so dream on. Being cheap and taking advantage will never earn you friendship. Escorts are friends with awesome clients who still respect our rates whilst getting to know us. Under any circumstances, that's the friendship we all want – supportive and considerate.

Be it a financial fix, a relationship that has been ripped apart or a life too mixed and messy to confess, many are in a jigsaw if not a pickle. I dare say that being human is not only being expert at muddying and messing up our own lives, but even the lives of those close to us. Assuredly, I have been that perfect pick-me-up, the anchor saving men from the gallows of life.

Time is precious. Most men I met have had that one moment in their life that changed everything, when they realised life is too short. Others have come close to death at some point of their life. Only when adverse life events happen, only then do we change our perspective of life and write-off the present with a different outlook and mindset. We came here to live, and many realise they are not living at all, just surviving.

***

MANY people are struggling with thoughts and the meaning of life. Some visibly frail and unwell, I have seen anxiety, emptiness, frustrations and scars on different scales. They know they have someone special in their life and it's an escort... Because... why not? Beyond the motive of money, I connected with my clients though love and purity. I had their best interests at heart always; we were stronger together. Each session was a mental floss of soul searching, yoga for the soul, because they were living through the mud and the muck caused by bottling up all their thoughts and feelings. Their mental illnesses were defeating them. You can't bottle it up and hope it fixes itself. We shared so much more, from traumas, strength, to healing. That was the therapy I needed too, hence my mental health did not deteriorate in my turmoil. As I walked through the fire, it did not burn me; as I walked through the waters, I did not sink, because I had the support group I needed.

The conflicts between our thoughts and emotions are so vigorous, hence why mental health and wellbeing were the absolute core of my decisions. Others were open with their struggles. Nonetheless, I don't judge a book by its cover; we are all human and depression doesn't discriminate. It sneaks up on anyone at any time regardless of their wealth or achievements, even more when people are exhausted, pressured and drained. Being motivated by money and commissions is not a terrible thing but if your work, family or friends are stressing you and causing constant fatigue, guard yourself, take a step back and gravitate towards people who have a fountain of living water.

Depression comes in many shapes and forms and affects everyone differently. Others have no idea who they are anymore. It does not give you any alert or indication as to when it will take a hold of you but usually its root is something 'traumatic' that has happened in our lives. There are some people with good physical health who have not looked after their mental health; all they do is judge and hate themselves. Others are off work, trying to get better; many are sick and on the long, hard road to recovery. Infected with paranoia and cynicism, dealing with anger and depression, the lack of kindness around them makes it worse. We can talk about mental health all day, but when the medical services are chronically underfunded, we can all do our part and make a difference to people's lives. To a legion of my clients, I was that light in their tunnel.

I had a gift to share with the world and that gift was me – a helpful and diligent escort with a new perspective. I did a course with Britain's leading chemist, on administering medication, should any of my clients need painkillers whilst in my care. It was about them. The world needs more escorts who are honest, smart, kind, confident, intelligent and open-minded and put the health and safety of themselves and their clients above all else. Many escorts are all about digging in the client's pockets to steal a few notes. My job is a choice and you will not bait me into conflict about my calling. Others dance their way out of their mess. Others paint. Others knit or sew. To others, an iron plays as an instrument. Sometimes you must find a way to let it out. I sexed my way out of my hardships and through that, I blanketed people with bliss and comfort. My job is not something I am trying to overcome. I love it, I am perfect at it, and it loves me back. My love for self is evidenced by the charging system, condom use and my frequency with medical examinations. I portray who I am, as I am. Accepting and embracing the real me has led to self-discovery and discovering my calling, in a greater measure. Some jobs cause destruction to physical and mental health. My job is my comfort zone and my life flourishes –

mind, body and soul. I got to understand the anatomy of life, how it works and most importantly, how to make it work for me.

Woe to those who sit at home either licking their blow-up doll, absorbed in Sudoku and their fidget spinners, nervous and miserably thinking that paying for an escort is pathetic. So selfish and egocentric, they would rather sleep with multiple pillows. The only comfort they have is from pills and none from people. I call them the less fortunate men, because escorts can be incredible humanitarians. Whilst some men prefer to roll a happy joint, an escort can take you to higher places. Those who have immersed themselves in this universe of escorts can testify that when skies are grey, on the gloomiest day, they found light when they picked the escort with special qualities. Men who book an escort are not, as others expect, the fat, boring, weak, pathetic and ugly one who will only get sex because they have paid for it. Sex is a beautiful thing; some just want to avoid the twisted drama that goes with dating. Both the buyer and seller are stigmatised by those outside the illicit world, but we can live with that. We are without fear of condemnation, where there is a good client/escort rapport. We shared significant challenges, traumas, and life's major milestones in a sincere way because I'm not dead inside; I have a soul. I get to know a man in a greater measure via that hour of sex than you do in ten dates or working with them for a decade. If a man treats a woman with utmost respect and consideration, that's the hour to detect, the soulmate by the hour.

Life is not a rehearsal play where the stage is all set, and you are supposed to know what your lines are supposed to be. Keep calm; you are not meant to know the lines. Depressed and anxious, no wonder I had a lot of nerves to calm and I am always reminded of my mentor Amanda, who suffered with it almost her entire life and that was part of the reason she ended it. She lives on in my heart. I see her mesmerising reflections in me. She was a tiger yet fed many hungers and fulfilled many lusts and desires. She is the filthy yearning flame that will always live on in my blissful heart. My deepest sympathy to her legion of clients.

It's amazing what odds, obstacles and loss can do for your gratitude and perspective. I never take a second for granted. I always remember that others are sinking in quicksand. Yes, it is painful, but always remember that no obstacle has come to you except what is common to humanity. Don't lose heart. You will overcome because you cannot have an obstacle beyond what you are able to bear. No matter how deep the hole is, you are stronger than you think. You can rise from the ashes and dig yourself out. You are stronger than you think.

***

Be it first time offenders or hardened criminals, the first thing a man runs to upon release from jail is not the jobcentre or a restaurant buffet. They want a hooker and I met many of the newly released. The top factor was the sex... but it was beyond that. They longed for someone who would not mock them, but would understand that they are no longer criminals, but ex-criminals. Their punishment fitted their crime and they had served their time. They just longed for someone who would sincerely wish them luck in their new life, because they knew they needed it. Some crimes and stains are deep red like scarlet. Can they be as white as snow again? We were settling matters and reasoning together. These ex-criminals had a soft and delicate side which was not a weakness but a strength which only I knew. They needed that basic instruction of reaping what they sow. "You wounded so much, go the extra mile and sow extra seeds of goodness." To someone, they were a great father, a wonderful son, an amazing husband; yet capable of committing the terrible crime they did. To me, I am yet to find a word that best describes them.

Their punishment fit the crime. They were not going to be punished again by me. Not by me. Some had stab wounds and scars in the most delicate places. I have met many ex-offenders and they are so brutally, sincerely honest about what they did. Revealing some horrifying truths, you confirm that 'love', 'money' and 'revenge' are the root of evil. Some people were sorry, others angry, others confused with life itself. Man is of a fallen nature and as I spoke to them, I knew those who had a criminal mind and waiting for the next opportunity to do something vile again at any cost, but most men I spoke to had truly repented and it was nice to know. I am not a masseuse, but I always gave the best massage during active listening and reasoning. The mind is the battlefield; it was an inside job and this genuine danger was beyond their control regarding whom they encountered. Within the mind, within the prisons, what has been done to the mind has to be undone upon release, and this was the significant hour to tell them earnestly that it is not an excuse for criminal behaviour to flourish. It is not what comes out of a man that defiles them, but what goes in. They met up with inmates who justify terrorism and its brand ambassadors. The appalling accounts of radicalisation within prisons were beyond my comprehension. These ex-offenders are calculating inwardly… fighting that tug-of-war that has been instilled in them, no one can predict where it leads. Spilling what was abundant in their hearts, others broke down and sobbed so much.

Those on a curfew or with electronic tagging devices attached to their leg, I made sure they did not break the rules further, so I watched the clock. We can all advocate for peace wherever/whenever possible.

For peace's sake, I avoided at all costs the unhealthy and unusual debates of religion, for it steals, kills and destroys quality time. What I hated with every fibre of my being were the men who booked an escort for the sole purpose of converting her religion into one of 'peace'. It happens a lot in the current climate. After sex, by their twisted conversation you shall know them… It gets intense and nerve-wracking. You feel vulnerable and don't know how to react. Don't let the door hit you on your way out! What a breath of fresh air, but still it left me angry because what the hell does me, doing the job I choose to do got to do with you?! Post-sex blues? I have had Bibles, Qurans and Torahs handed to me. I learnt the world 'bollocks' because of clients like these.

With technique and passion, sex was an artistic form of healing and recovery for me and my clients. After all, it takes four text messages to make plans for sex with an escort, but it takes forty-seven texts to plan for dinner with lifelong friends. Some men collect stuff, bric-a-brac; other men collect experiences. Whatever enhances your life, moments or items is a matter of choice. In what way, by what means, can you meet a total stranger and connect and have the most amazing sex in this way within ten minutes? Real chemistry cannot be faked.

Nothing changes unless our mindset changes. Life moves fast so we need to think sharp and rapid – and accept that sex and intimacy are amazing and underrated therapeutically. Picture two strangers, both completely different generations and backgrounds, instantly having the most incredible sex. It's a medical miracle when a man tells me they were told they may never achieve an orgasm again and then they have the first one after five years or so. What a privilege it is! So inclusive and diverse, I appreciate these special moments where I go to amazing lengths to help a stranger.

***

Walking in the corridors, usually in my perfect little black dress, the disapproving look I often get from the housekeeping lady standing in the hotel hallway with her trolley, cleaning the room next-door to my destination. She is there to do a wonderful job, and so am I. She chooses to work as a cleaner. I choose to work as an escort. As my client awaits my arrival, there is normally a 'do not disturb' sign on the door and it speaks volumes of my work. Is she imagining me taking some stranger's cum on my face for money? Well, I found a way the awkwardness is adorable. I get an extra towel from her trolley as I smile gently and wish her a wonderful day.

She is usually within sight again as I leave the room, and considering I always put some cash on her trolley. As she cleaned a room or two, I probably just earned myself what could be her weekly wage. Again, I smile as I walk away in long strides before she declines it due to work ethics. I told her earlier to have a wonderful day. Rest assured she will.

Be money-motivated but don't let that be your only concern. Whatever your field of work, wherever you have been positioned, you can make the day extraordinary, by giving something back. Put on a smile, for it is more blessed to give than to receive. That random act of kindness could be just the miracle somebody needed. There is a reason your paths crossed.

***

One man booked me overnight. I was disturbed throughout the night, not for constant sex demands but due to his frequent urges and urgency to urinate, and he told me of the difficulty he was experiencing in starting urinating and the pain during urination. Sometimes he spotted some blood in the urine. In the morning I told him about the common symptoms for prostate cancer, considering I had met a few men with it, and many had won the battle… but early examination and detection was crucial. I did not hear from him after he left, but he was in my thoughts. In 2017, a few days before Christmas, he came to say thank you with an envelope containing £200 because I had saved his life. He had been ignoring all the symptoms until I drummed it into him, and he went to the doctor, who gave him urgent help to try and shrink the prostate. "I had not gone to the doctor in eleven years until you suggested I go," he told me. "You sent me a text the following day to remind me to access medical help, and that was when I went. That text message showed me how you cared. Merry Christmas and thank you."

***

No woman appreciates a man who is done and dusted in two strokes, but I met men with a rare condition which leaves them on the verge of orgasm all the time. It's literally too much of a good thing and a horrible way to live, because they are in constant pain all the time. They have an erection all the time and I have counted myself lucky that I am not their spouse. It's not mental like sex addiction; it's beyond that. It's a malfunction of something. It is a horrific disorder of pain and discomfort and some men have felt suicidal because of it. Others have gone bankrupt because of it, constantly paying for sex. They search out sex anywhere and get involved with anyone that accepts their condition, which often leads to some bad choices. The constant need for relief is exhausting and causes them massive depression. They wish they could clip that nerve, but instead go on believing that they will probably grow out of those hard-on old days. It's hard to function. They tell me how many times they must masturbate at work, to try to hold down a job. They ejaculate just by thinking about it… it's insane. You just cannot conduct yourself with an erection in many circumstances – meetings, talking to your children, visiting your parents.

I started my work in my late twenties, so I am now well into my thirties and intend to work well beyond my sixties, because pussy is like wine. It gets better with age and my clientele age range is getting younger: usually men in their twenties all squirting their way down to me; it's exciting. Most importantly, attitudes have changed. They are not as cheeky and as rude as they used to be. However successful, stylish and sophisticated they are, most have been humble and kind. They are always happy to listen to me and let me have my way with them.

Taking men out of their comfort zone in our explorations and escapades has been my greatest speciality. I enjoyed luring them into what they once never even thought they could do.

However, my most annoying frequently asked question has for years been: "Do you squirt?" No, I don't. Apparently, I'm not one to cum gallons on command. If it's pee, then I can pee on my own. Thank you very much. Is it anything to do with the guy and their vast experience? In a relaxing atmosphere, I love to show a guy what I need, because I am so in touch with my body, but my need has never led me to that destination, so I guess I am not programmed to squirt. Sex is an art a woman should learn and please don't say ignorance is bliss. A lot of women do not know their bodies well enough and many have never masturbated, so how in the world would someone else know your body better than you?

Men don't make women orgasm, but they help them make themselves get there. Women! There is a space within you that is not discovered. That orgasm is already there within you; you just must have a desire to seek and find it. No one must climax all the time but it's liberating and empowering to know that you don't need a man to achieve an orgasm. A closed mouth is never fed… Have a thirst and hunger for creativity because that amazing combination of greatness will bring tact and strategy and eventually, a genius, mind-blowing orgasm.

My battery-powered toys bring desirable outcomes, but some adventures are best undertaken with a partner… Oops, I mean a client in my case. Admittedly, I am a greedy girl because the best orgasms are those with more than two men at once… sometimes it takes group effort because they are not brilliant at multitasking. When one is sucking my nipples hard and the other man is sucking my pussy – not licking it like a yoghurt lid, please! I said suck, with a finger up my bum; if that is not heavenly, then what is? It takes two men to tango me to cloud nine.

At this rate, the superstitious folks said I was going to ruin my life and develop hornlike spikes in my pussy, caused by too much fucking. My experiences are overflowing, but it didn't ruin my life. Suddenly, others were scared to visit me, as there were rumours that I collect rare items of amputated dicks that I chopped off my clients. It was purely moral policing, triggered by pathological jealousy.

Sex work is real work. The utterly baffling myths no longer serve us. Beyond the threats of eternal damnation, we already must deal with the stigma that society unjustly throws upon us. It is courageous that we overcome and teach the world that we are human.

Do I need a man to make me squirt or can that be achieved solo, like an orgasm? And is it much more fun with a partner? I wonder. Has it more to do with the woman knowing her sexuality than the skill of the guy? I have done many threesomes with women and I am yet to see the original one, but I have friends who have rebuked me for honestly saying that I do not squirt. Well, I come as I am, but I salute those colleagues of mine who do a fraud squirt. Wonders never end. It's not on my wish list but when I do squirt, I won't stay silent. Hold on, is that why in the middle of sex I want to pee? I guess that can't be related to squirting. Oh well, never mind.

What about another frequently asked and most loved question? "Do you have a strap-on, a.k.a. dildo?" Of course, I do, especially now that anal is so in fashion, all guys crave anal and a woman who does it is even more adorable. Dildos are the trend. Anal is the goal, so never ask a man which hole he would choose. Just tell him to 'go for it', there is nothing bum fun cannot fix. I have never seen a man's eyes sparkle so brightly than when I put a dildo in his ass. There must be something up there that rattles their delicious spot.

Now that it's so common and everybody wants it, even though I always put a condom on my aids, I wanted to avoid cross contamination, so I went a little bit 'fruit and vegetable' and asked the client to bring either a banana, a courgette or a carrot of their desired shape and size. Disposables are the new trend. Health and safety are paramount. Let's enjoy sex, but safe sex. Let's get kinky and dirty without the contamination.

Men who book an escort for the sole purpose of asking how they can become a male escort, a gigolo – "You wouldn't be fit for purpose. You would make a dreadful escort; just stop."

I know a man is a savage when he asks me, "How many times am I allowed to cum in the hour booking?" Seriously, what happened to 'one perfect shot'?

My regular client for ten years, deeply in debt because he samples hookers all year round due to his obsession with worshipping feet and gagging on toes. Especially when his dog Xara died. The only thing that gave him comfort was feet. His whole life revolves around women's them and he remains a virgin at fifty-two.

Others think others have gone through life the wrong way but to each their own… some like peeling bananas from the bottom; apparently, it's the correct way of eating them. Others eat pussy only from the back, that's their correct way. Who is to decide that you must not have your steak well done with ketchup?

Chapter 27
As I Am

I love the beach and growing up, Lake Malawi gave me some comforting power and rejuvenation. If you could describe the sound of hope, the waves soothed my anxious soul and filled me with it. With many tourists there, I developed a special fondness for white skin. Although not intended, coming to England and being a sex worker, I preferred Caucasian clients and expressed it on my website. I love black and white skin naked together. If you look the right way, you will find that colour contrast is magical in and of itself, so much it influenced my choices.

Let's talk about generations... I used to prefer much older clients but there was a sudden shift in perspective. I thought they were fantastic, realistic and soft senior citizens. Miserable than ever, they are often too cautious and cynical, it made me anxious. I am playful and sensual with a hint of naughtiness... I love to tease. Sex is called play, yet they don't want you to fool around in getting the job done. They want you to fuck them until their hinges fall off, and when you do, they mourn to say you are hurrying them off and speeding them out of the pitch. They want to prove that they have still got it, even though they never had it in the first place. Like an old pot-holed road, they can be noisy with instructions. It kills the passion because many don't want to think outside the box, and they don't take kindly to restrictions.

Phrases like "once you go black, you don't go back" and "the darker the berry, the sweeter the juice" are so out-dated and annoying to me. Don't reduce my identity to a skin colour. Once upon a time, it flattered me, until I realised it was frequently said by the older generation, who would always say this to prove their ancient philosophy of "I am no longer racist but..." They feel the need to highlight that I need not worry; they're not going back to their own. Sigh, the older generation just don't get it. With crippling insecurities, they can't cope with getting old, they get it so twisted they blame you even for their erectile dysfunction and throw their toys out of the pram.

The younger generation had much greater levels of understanding, it was an honour playing with them. They allowed me to fool around whilst getting the job done, without the need to constantly remind me "but I have paid1". Let's put it this way, the modern and refined roads are usually a smooth ride and reasonably intuitive. They have gone to school with diverse and multiracial numbers, so talking about our colour is never the hot topic of the day. They don't need to add emphasis that I am the be-all-and-end-all. saturated with enthusiasm, it's fun time and that's what matters to them. Also, there is no doubt that they are more comfortable and confident around battery-operated technology such as sex toys, without getting suspicious. That will only continue to increase as time passes, because toys are better when used together.

Devouring me like candy, these youngsters know that pussy ages well like wine, either. They want something sinfully mature and delicious. The last thing they need is a girl who will feed them milk as though they are infants in elementary school. The magnificence of maturity goes the whole distance. We aren't going to hold back. What if we are living on borrowed time? He who dares, wins; these daring young adults are ready for solid food. In fact, they want to rise to the challenge to chew strong, mature, experienced beast meat. By this time, I was a teacher and some young men came for training and a starter pack for when they were dating an older woman and wanted to prove to her that they have what it takes. That they won't disappoint. So, they tell me their reason for the visit. I taught them the first principles of the oracle of sex and how to be unbelievably great at multi-tasking to pleasure a woman. I enjoyed daring them. They enjoyed manifesting the dare. Sex-work, no matter how risky, is what I did best, and I enjoyed the thrill, so nothing and no one could supress my passion for my work.

Sugar daddies were in the limelight for a while, but seasons change. What couple's age gap has received more attention around the world than Ben10 and the Cougar? French President Emmanuel Macron and his wife Brigitte Macron, who is twenty-five years older than him, she gets me excited about my future. She was his drama class teacher during his teenage years, and they ended up pursuing a passionate affair before she left her first husband. I noticed a cougar trend after his presidency. After seeing the true benefits of maturity, he set an "Aged wine is best, old is gold" precedence. Others are bullish about age but with this trend of maturity, magnificence and magnetism, I'm not packing my bags yet.

Macron's parents were flabbergasted when they learned of their son's romance with his teacher, and they removed him from the school in Amiens, northern France, sending him to finish his education in Paris. When they told her to stay away from him, she told them she cannot promise anything. Happy days.

Still in the box, untouched. The sheer terror in their faces… Other men just wanted to lose their virginity. They have masturbated so much so long and used blow up dolls, it was time for the real thing. Others I have had to teach how to handle a woman, even though it's not one-size-fits-all; at least I tell them that a clitoris is delicate and not to be scratched like a scratch card and nipples are not to be tuned in like a radio.

Chapter 28
The Crown Title

Edward was an excessively lustful and wealthy man in North West England, who previously worked under the crown. Through my sex-work, our paths crossed. We often went hiking because our insanely wild ideas and adventures included eating me out and sucking him off on the mountains, in his caravan and many nights together at my place or his home. He lived in an intriguing mansion of ancient architectures and exquisite artwork, which was explored and appreciated by many tourists. Some families had a vacation there. It was passed on from generations, as his background was that of admirals, the most senior commanders of a fleet or navy, whilst his late father was a Church of England clergyman. A tour of his unique mansion took us over an hour, as he introduced to me the family portraits, including that of his ex-wife. The tour outside his huge land of perfectly manicured gardens, included generational graves and the most recent one being his beloved son who had just lost his long battle to cancer, just a month before my visit. His son's wish was to turn forty and he held on to life so tight, until two days after his birthday.

Edward found me to be an absolute package of delightful mischief because I always thought up some ways beyond his comprehension, to keep him balanced. I was the essential condiment that gave his life flavour. Nonetheless, I was devastated beyond words how he would never pay me the asking price. As I looked at the money in shock… "That is enough for any girl," he would shout with a fiercely notorious temper… to end the story.

His wife, Fiona, went to visit her daughter, whom Edward confessed he had always sexually fantasised, and their marriage was on the rocks because of this. Whilst there, she had an argument with her son-in-law. Storming out, she drove back home after midnight. She needed a shoulder to cry on, but Edward was in my bed having an overnight booking because he had decided to make the most of her night away from home.

Because of the rare snoring, I had left the room and gone to sleep on the couch, so it wasn't much of a valuable time for him. When I woke up, I went to the bedroom to ask him if he wanted a hot drink, but he was sat upright, almost frozen like a statue, in shock.

"What is it? Are you okay?" Words failed him, but trembling, he showed me the text message he had just woken up to, which had been on his phone for hours. "I'm in our bed, with myself, by myself. Where are you?"

A man in his late sixties, with erectile dysfunction, every wife would be worried about his wellbeing before even suspecting him of cheating.

When I finally opened my mouth, trembling, he said...

"Darling, this is it. I'm thinking what I'm going to say to her. Please be quiet."

To save his marriage, his sanity, I cooked up a compelling story which worked wonders. Christmas was around the corner and she had always wanted a pizza oven. "Well, tell her you wanted to surprise her with it and took the opportunity whilst she was away, to come and buy the oven in Manchester."

Fiona welcomed the excuse and went as far as apologising to him. Our illicit encounters continued but he was too tight-fisted to say the least, it was not a pleasure doing business with this extremely wealthy man. Nonetheless, after devouring me for two years and indulging in all manner of kinks, he enjoyed reading this book so much prior to its publication, his favourite and most relatable chapter being the Presidents Club, which he sent to media outlets and was immensely disappointed that they disapproved it because I, a black woman, was shining light on bigotry at its absolute filth and condemning entitlement of the societal upper crust. One day as we relaxed in his outdoor Jacuzzi, having some heart-to-heart talk, he came up with this idyllic title: 'Confessions of a Justified Hooker', for which I am eternally grateful. Apart from the eggcups and lampshades that he made me buy, to make his visits that much more pleasurable, he leaves his huge mark right here.

"Unlike many hookers, you undoubtedly love what you do, and you defend your position with passion. That's what I love about you. You are justified, irrespective of what others might think or say. I have been with many hookers and they are not all delighted to delight a client," he rightly declared.

Chapter 29
Risky Planet

Me: To an extent, always be paranoid that it may contain nuts. Realistically, always look at everyone as the devil in disguise, unless they prove you wrong... Me also: It's wise to be vigilant, but paranoia gets you nowhere. You trap yourself when you are constantly thinking that everything is a trap.

To fulfil secret sexual fantasies, some proposals required great boldness, great hardiness of the heart and pure daredevilry – I loved the thrill. We can't possibly live without risks. Being a hooker does not automatically mean we look for trouble and we are playing Russian roulette with our life. Trouble finds us like it does anyone else, but it is perhaps easier to say of a hooker, "Look now, you brought this upon yourself." It is downright tragic when people think that we go blindly without any thought of risk or decency!

Moreover, who knows when the hour will come? Fish are caught up in a cruel net, or birds taken in a trap, likewise, people are caught up by sudden tragedy. No man knows his time. Something unexpected and evil falls on us all, so let us just enjoy our portion in this life without judging and condemnation. "Keep surveying your surroundings and always be ready to act" .... Neat advice, thanks, but all of us can be overtaken by calamity, whatever job we do. When you do the job you love, you defend it, hence why I find it strange when ignorant folks say sex workers don't like sex; they need to put themselves in high risk environments in order to survive. Sit down. You, a non-sex worker, are telling a sex worker how she feels and ought to feel.

Not all jobs are created equal, but they share something: risks. We all encounter desperately dishonest clients, lunatics and crooks. There is always that bad apple with dangerous and terrifying intentions, so yes, I have had one or two near-death experiences. The wild web is made up of the good, the bad and the ugly, with some insanely high potential for aggression. Sinister clients with some shady shenanigans, particularly look for a gullible, unsuspecting escort, in the hope that she will let her guard down. Swindling is all they know. Their pleasure derives from evil. When you go back to the tape to see where you went wrong, stunned and upset, you realise that for your own good, keep up to speed and steadfastly suspect everyone.

Because I am a hooker. Next question.

Nobody told me the road would be easy. I always knew there would be trials and tribulations, but that's the reality of any job. Everything is a gamble… The decision is in how much you are willing to risk, and one must remember… The higher the risk, the higher the return, but never risk more than you can afford to walk away from.

Trust me on this one. This was my sphere. I was not an escort by tragedy, so there was no such thing as risking my integrity and reputation. This was the industry I chose, a job title I loved with many aspects I enjoyed. I was a justified hooker. I have never sat down and lamented my 'stupidity' nor felt guilty or ashamed. I just wish I had come out earlier, because hiding it has been a distraction. Some days in your lifetime you must put in a frame and hang them up, but I frame every one of my days, because they are all like shining portraits, shining brighter and brighter each day, illuminated with grace and glory.

Above all else, when sex work is illegal (in most parts) and humiliating in others, personal freedoms are systematically and grossly infringed. This aspect is not only despicable but makes equality impossible. Women's bodies and their choices remain a riddled debate, as though we are limited to being. Rather than be grateful for one another, it is beyond belief that we must perpetually defend diversity and the job we love.

I have met some dangerous clients, as this profession is all about being alone with a stranger, doing some crude nasty things. A few times, I have revoked consent and walked away when I have felt uncomfortable. We can never be too careful or extra vigilant.

The most careful will not always be safe and sound. The fastest runner does not always win the race. The strongest warrior does not always win the battle. The most skilful or the best-educated are not always the wealthy ones leading successful lives, just as the most dedicated ones will not always be in line for that promotion. It's all about timing and chance – Being in the right place at the right time or being in the wrong place at the wrong time.

Any tool or service can be misused. Not every enquiry is a genuine interaction. Even those with a filthy heart have access to the internet, so I always hoped that my profile did not attract these terribly evil, wicked men whose plans are to steal, to kill and to destroy. Even convicts have threatened me for nudes and video chats from their jail cell.

***

Who declared that the piece of skin on the end of the penis is useless? Shame on them. Unless it's for a medical reason, it changes nothing for better but for worse. Male genital mutilation removes a significant percentage of healthy penile skin. It's a permanent and dramatic alteration of a healthy anatomy on a functional organ. I pardoned those who did it for medical reasons but for the majority, it was a cultural, superstitious and religious tradition. I had little patience with them. The only reason it doesn't feel like mutilation is because people are used to it, but I have been with them and experienced, first-hand, many of these men and some have been left with zero sensation. They are so damn hard to please and certainly not for the faint-hearted. As the skin is so exposed, constantly rubbing on the underwear and jeans, it becomes sun-dried, wind-dried, leather-like, rough and coarse and loses its sensation. Each circumcised man is suffering the consequences differently according to the measure of skin that was removed in the process. In most cases, it was obvious at first glance that a crude traditional knife was used to amputate the foreskin and certainly not done in the hospital.

Healthy penile skin being destroyed, thus affecting sex life massively, is what I'm talking about. The loss of nerve endings and nerve damage… a penis with abnormally dried out skin. You can huff, you can puff, you can blow the head out and do what you do best, but nothing happens. Many a time, frustrated for trying to square the circle, I have thought to myself, *I have done it all now. Do I need to get a bulldozer to the rescue? Am I going to get paid for overtime?* When you look up at their face, it serves as a reminder that they are meant to be enjoying whatever you are doing. Acting is a talent. Looking distracted and disinterested, the have clearly lost the sensation. They act how they think they are supposed to act, making sounds only when you look up or down at them. Some might as well do some knitting or sewing whilst a woman performs sexual tasks on them. Those who call it the Holy Grail are just crying out loud. They say the modified one makes you a better lover, makes you hygienic and reduces premature ejaculation.

Let's go foreskin! I call it the great and glorious foreskin because it protects the head of the penis and keeps it supreme and sensitive. That foreskin moving up and down the vagina makes all things bright and beautiful, heavenly for stimulating the clitoris; what's not to love? So why the hell would someone downgrade their sexual pleasure experiences with a woman? That feeling when the foreskin is drawn back by the pussy lips, indescribable. So just give me that skin. I want to stroke it up and down. It's not unhygienic.

Like any business, being a sex-worker requires strategy. Pubic hair, clean-shaven or trimmed? Always be cautious of what the market wants, and you will stay on top. A beautiful, big and fluffy bush is the current trend. Being conscious of the social climate, the trend and catering for it adds to the fun.

Although still in progress, well done to Iceland for having the moral decency to ban this despicable procedure, which is equally as bad as Female Genital Mutilation. Reaffirming that the practice violates the child's rights, Iceland has imposed a six-year prison term on anyone guilty of "removing part or all of the child's sexual organs" unless for medical reasons. Jewish and Muslim leaders have called the draft bill a form of extremism and an attack on religious freedom, claiming that Judaism and Islam will become criminalised religions.

As one who has worked in massage parlours, brothels or romping shops as it were, those who circumcise on religious grounds – the extremely religious ones – continue to fill these places day and night, all year round, whatever the weather. Hypocrisy at its finest is the theme in these unique times, but I will just leave this one here. These are truly trying times for all.

As though we are artificial, contrived people, some have often asked me, "Do prostitutes climax?" Yes, we do. If there is anyone faking orgasms, it is usually the wives and girlfriends. Sometimes it's easier to be ourselves in the presence of a stranger, despite our nakedness and while we are at it, we might as well enjoy our time, right? We are real and passionate, and yes, more loving than you have ever anticipated. Orgasms and laughter are the two things I can't fake… some men trigger both and they are absolute treasures.

Most men are clueless about how to make a woman climax, but anyhow, I have often been tactful and strategic to avoid a climax, and this is how I do it…

It is I, the hooker. It's not mandatory that I climax with every client, so I derail myself immediately when it's best not to, because when I do, it takes an enormous chunk out of me. Although it's beautifully exhausting, I bear in mind that I have a long day ahead of me and I don't want to be all wobbly and lethargic. When I worked in the brothel and there was no compromise, at times I would have a climax and wish it could be undone. That loss of energy is bad for business. The sessions are timed, so it's hard to let go and relax on the job, because time is money and most of the money was for the brothel, so I caused many derailments to avoid reaching an orgasm.

However, there are times when the clouds are so full of rain that they must empty themselves upon the earth… they can't hold back. It's utterly impossible to put the brakes on, despite being an expert in derailing a climax… so I just let go.

Well, from the horse's mouth, most times we don't, and whether we do or not really depends on how we flow with the client, because that would be like drinking on the job. But there is chemistry on the job too. I don't have an acting job, so I don't fake orgasms; after all, I may as well enjoy my work while I am getting paid.

Prostitutes, hookers, escort, models, sometimes actresses, the terms are interchangeable. Nonetheless, whatever you identify as, I have been viciously attacked by some colleagues, for using the term they don't prefer. Some hookers in and outside the brothels have told me that they like to be called actresses. Oh, the predicaments! I am still scrambling with the adjustments for the right term, but one thing is certain: we don't claim to be indispensable assets, nonetheless, we are certainly spectacularly talented folks under one umbrella, with similar big boots to fill when we leave.

Cultures and traditions aside, like most people, I am still trying to do away with the stereotype mindset. White men can't jump. Black men have bigger dicks. In fact, black men thrive on the thought that white men have tiny dicks and many a time I have burst their bubbles when I told them that it is not true, in any way, shape or form. Some men make me cringe. I can handle all things through the inner man that strengthens me, but some dicks are so disgustingly huge, and I tell a man, "Don't even be proud of that. It's not even funny and I feel sorry for your impairment." It is cruel to boast of an abnormally huge dick that will cause pain and torment. Twelve is meant to be a dozen, not inches between the legs, so please take that and your money elsewhere. One woman's food is another woman's poison; someone else may drool over you. I won't.

We live and learn. Sometimes we learn things the hard way. Language is about respect, so I always try to recognise how people wish to be addressed. I do my best to adjust to changing times and terms and address people the way they ask me. Like most things, language has evolved and sometimes I can't keep up, but ignorance of such things leads to offence, unless you want to spend your day arguing and explaining that, "I didn't mean it that way. I am traditional and old school. Please pardon that I am out-dated." The overriding principle is to treat people with respect; after all, chances of the offended person understanding your ignorance everyday are slim to none. My clients are meant to be under the waterfall of my love, and love does not offend.

Just be a kind human and call trans people by their correct pronouns! I still embrace being female.

Be an oasis, that those who are weary and burdened can find rest, strength and comfort. As a route to happiness, it is amazing and a wonder how many men refer to an escort as the first point of contact in joy and sorrow – to celebrate or to mourn. To some, I have been a sex object but to many, I have been an oasis. A river in the desert, a roadway in the wilderness. I have unlocked potentials and saved people's lives. Some men simply rang me as a precautionary measure against heartache. I felt like a first responder in an adult playground. I offered counselling to reckless men who needed extra reinforcement. I have men contacting me because they are deeply hurt, having discovered that their wife is cheating on them and they just want revenge without having an affair. I tell them, "What she does not know does not exist to her, so what is the point?"

"I will feel better in my own mind," many said.

Chapter 30
Stolen Water Is Sweet

Stolen water is sweet. Food eaten in secret is delicious!
The public, the private and the secret; a man has three faces. One he shows to the world and does what is expected of him. The other he shows to close friends and family and just does what is expected of him. The third, he reveals his true perspective, only to a hooker and he loves the person he is then.

What one does not know, does not exist, but is there love after betrayal? You're trying too hard to catch them out, and it shows. Even when your man is a certified cheater and you somehow know what's coming, you still get caught off-guard when shit happens. You can huff, you can puff, but remember... That it is only a tiny fraction of their secret deeds. There is more... so much more and you can't control it because man is a free agent. That all-too-painful experience and exceptionally hurtful moment when your significant other has cheated on you and you ask, "What does she have that I don't have?" and, "What does he have that I don't have?" and, "I'm the insufficient one?" Hold on, don't pack your bags just yet. A rollercoaster is when you dump your partner because of cheating and get another partner who has been dumped because of cheating. Now, with the trendy notion of 'finders' keepers', it gets even more dramatic. Like a car, you want to remote lock and unlock your partner and constantly locate them with Google navigation.

Hold on; because I will share what I have observed. Every time something is banned, it promotes rebellion because that which is forbidden is more pleasant. "Don't touch – just look". One instruction and you're tempted to touch. How many people would have read *Lady Chatterley's Lover*, a novel by D.H. Lawrence, had it not been banned? We are a rebellious breed with a dark secret. Is it even fun if there isn't an element of danger involved?

When you are told not to have the cookies, they become irresistible and the temptation so tormenting, be as prepared as possible that rebellion is inevitable. If caught red-handed, ask the child, "What have you got in your mouth?" They will stumble and fall on their own words: "Nothing is in my mouth. I didn't take the cookie…"

"Yes, you did…"

"No, I didn't."

There is always someone sharing a new perspective with your significant other. No matter how diligent, you can't guard against that, and they are only sorry when they get caught. "I'm disgusted with myself." No, you're not. This 'dirty arrangement' was in your carefully planned diary and yes, you were counting down to it.

There is always that group of men who love their companion to the moon and back, and many people do cherish what they have, and yet stolen water is sweet, and bread eaten in secret is pleasant. It takes art, skill and some strokes of a genius to accomplish a prohibited mission. The thrill of getting that forbidden fantasy brings a euphoria of curiosity which adds to the pleasure. Once, twice undetected, the rebellion becomes addictive. That's it; they depend on the kinkiness of strangers.

They may have a spouse at home, and I see their eyes literally light up when they talk about their significant other, whom they wouldn't want to lose for the world. There may be a feast of succulent satisfying sex on chandeliers, but still, they absolutely love the thrill of sneaking out to a forbidden liaison because what is eaten in secret is more delicious.

Richard, the man who introduced me to the swinging scene, described how he had successfully hidden this from his wife, for well over seventeen years. I am a bit of an inquisitive hedgehog sometimes, especially when I'm doing my research on human nature and getting to the nitty-gritty of excessive lust. "What if your wife would enjoy it too?" I asked him.

"It wouldn't be fun if she came along. It wouldn't be my dirty little secret anymore." She is a conservative wife, so breaching the restraint makes the risk danger more thrilling fruitful.

Those with an awesome sex life at home can still want the stolen water because it tastes best.

Most can relate to having something stolen that becomes a favourite. That towel you took from the hotel which you know you were supposed to leave behind, yes, the stolen one… It suddenly becomes the favourite out of all the towels you purchased.

A few times I have met a couple in Cheshire which all started when she noticed on several occasions that her man had been watching pornography that each time featured black girls. She was surprised because he always claimed that black girls never appealed to him. He was either lying, like most do concerning this, or it was a newfound appreciation for *ebony*. She sought out a black escort and found me. She said it was his birthday soon and all she wanted to get him was me. We discussed what outfits I had and planned the surprise. I turned up. He was in shock and initially went into a tantrum. "You can't do this!" he shouted.

"You know you want to," she said as I gave him a striptease. In no time, we were all on cloud nine. I have been back three times since and it seems they are happily in love, and I'm loving it too.

Some women have had the privilege of an open and honest chat with me after they have caught a text or similar clue. One such time was a confirmed booking for a Tuesday and my client's text message was caught by his wife. I never knew his real name, but he always referred to himself as 'Man in the Mirror' because as we fucked, he fell in love with our naked reflection in the mirrors to such a great degree that it became a fetish.

"Hi, it's Man in the Mirror. I'm up in Manchester on business on Tuesday and wondered if you are available."

Upon seeing that text, knowing her man was due in Manchester and that she would be packing his case for the trip, her temperature evidently hit the roof.

"You are meeting Man in the Mirror on Tuesday at two o'clock, you bitch!" She went on and on and then burst into tears. I could have hung up, but I am not a horrible person. Alarmingly, I have never broken a marriage, but I have fixed many. I told her to ring me back when she has calmed down. And to my surprise, she did.

I told her the trait of corrupt human nature. Unfortunately, the forbidden fruit, the stolen water, adultery, however momentary the pleasure, is more enticing. The lawful enjoyment of his own wife is different to illicit sex, so she should not think of herself any lower than she ought to, and likewise I would not think of myself any higher than I ought to.

Most men love porn and it is more enticing in secret from their partners. A few addicts I have met have said to me, "She would kill me if she knew I love porn."

Often, I have asked, "What if you realised, she doesn't mind you watching porn after all; what if she loves it too?"

"Oh, I won't even go there. You don't know what she is like. If she saw it on the internet history, that would be us finished."

The answer has always been the same.

"That's my private sin, my secret lust, unlawful lust."

I love to watch a man wank. It absolutely turns me on. The way they hold their penis is a fascinating art. Each man is unique in their grip, some at the tip, others the base, some prefer dry, others demand baby oil, others spit on their hand and decline baby oil – I love it. They love a good masturbation session. Asked if he would let his wife watch, the answer was the same. Never. "If she knew I masturbated, that would be it. But I wank once or twice a day. She would never allow it." If you really love him, you will watch him wanking.

Indeed, sex is awesome, but have you ever masturbated? I mean… masturbation is underrated. Be not devastated. There is no shame in admitting that you are addicted to masturbating either; it's in your daily schedule. You set aside a slice of time each day… to make love to yourself or your imaginary lover. It's okay; be your own best lover. It is refreshing and stimulating. Despite all the sex I have in my busy schedule, I pause for a moment, specifically to spend time with my body and relearn what feels good.

I can tell straight away when a man is addicted to masturbation: Sex is virtually impossible. Their tight grip of the hand surpasses the grip of the vagina or the anus. These boys are a total waste of time. I just put on some porn and tell them to masturbate or tell them to stand over there, have a wank and watch me play.

Who, in real life, is squeaky clean? Holy shit! I met some goddamn pastors, predators, bishops and traitors and priests, and they savoured every moment, thanking god that we found each other in this lifetime. What a gift! Some miracles find you if you revel them with gratitude.

How much sin does it take to be a sinner? We are all sinners judging other sinners for sinning differently. Those who were in the Holy Month of Ramadan, it must be the hunger that makes them extra horny, because go to every brothel, do a survey and find out who goes in the most. It's shocking and yet not shocking at the same time, because I know the reality; stolen bread is more delicious.

Its consequences are another matter entirely.

The sweet stolen waters and the sweet pleasant bread may become bitter and painful in the end – that will be then.

The grass may not be greener after all – that will be then.

The forbidden field may not be as enticing as it once looked – that will be then.

The wreckage and aftertaste may be regrettable – that will be then.

We are a 'now' generation who just want to crack on. Our motive is today.

We are all at it. Everyone has a log in their eye, so no one real says anymore, "I Saw What You Did There; I'm Keeping an Eye on You."

What about the not-so-smart women who wrap themselves in barbed wire for days and weeks… to restrain their man from getting in? They sit on the couch, in barbed wire. They go to bed… in barbed wire… Sharp objects, out of bounds.

In such an atmosphere, you deprive and drive him to a hooker who will open wide and let him in, wearing inviting lingerie. I had a special PRIORITY folder for these 'deprived' men.

The bed being the most basic route is somehow boring. You'd be forgiven if you thought car-sex was only for people who can't fuck in the house or for the homeless. With sex on the brain, what if we can't wait any longer? Truly dedicated to being adventurous, I was happiest when I got a request for sex-in-the-car and was rightly proud of the outcome achieved in the uncomfortable, confined space. It takes art and shows off flexibility and talent on numerous levels, to deliver amazing sex in nearly impossible places. It felt like something that further improved my already amazing CV: "I managed to do various sex positions in a tiny sports car."

A sex-on-wheels client asked, "Are you sure this will happen?"

I confidently replied, "Leave it with me, darling. It's the only struggle I enjoy." I have even managed some sneaky test drives in my clients' cars!

Emphasis added. The vehicle must be stationary. Do not try the ladder…it is a disaster. Sex down their allotments can get beautifully wild and exciting, its demand has increased.

As ever, there was always something adventurous going on with me. Being pulled up into a truck was always kinky too. Others have a phobia for confined spaces, but the tiny space thrilled me, and I can proudly say that I have fucked in more trucks than you could know, but no, I have never driven one! Truck drivers worry about their work/life balance. Apart from feeling isolated, they hardly have the time to do things that we take for granted, such as going to the gym or cooking healthy meals. Their work habits of long-distance hauls have a negative impact on their physical health and after a day of fatigue, most drivers resort to watching pornography and masturbating. The lucky ones had me, a saviour to drive up to their truck stop on the M6 Motorway in Lymm, Cheshire, and I felt lucky too because these meek and lowly truck drivers always paid me much more than the filthy rich. In my coat and nothing underneath, the best part was always when the driver pulled me up into the truck as the nearby drivers watched on. When we closed the curtains, they just knew that we were about to stir it up and the clever ones always targeted me on my way down, which was usually after just a few minutes. Then I would be pulled up into another truck.

I suffered from the incurable disease of curiosity. BDSM; having the power to deeply arouse and torment, I loved to be at the helm. I loved to be the head, not the tail. To be above, not beneath. For a change. I needed a dungeon for bondage and after pondering where to have it, I came up with an idea. A self-storage unit near me, with excellent value and flexible agreements, came to the rescue. I was given the brand-new cabin and put a lot of thought into the layout and turned it into a fit-for-purpose place with chains and whips, and it was convenient too. I took pride in my job and looked after my cabin. It was just what my clients and I needed. It was lovely to go to five-star hotels for out-calls, but these kinky, fetish places were awesome.

When pride comes, disgrace follows, but the lowly and humble in spirit gain honour. Even the greatest eagle can be forgotten if it flies very high. Pride is social poison. Life will fuck you up! When your wings start getting too close to the sun… the moment you think you have grasped the world, is the moment when you surely haven't, and failure is on the horizon. We can all cite an example of that selfish, vainglorious person who was reduced to a laughingstock. Made a public spectacle because of pride, turned from solid ground to liquid mud. So full of themselves, they were brought to nothing, their powers stripped, disarmed, publicly shamed and disgraced… Only sadness and pain keep some people humble.

Humility… even just a little of it, saves you from the monstrous terror; but the moment you brag how humble you are, you are no longer humble. Some people have seen that they have made it in life, so arrogant, even a handshake was a problem to them because they look narrowly down on everyone. When life humbles you, those you called the nobodies… the downtrodden… will soon triumph over your downfall.

***

Lost and found, I managed lost property too. If you think you have lost property during your visit to an escort, just make a U-turn if possible, because I only store them for seven days, after which it's finders' keepers – socks, neck-ties, scarves, caps, watches, especially boxers. The long johns, I binned. If you want to put me off with the clothing you wear, just wear some long johns. Oh, how I hate them! I would not even store them as lost property. Men always left them behind because they came in cold but left hot, so hot.

Be good to people on your way out. You may find them on your way down, because life can bring you to nothing. Be good to people on your way out because you may need to contact them for lost property. The parting point is always crucial. Did you slam the door behind you and say, "fuck off"? People will always remember how you treated them, so why not leave some good footprints and part in peace, so that goodness and mercy follow you? One businessman who came from Geneva, Switzerland, to watch a Manchester United game learned this lesson the hard way. As they do, an escort is on the itinerary, as soon as he landed at Manchester Airport, one winter night, he made his way to me and the football game was the following day. He was nasty throughout the booking and even more horrible on departure. Whilst in the taxi to his hotel, he realised his Italian designer scarf was not on his neck and he rang me in panic. It was not about the price tag on it, but it was sentimental to him. The more he told me it was a present from his late grandfather, the more I told him I'm about to burn it with a lighter because of his terribly wicked and filthy heart. Please don't feel sorry for him. He has probably been nasty all his life and was sent to me to have his heart circumcised. True circumcision is of the heart. "Don't even bother making a U-Turn, sir. Just proceed and get yourself a scarf at the football ground tomorrow."

Everywhere you go, it matters what footprints you leave behind; you might want them to let you back in. In all fairness, those who parted with me in peace have come back and others have had their cherished items posted to them at no cost.

***

By their body art you shall know them. I have seen more tattoos than you'd believe, and usually I have teased men into explaining why in the world they would put beneath their belly button a tattoo such as: "What would your mother tell you to do? Spit or swallow?"

Currently, so many have tattoos of vacuum cleaners because apparently LIFE SUCKS! To those who have their names inked on their lover's penises as a deterrent and to prove ownership. Be reminded that it still gets erect and deep into others. We are in deep trouble if we assume that ink will change anything or deter anyone. At this point, it's no longer called cheating. It's simply called sharing. Just ask your partners to use protection. I have read out many names in my line of duty. Your name on their centre piece only opens the floodgates of ridicule.

***

I never promised that everything I touch comes to life! There is no shame in confessing that you are diabetic and/or have erectile dysfunction. Vileness is when you make out as if I'm doing something wrong or I don't know my job. Like a branch cut off from the vine, there is no life in this penis. It's dead and it's not my fault. But some men were told early on in their life, whatever happens in bed, "always blame the woman".

***

Being in bed with socks on is bad manners. I love white men's feet. It's a fetish, so I hate when I must remind them to remove their socks.

Occasionally, I feel I should meet a man to grow old with, but then I suddenly meet a client who heals me – mind, body and soul, and I'm all better.

Some men book an escort just to get to know her drama and if there have been any famous clients. I don't mind that, but it's the stalkers I loathe.

I met some men who are perishing, so messed up that they believe they are in this world for misery and it was nice to remind them that, "No, you are here to enjoy life." There is a raging war in their mind, but when I appeared in their life, the darkness disappeared. They received strength and a sense of unconditional, irreversible, everlasting love which simply never existed until they met me. For me, this was beyond a job. It was my platform to dispense love, stimulate their faith and activate the joy within them, which they never knew they had.

Smart clients know that if they treat me with respect, it will pay dividends. Every action brings a reaction. With others, I'm watching the clock and many I have met once, and they have been banned from calling me again. When they change number and pose as a different person, my intuition tells me not to give them the benefit of the doubt. Each time I have relented, I have always regretted it, because they have been more horrible and dangerous than the previous time.

***

Love at first sight, I have experienced some great chemistry with my clients and sometimes it's unreal. Giving a love bite is against the rules in the code and conduct of an escort, but it can be easily done.

With Alan, it was just the little kiss that he gave me every time after sex that made me feel appreciated and respected. He almost won my soul over. Such a simple yet erotic gesture but it held so much love and tenderness for me. I treasured these brief but memorable soul-to-soul bonds.

With Brian, the kiss and tight giant hug he gave me at the door on his way out made the parting sweet sorrow. At times, I was in desperate need of a hug. Nothing more. Just some arms around me and a chest for my head to rest against.

Chapter 31
Honesty Box

On Halloween, I often left some trick or treat money at my front door for the kids and when I came back, there was always some sweets left on my doorstep. They didn't have to leave anything, but it feels awesome because it's a sign of kindness and honesty. Not everyone puts something in the honesty box.

I have seen some people dip their hand in the offering box at church so that they can be seen to be giving, but they have put nothing in. Some will put rubbish inside and feel successful in their intention to save a penny. They do that so often; it becomes a habit.

Good grief. "See a penny. Pick it up. All day you have a penny."

The first time I ever went to the rural areas of Britain, I learned of something I'd never heard of before, the 'honesty box' at the gate. You pick your items and choose what to pay, as you see fit; it's about honesty. I found it fascinating. There is no CCTV in operation. It is all based on *honesty* and a strong belief in humanity.

I thought it was a brilliant idea, so I decided to experiment that style on my services and left an honesty box at the 'gate'. It left me even more fascinated… or rather, angrier. Not only did the takings not match the 'takings', but it was sad to see how those who were wealthy, demanding more than the usual, always gave what cost them nothing, in return for a succulent service.

My frustrating experiences: men who worked as window cleaners or taxi drivers paid me more handsomely than the high earning Premier League footballers. It left me devastated. There is a thin line between bad economics, dishonesty and bad behaviour. How do you work that one out? Even when you specify the rates, with some people, you must be robust and that was sad because I just expected them to be fair. Even that is too much to ask from some folks.

To give without sacrifice is not to give at all. To calculate how little you can give and get away with it is shameful and morally bankrupt. Innovative, creative and relentless. I and many hookers out there, have often witnessed the correlation between exorbitant wealth and selfishness! Unfeeling, pompous, tight-fisted termites. They retain their privileges from cradle to grave, but still, we, the hookers must plead with them to RESPECT OUR RATES!

Chapter 32
Celebrities

I was repeatedly contacted by the grand sportsman. I repeatedly told him I was unavailable, although that was not true. I could tell from his accent that he was African. I did not usually take on black or Asian clients and I stated on my advert that I preferred to deal exclusively with Caucasian men, although I often still got enquiries from them. He continued to repeatedly phone me, perhaps up to ten times a week, so I became annoyed and contemplated blocking his number on my phone as he was so persistent. However, on one occasion, he called me after midnight and asked me whether I had refused to meet him because he was black. He pleaded with me not to refuse to see him and said he was different and would treat me with respect. He asked me to visit him at his home in Cheshire. I relented but told him that I was not prepared to travel all the way to his home that late at night, and instead asked him to come over to my flat the next day.

The next morning, I went about my usual routine and I received a telephone call from him, telling me that he had arrived at my home address. I was furious and told him off for not warning me that he was on the way, as I needed a shower and to get ready. I gave him a choice of either coming in or waiting in his car, so he decided to wait inside, and I made him a coffee while I got ready. He was courteous and well-mannered, even taking his shoes off at the door.

When I was ready, I called him through. He was not particularly talkative, but I complimented him on his physique when he undressed.

When he rang me again another time, I still recognised that French accent. I was pleased to hear from him as he had made a good impression the first time we met. He asked me if I was available that evening and I told him I was. Again, he was wearing the same hooded tracksuit. This time he was more talkative and when he undressed, I noticed a fresh tattoo on his arm and told him that he had ruined his nice body with it because his skin was too dark, and it looked like dirt instead of a tattoo. I remember his face was that of regret. He became a regular client. Little did I know that he was an epic sportsman. Until, one day I saw him doing an interview on television after a game. But we still met up for our sex rendezvous. This time scared that he would be recognised in the neighbourhood, we started to have steamy and succulent sexy romps in the back seat of his left-hand drive car; for easy access, I had just a coat on with nothing underneath. With an erection, he drove around for about half an hour as we sought the ideal spot to fuck. That was not a romantic drive. I was anxious because he's not a smooth driver... Perhaps he was too horny to focus – worse still, it was raining. He had his TV on with some Afro beats.

Unless it's criminal, there is no weird place to have sex. We finally found a spot, but as soon as we got out and into the back seat, desperate to get started, the car alarm went haywire... He got nervous, but we got there in the end because forget the flirting and foreplay, car sex literally gets straight to the point, and it was amazing. At least nobody knocked on the window to say, "Please step out of the vehicle."

I didn't take money upfront as I reasonably expected him to pay me handsomely this time, but when he gave two fifty-pound notes that he pulled out of a wad of cash, I was too flabbergasted but managed to conceal my shock and disgust. I drew the line. That was the end of our escapades. Because he loved a bit of anal (which man doesn't!), he always asked me to send him pictures of my juicy ass until my phone bill was sky high. That was the end too.

***

He passed on my phone number to his brother. Sportsmen love hookers. I visited his mansion in Prestbury, Cheshire.

Upon my arrival on the first visit, he continued attempting to disguise who he was and tried to justify being in a mansion, as if he owed me an apology for being rich. In dimmed lights, he started explaining that his parents had gone away and literally left him home alone, so as he was bored stiff watching porn, he had decided to ring an escort. Fully aware who he was... I ignored him and let him talk away. I didn't wrestle with his story. He felt silly when he eventually discovered that I knew him all along and was flabbergasted when I told him that my fantasy is to have them in bed together. He said they had done it, in another country and that he would suggest the thrill to his brother later that day.

He was craving me harder and harder; I drove him insanely wild. Perhaps it was the sexy neck kisses I gave him? A hint of his cologne always lingered on me. Anyhow, he hit a different nerve which made my clit come alive each time he rang. I was dripping with nectar on my way to him… the thought of him sliding his jaw-dropping, lovely length deep in my honeypot… he got to my hard-to-reach places. Somewhere between making love and fucking, we did it again and again, leading to some electrifying moments. He figured that I love to be fucked fast and often. Oh, the strangeness of life! The beautiful eye contact with clients! Who said that sex with someone you love is the best there is?

The only downside… Just like his brother, he didn't respect my rate.

He caught me red-handed taking a picture of him and it made him so angry. He checked my phone and deleted it. I buried my head in shame and thought that was the end of us, but to my surprise, he contacted me again a few hours later to go back for round two. I arrived around 9 pm. He had no consideration that it took me forty-five minutes to get there and forty-five minutes back!

Always horny, and ready to play, he turned me on without touching me. Waiting and wanting, I never met a man who looked so sexy wearing a onesie, but he did and even better when he removed it. My oh my, boy oh boy! Come and get it. What a body and a delicious succulent throbbing dick to go with it! He had guests at the house, so he switched off his CCTV and he devoured me outside his house. He told me he was looking forward to the *Mayweather v Pacquiao* boxing match, which was being broadcast live from Las Vegas that night.

The way we fucked was art. He even suggested that I should be their nanny because they were looking for one, and he wanted me under his roof, but the controversial question was, "Where would I say we met? Because it is my wife in charge of that vetting process." That thought turned me on as much as it did him. It was just fantasy, I suppose. Wishful thinking.

He enjoyed savagely indulging my curves on the grass, so we did it again. This time I had the courage to complain that the distance is costing me a lot in petrol. I told him, "By now we are supposed to be friends and you are supposed to keep me happy." He asked me how much petrol was, and I was disgusted. Are you going to fuel my passion or calculate the petrol and mileage?

On one visit, he asked me what shoes I was wearing, and I told him I had heels on. He told me to remove them and sneak in the house. This time, he had included an extra £20 in petrol. Charming.

As much as I deliver all the playful promises, some men have special qualities. They will tease you and make you want and need them. The scene is hailed triumphant each time. I have never been so horny in my entire life. At his mansion in Prestbury, upstairs in the self-contained guest bedroom, downstairs in the dining room and sometimes outdoors on the grass, that is where it was most pleasurable and that became his kink and fetish. Needlessly competitive, on each meeting he boasted how he had a much bigger penis than his brother. "Who fucks you better, me or my brother? I know it's me." He wanted me to assure him that I was loving sex with him better.

I did not accomplish my fantasy because the compensation for the intimate services was outrageously low; it was so unfair. I loved how I was fucking two sportsmen. They loved how they were fucking the same girl. What's not to love? The excitement was mutual and surreal. If only they were generous, our escapades would have lasted longer. But they were the most tight-fisted men alive. They paralysed my faith in rich people. They never, ever wanted to part with their hard-earned cash, and they are eagerly waiting for that moment when they save a penny, because it's better in their pocket than somebody else's, which I found rather annoying and hurtful. The sexual activities were enjoyable though; I miss them, and I know they miss me too.

What was it that set him apart? Why is he the man who comes to my mind when I am super horny? There was something incredibly erotic about him that I loved and still miss. He still gets my juices flowing and I fantasise about him often. His brother was not idyllic, but there was something undeniably delicious about him that made me want him more and more. This was unprecedented, considering I am obsessed with Caucasian men and colour contrast, but like a slippery slope, he was so easy to fall into. If not in his boxers, he was in his onesie. Let's face it, not all men look good in a onesie, but he always did, always ready and excitedly expecting me, in his onesie with nothing but a fresh smell underneath. Moist with longing, I unzipped it all the way down, and sucked his dick… knowing he's about to fuck my soul out of my body.

I always left him eager for more. After each meeting, as soon I arrived home, he would ring me. "Guess what, I want you again now. I'm so hard and horny. I wish you would come back. Please come back, babe." We spoke on the phone quite a lot and he would say, "Look, you would have been here by now. We would be fucking."

Gradually, the thrill was lost because he was very tight-fisted, so I declined, even though I was into him. If these people are happy with all this money, why can't they deploy it to their advantage so that it's a win-win for all? From Manchester to Prestbury, it was close to two hours' round trip and I had to beg him for petrol. And even then, he gave me just £20? There is nothing more refreshing than a generous, considerate man. All riches come to nought when an escort must beg and explain travel costs. He rattled my cage and I never went back. Despite constantly reminding him that this was not a pizza delivery, it was sex, delivered to him in the comfort of his home, sometimes in his garden, he still gave excuses. The awesome escapades were cut short too early and the gap we left on either side is too huge to fill. I still crave his essence and caress.

Chapter 33
Cheshire

I went without a penny. I came home without a penny. It was the biggest mansion I have ever visited in all my years as an escort, yet and the biggest lesson learned. Don't judge a man by his house. Located on a street with extra security because it housed the rich, famous and footballers... and I came back to my impoverished ghetto penniless because the filthy rich bastard had gone back in my bag and stolen all the money that he had paid.

Upon entry, I gazed in wonder, at the luxurious house of breathtaking beauty and grandeur. I felt an excitement in me that was uncontrollable; the beautiful decoration embodied my dream. This was but a mirage to some of us!

With his poorly disguised IQ test, he decided that women like me have no decorum. Whilst I was complimenting the phenomenal house, he thought I was cooking up a way to stay ever after. So full of himself, glorifying himself, he warned me not to fall in love with him because I am not his type. I sure as hell was his type to give him golden showers, use my strap-on... and fuck him in private. Feeling humiliated, I showed him my engagement ring, which always came in handy for rude, vainglorious men like him.

I was given £300 for outcall and came home with nothing. I had visited the toilet before leaving, taking my time, and this very rich man went in my bag and took all his money back! Unfathomable. But I came back with a monumental lesson.

Admittedly, I had trusted him because he was in a mansion surrounded in marble, so perhaps this was deserved, right? If I had gone to a council house on a run-down estate like mine, I would have protected my bag and taken it to the bathroom. It taught me to honour my honest regulars from ordinary places. Truly appalling how the well-heeled can be so heartless and rotten to the core. Those I met either needed to circumcise their hearts or at least get a personality transplant. They usually wanted two girls for the price of one. They always paid for an hour and wanted the other for free. Shocking and annoying.

Gentle reminder: don't be afraid of the less fortunate; having little is not a moral flaw. Also, never judge a man by his fortunes, nor a book by its cover. After all, it's societal upper crusts, who destroy a country and continue to gain so much more fortune for themselves, by their morally flawed actions. They only scratch each other's back, so don't even think about it. If these selfish people ever came near an 'honesty box', it would be ransacked; money tubs burst open and robbed blind.

Apart from the stimulation, I love what working in the sex industry has done to me. It has given me some perspective, sharpened and enlightened me; that it is usually the rich lunatics who pursue some cheating strategies. They bend reality to their perspective, rather than using their perspective to try and understand reality. In this case, the reality being he was meant to pay for the sexual services. Some people only ever have their own interests at heart. Some hearts are like filthy rags. When I rang him back to say my money was not in my bag, he laughed rudely and said, "Well, don't be coming back here because I will ring security."

Some hearts have such a huge foreskin of selfishness and insatiable greed, it needs to be circumcised. Their very souls are malformed, in harmony with their entitlement. Be fair, give something back and share the spoils with those who fulfil your dark, deepest desires. Naked we came into this world, naked shall we return. Your credit cards won't work up there, or down there!

It is I, the hooker. A lot is thrown at us, but still, we let it roll off and knit compassion and kindness at every turn. Our services are very much needed, yet we are taken for granted. Being emotionally invested is a gift in our field and it doesn't make us less of a hooker to express our feelings. I allow myself to feel the pain and the joy; as an affirmation that I am alive. One thing is certain; being a hooker augmented my outlook and taught me some crucial lessons in humanism, risks, critical thought and reflection. I get a new perspective all the time. I have learned, not only from other sex workers, but from my clients and, surprisingly… myself. Beyond work, it is an opportunity.

Chapter 34
The Irish VIP

People form assumptions about others on face value, but that doesn't mean that they know you who you are.

They *think* they know him – wealthy, influential and prestigious. They may know *of* him, but the world doesn't know him like I know him; I know him personally. My story is a collection of truths, an authentic chronicle of a tycoon falling apart, deteriorating and in need of rescuing. A paranoid man, troubled and unhinged, who happened to have a home in my heart.

Sometimes, the only thing one needs is encouragement. I saw him through the constant stormy clouds; I understood him with love and compassion. I felt his trials and tribulations with a sincerity that the world does not always give.

Hearing his fears first-hand was almost haunting. Even the strongest, wealthiest and most illustrious human beings go through great difficulties and struggles. They have invisible wounds that the world does not see. They experience times of distress and call out for help. What he showed me was that money, fame and fortune do not guarantee you immunity from the fiery darts of life. He was his own worst enemy. He would say, "I am not my own. I don't even trust myself."

Apart from being one of a kind, there was a woeful irony from the moment I met this man. On the spectrum of wealth, it was clear that this friendship had broken convention. Him… a business magnate who carried a lot of clout. Me… a downtrodden pauper from the council estate. My simplicity and empty handedness happened to be the vital instrument to overhaul his mind, body and soul.

Being Irish in the conservative Roman Catholicism culture, society expects you to function in a certain way; any hiccup means you are frowned upon by moral high grounders who think themselves higher and more holy than they ought to. I think we can all agree that no one is without blemish.

By whose standard is anyone holy? Everyone is fighting their own battle on their own terms; no one is perfect. We can learn from Pope Francis and his visits to a psychoanalyst many years ago for the purpose of shedding light on a few things. He has also criticised 'rigid priests who are afraid of communicating' and has always used his Christmas address to deliver undiluted truths of hypocritical double lives, terrorism of gossip, traitors of trust, spiritual Alzheimer's, virtues of honesty, humility and sobriety and urged people to examine their consciences. He acknowledges that patience, dedication and delicacy were required to reform Rome.

The Irish millionaire came to Manchester on business and, like most men, all work and no play makes a man dull, so he contacted me after spotting my escort advertisement online. Balancing work and play, that's the key to life. I woke up one morning and noticed I had missed six calls from the same number. I returned the call, but the man told me he had already been with another escort. Despite it being too late, he appreciated my getting back to him and said he would contact me when he comes back on business. We ended the call and to my surprise, he rang again and asked how long it would take me to get to the hotel. He said I could still go and meet him briefly before his departure at mid-day. I made sure to tell him that I was expecting to be paid; I have dealt with some selfish men in the past that felt I should be honoured to even step foot in a hotel of this class and therefore not be paid for my work.

Everyone wants to matter but the facts speak for themselves. Ordinary is not insignificant. From my council estate in a run-down part of town, it was a new day for me. Ecstasy awaited when I entered the five-star hotel in the city centre.

It was a dream or perhaps even a nightmare, as I was welcomed by an unusual man with character. A tall, talkative and charming Irishman. Glancing at the rolled-up bank notes and cocaine on the table, it was obvious that this man had had a party with the previous escort and was now ready to fly back to Ireland to live by the house rules again.

Most of the Irishmen I met usually came to Manchester for the Premier League football games and would normally stay in the budget hotels, sharing a room between three or four lads to cut costs. Because of their lively spirits and my passion for adventure, the chaos of sharing one room between us was all part of the pleasure; they just wanted to lock the door to the outside world and have copious amounts of fun.

This man, on this blessed day, was not my typical day-to-day client. He was peculiar. Seeming like the sort of man who would let me have my own way, I seized the moment and found myself running a hot bath as he talked away and devoured more cocaine. My flat on the council estate only had a tiny shower, so one of the perks of going to an upscale hotel was indulging in a lovely hot bath, not something I would dare do with stern clients.

We chatted away about Africa; that his son lived in Cape Town and was planning to come back home to Ireland because of the rise in crime. With a pitiful tone, he said his son was very ill and they feared he *may* have cancer. Then he handed me some money, which made my heart skip a beat. I didn't count it in his presence because it was clearly a lot more than my standard rate. I gazed at him in awe and gratitude. He excitedly showed me his passport, boasting about how much weight he had lost. I was flabbergasted! The man in the photo had worked extremely hard to become the man who stood before me. I asked him if he had had surgery, but he said he had achieved the weight loss just by eating right and doing exercise. He was half the size of the man in the picture. I told him, "You need a new passport now because you are a different man."

He told me he was bisexual. I said, "Aren't we all…or at least, if we are honest… bi-curious?" He laughed. I was curious as to whether his escort from the previous night had been a man or a woman, but when I asked, he didn't give me an answer. Instead, he dived between my legs and gave me oral sex in the only way he knew how, and he kept telling me how brilliant he was at it. I told him to relax and listen because it's not one-size-fits-all. Every layout is different in size, dimensions, sensitivity and taste, amongst other things. There was no room to be stubborn with me, so he calmed down and allowed me to instruct him on exactly how to delight my unique pussy. With a combination of patience and guidance, we got there in the end. I get the most exciting thrill in showing a man another side of himself.

He took me by surprise when he asked me if I knew anyone who could come and join us. After some minor debate and on such short notice, I said certainly not, especially if he says he's about to check out and leave soon. He pleaded with me, but I said no.

"Should we check who is in the next room?" he asked.

"Don't be silly. How in the world would I go and knock on a random room? And anyway, what if there is nobody in it."

"Then try the next room."

I realised he wasn't joking. I told him to stop being absurd because after all, he had to checkout and head for the airport.

It was at this point that he mentioned another deep and shocking fantasy if not confession… to which I naturally cringed and pleaded with him to stop; I was relieved that he never mentioned it again, ever. Sternly, I emphasised to him that I am all about kink and fetish, but ONLY between consenting adults.

He assured me he would be back in England soon and that this was just the beginning of the fun. *It's me he will ring on his next business trip*, I thought. I was delighted, and I saved his number. I assured him that I would arrange for someone else to join us next time and that he wouldn't be disappointed.

No sooner had I left, than he rang me and asked if I could come back to the hotel room. Because he had paid me handsomely, I felt it rude to decline. I turned back to the friendly concierge to whom I had just said goodbye and declared, "I have just forgotten something, silly me."

Upon re-entering his room, he gave me more money from a bundle of cash and started the conversation all over again. Money talks. It answers many things.

"Do you know any man who can join us? Surely you must know someone," he begged.

I was not revolted by his erratic behaviour... just grateful to receive more money. I looked through my phone contacts but everyone that I approached was busy. I then suggested that we go online and get a male escort we both liked. As we scrolled through the male escorts, he started to get agitated and suddenly said, "I have no time. I must be going soon. Let's do this when I have more time. You go and make sure nobody sees you leaving the room."

"Okay," I laughed, "I will make myself invisible."

As I was leaving, he was scraping the table for leftover cocaine. I took a wet facecloth from the bathroom, cleaned the table and told him, "The party is over. Get ready for the airport. Goodbye."

He looked at me, gave me more money and said, "Go and please don't come back now. I will be gone." He repeated, "Don't come back."

I promised I wouldn't. He gave me a little bit more money and led me to the door. As he opened it, I shut it once more, squeezed his hand and thanked him.

"Don't worry," he said, "I will come again, and we will have a good time."

Elated, I could have easily danced all the way out of the hotel. I had never been paid so much money in my life. What a feeling! I got this money without having to be fucked from every angle in every hole. I didn't have to do any somersaults or perform acrobatic porn sex that some men demand when paying a fraction of this cash. Was I dreaming?

On my way home, the world seemed to be in the way. I just wanted it to leave me alone to count my cash. This was an unprecedented amount of money. I got in the back of the taxi and, as I discreetly attempted to count my cash, I was continuously interrupted by the talkative driver. I didn't want to hear about his love life; I just wanted him to shut up. I wanted to take this time to reflect on my curious encounter.

After that, we kept in touch and on Tuesday, 15 July 2014, he arrived at the same hotel.

He explained that the usual pattern of his business trips was to arrive on Tuesday and fly back on Thursday, unless he had to travel out of Europe. I was overwhelmed.

I arrived at the hotel just after 8 pm. He made a phone call to his wife, brief and to the point. All he said to her was, "I have just taken my Zopiclone and I'm about to sleep now." Only I knew that my client was wide-awake, excited and ready to party. He had his cocaine delivered from his trusted London source, so I let him get on with it. The night had just begun.

I told him that I wouldn't just live up to my promise, but I would go far beyond. I called a man with a fabulous, delicious, mouth-watering package that I had met the previous month as a client. He told me to make sure he didn't have HIV because he hates condoms. I told him that I cannot guarantee that, so it will have to be condoms; better safe than sorry.

Mike was a taxi driver. He was not gay or bisexual but was ready to switch and identify accordingly, if the price was right. Money talks. Money speaks. Money answers most things. You can't be too rigid in life or you miss out. I had previously discussed with Mike on his last booking that I may need him and his nine inches soon. I convinced him and finally he said, "If the price is right." Cash is king. This was the night and he made sure he was within reach.

Mike was happy, considering there was no way he would have made this amount of money, even if he charged double for his taxi fare. As for my VIP, he was happy that I had delivered. I was pleased that everything went smoothly. Such arrangements can sometimes go disastrously wrong and there are a few times I have regretted making them.

My first threesome with two men was a disaster; one was stubborn and greedy, and the other one rich and selfish but unable to perform. Their personalities clashed so much that I was caught up in the middle having to mediate between the two inadequate men.

With Mike and my VIP, it was wonderfully different in that both men let me take the wheel and control the whole process. Mike being new to that sort of scene helped greatly. They both knew they were in very safe hands. All ended well and us three would certainly meet again.

When his classic paranoid cocaine behaviours started to ease off, I left just before midnight after he had taken about six or seven Zopiclone sleeping pills. In utter shock, I asked him how many pills he was taking. He said just four. He wasn't happy when I expressed my shock, so I changed the subject immediately; perhaps I was overstepping the boundaries. I was always re-evaluating my place in these relationships. The following day he went to Liverpool and we had plans to meet that evening, but he cancelled, and I guessed why.

In truth, I was angry that I didn't hear from him that evening before he flew back on Thursday. I told myself that he felt shy about our escapades of the previous night and wanted some time before we met again.

After this meeting, and despite not seeing him on the Wednesday, we kept in touch a lot more. He was not one for texting, but he rang me many times. He rang once to ask if I preferred white gold or yellow gold because he wanted to buy me a necklace while he was abroad before his next trip to Manchester. I told him, "You choose. I have no idea what gold I like. I have other specialities, but gold is certainly not one of them. I don't even own anything in gold." He laughed.

His next trip to Manchester was cancelled due to illness after a long-haul flight; he believed it was because of the germ-laden cabin air. He complained to me that they should have changed the air on the flight, but they didn't and now he feared for his life. He kept asking, "Am I dying or what?"

Purpose is powerful. It keeps death away until life is fulfilled. I kept him focussed on living by saying, "Don't pack your bags yet. Hang in there. You are going nowhere until I get my gold necklace, so keep telling yourself you have an important parcel to deliver to me and you will live."

The doctor was visiting him at home regularly and he kept me updated about his recovery until he was given the all-clear to travel again.

After speaking for so long, my words carried love and healing, and I was longing to be close to him, to have physical contact after such a long time apart. It was Tuesday, 4 November 2014. He flew from Dublin to Glasgow and took the train to Manchester with his friends. I texted him a few enticing messages and videos when he was on the train, some of which he was careful not to open because he was in company.

I received a warm welcome at the hotel bar. He walked over to meet me and gave me a hug and his three friends all shook my hand. Everyone was pleasant to me and I felt on top of the world as he introduced me as his special friend. He apologised for wearing some light Skechers with his smart clothes. I couldn't even hear what he was saying, I was in my own little world, both excited and terrified that I was with these extremely rich, yet humble people. He laughed at the size of my bag and asked if I was moving in. When I told him that it contained my 'work-gear', his friends looked at each other, alarmed and intrigued, and laughed too.

"You won't be laughing when I open it," I said.

I sat there whilst he showered me with compliments, and his friends asked me where I was from. It was a surreal experience. I asked for a sparkling water when, abruptly, he asked if we could get that delivered to the room. It was as if he had suddenly remembered who and where he was. I was only in the bar another two minutes before, rather ironically, I was 'escorted' upstairs.

He had put on some weight since I had last seen him, which I could tell bothered him because he mentioned it when we got to the escalators.

"I promise I will be slimmer when I see you again at Christmas," he said.

Even though I understand the challenges of maintaining weight loss, I asked him what had happened. He said that he had been heavily burdened with problem after problem and his son's ill health was taking a toll on him. I can't recall whether he said his son had kidney problems or if it was something else, but all these issues were weighing him down and had derailed him from his healthy eating. I asked if he had stopped walking his daily six miles. He promised again that he would be slimmer when he saw me again before Christmas. I told him I was just happy to see him.

We reached the 12th floor and, after a long walk, I realised we were going around in circles. He was certain it was the 12th floor, but because of his dyslexia, he had forgotten what room number. "Be patient," he asked. I'm so used to hearing false excuses from men for their behaviour – when they can't perform, they blame it on muscle cramp, to prove it's a random malfunction – that my first reaction was to doubt whether he'd even booked a room here. Finally, we reached our destination, Room 1203, and I laughed.

No sooner had we opened the door to Room 1203, than I received a phone call from a friend who was also out with a client. At that moment, we found ourselves in two different worlds: Her client had taken her to a demolition site, and I had been taken to a five-star hotel. She only called to vent, but it was hilarious. She's one of those people that can make the saddest experiences sound funny. We were all in stitches, including my client.

It was just before 10 pm and he asked me to turn off my phone so he could ring his wife. After some initial greetings, he asked her if she had heard anything from the kids; I imagined he meant their children as well as the grandkids. Whoever. They swapped updates back and forth, and then he told her he was going to bed. "I will ring you in the morning, but my phone will be on vibration as usual." He talked to her about going to Liverpool the following day and about how he would be back in Manchester early enough to beat the football traffic that evening. I put myself on mute as they chatted away. It was lovely hearing the conversation. Temporarily being put on mute is part and parcel of the trade, so this was nothing new.

I can usually summarise a relationship immediately. This one consisted of a man who has already messed up multiple times, but their offspring and religion keeps them together. He's frightened of her; she is a tough woman. She needs continuous reassurance; she has been hurt too many times to ever truly trust this man again. That's why she calls and asks whether he has taken his sleeping pills; she needs to know he's going to sleep so that she too can safely retire to bed. This is a woman that has had enough of her man's scandals. These late-night phone calls were a way to prove faithfulness, not expressions of love. They were a rule because there was too much at stake.

After his phone call, I knew what was coming next, the necklace. When he handed it to me, I said, "How could you even think of dying before I got this? No way that was happening!"

"I did as you said, and it worked."

"Well, congratulations on not dying."

We laughed together, and I told him that I want my next gift to be a friendship ring. The necklace felt like an anchor that kept him safe at shore, within my reach. We had a good talk and I asked him what kinky things he had been up to recently. He told me about his last escapade in Hong Kong with a transvestite escort with fantastic breasts and a mouth-watering penis. For a second I was envious that I had missed out, but he quickly changed that when he asked if I could bring company the following evening. I told Mike to be on standby.

After a good face sitting, I left with my necklace, money and all smiles.

The next afternoon he rang me a few times and asked how long I would be; he was impatient, eager and waiting in anticipation. His cocaine delivery had just arrived, so although he was happy, he would be even happier when I got there.

Upon arrival, he rebuked me for leaving my earrings behind the previous night, so he had bagged them up for me and made sure I put them away safely in my bag. He was in the hotel dressing gown and his Skechers, so I wore the other gown, as it was pointless changing into my sexy lingerie. High and bewildered, cocaine on the table. Besides that, we seemed to have a problem. He had taken laxatives and had watery stools. This wasn't going to be an easy night.

"Why did you pick this time to do a colon cleanse?" I asked. And yet some hold on to the idea that millionaires are rational.

"Please don't shout at me. I needed it, that's why."

"I am not shouting," I said, "but that means we won't be calling Mike tonight." I rise to the occasion, but at times it feels like men can be kids and women are tasked with caring for them.

He insisted that we must call Mike to fuck the stress out of him, so I said I would in an hour or two, once he had composed himself. I spent this time clearing away his drugs from the table and convinced him "enough"! Drugs seemed to be the only way he knew how to cope in his wild and lavish world. He must have watched carefully because in no time at all, he went in my bag and took back the cocaine. This was gluttony on another scale, and I pitied his inability to control himself. Addictions are an actual health crisis. A pestilence. It was worse than babysitting and painful to watch. He was a tycoon in a contorted mess; it would have haunted me to leave anyone in that state.

I whistled, and Mike came running. Still in my dressing gown, I went downstairs to meet him and briefed him about the situation.

We entered the room and he saw it for himself. It took a dark turn when the client opened about his dark fantasy for minors. I rebuked him with raw disgust and anger and was never discussed but it left me shocked. He apologised as he tried to justify what he really meant, but the evening was ruined.

He was in such a state that I told him to pay Mike now, in advance, and he did so without counting the money. It was a huge chunk of money.

We did all-sorts that night, but it wasn't a good session. Too many things had happened, and the mood was gone. He demanded I take a video and send it to him after. Mike agreed to this if his face was not in it, so I did.

Mike left with his jackpot win. It may have been about four thousand pounds. That was the last I ever saw or heard from Mike.

Now it was just the two of us again. He demanded the rest of the cocaine that I had removed from the table. His addictions knew no moderation and it was a devastating battle that consumed him. He was sweating, had diarrhoea and was urinating in the sink. I wanted to go, but there was no way I could leave him in such a state. He was losing his spectacles every five minutes, asking for water every ten minutes and continuously wanted the lights changing from dim to bright, dim to bright. It was a historic encounter that proved even the elite need looking after, regardless of how they boast.

The money undoubtedly influenced how much I sacrificed but escorts don't swear a 'solemn oath' to put their clients care above all else. In this case, my love was all that was needed to go the extra mile. Withered and wasted, he took his seven Zopiclone sleeping pills, a dose far beyond the highest dosage, and still had no shuteye until dawn. The bed was a mess, so I put the pillows on the floor and sat there. I left at dawn and prompted him to get some rest to feel refreshed for the day. He agreed and told me to come back in the morning, after his breakfast, to collect my cash. I left penniless with no doubt that I would be paid the following day as promised. I always keep room in my heart for the unimaginable but not on this day. I trusted him. He was worth the devotion, or at least I thought so. I was exhausted and looked forward to a restful day.

I had a bath as soon as I got home, got ready and waited for his call to go and collect my cash. Little did I know that what was cooking on the other side was unimaginable. Having served as his midnight nurse, fulfilling his kinky fantasies, and witnessing his inexcusable floppiness, who would have thought that he would unleash his inner beast and trample the rose on the ground!

When the VIP had sobered up and was now coordinated enough to reveal his arrogant nature. He was furious that his books were not balancing by three thousand pounds. He accused me of stealing, having chosen to forget that he had overpaid Mike at my expense. I tried to explain to him that he had given Mike too much money, which obviously included mine, but it was pointless; he had made up his mind.

I tried to ring Mike, but the number was not in use. Christmas had come early. As a family man, this money would have meant a lot to him. It wouldn't surprise me if he went on to become an escort after this experience, having realised the commercial value of his succulent penis and the stamina to go with it.

Whether my client truly had no memory of the previous night or that he was just feeling shame for the state he had found himself in, he had hurt me either way. It was a new day, and he wanted to demonstrate that he had power and strength. He was brave enough to go on a cocaine binge because he knew he had me beside him; he was in safe hands. What I went through on that grim night was unforgettable. I didn't care how low he stooped for his thrills but a thank you would have been nice!

The financial imbalance was insignificant in comparison; it cost me my sleep and my sanity. To discard me like that without a second thought, as though I was the dirt on the bottom of his shoe… Surely, he could have parted with me in a more peaceful and respectful way, rather than slapping me with accusations. How distasteful coming from a respectable figure in society.

Gratitude and humility – even just a small amount can save you from monstrous terror. His vile behaviour backfired. When he arrived back in Ireland, he asked me to send him the videos he asked me to take the previous night. I sent them all signed off with his full name.

We are all in need of change, to grow to become better to ourselves and to others. You can have all the money, power and possessions in the world, but if you cannot keep your word, you are poor in spirit. When your words exceed your heart, they are empty words. They are lies and heartless apologies.

There is so much in a name. Upon receiving the text, he knew that this would backfire in a huge way. He suddenly became very apologetic, only because he didn't want to deal with the actual effect that this would have on his world. A bogus apology for his name's sake, as this would expedite the downfall of his household. If I hadn't quoted his majestic name to him, he would have, undoubtedly, lived without an ounce of guilt and never looked back at the revolting way he had treated me. He told me he would come and make amends before Christmas, so we planned to meet, but he called to say he thought he had arthritis and wouldn't be travelling. His son had also had a kidney transplant, or so he said. Excuses, perhaps.

In the end, it was clear that a rich man does not want the responsibility of reality, so he will not work towards reconciliation and forgiveness. The tables turned in his favour when I became gripped with fear. He had money and power, and who was I to challenge this with his name and videos. I felt like I was at the bar of justice, pleading for mercy that I didn't need. He felt better that the power was back in his hands. Money is power. We all know what it can and cannot do. It takes money for one to carry out a gruesome task for another, so I had to revive the friendship to feel safe. Lack of money makes one a victim. In this scenario, he was the victor and I the victim, and I became weary of the clients I met thereafter. What if he had sent them to me? I had to be vigilant.

One day, he rang me in some distress. His good friend had died at the wheel from a heart attack. He used the biblical phrase "He's crossed the river Jordan", entered the promised land through death. He was convinced that this man, although now absent in the body, was alive with Christ in Heaven because he was a changed and repentant man in his latter days. That sudden announcement felt to him like 'the party is over', without a warning. He was devastated; death stings and I felt his pain. Death and tragedy do not discriminate, and he started to live life with the fear of dying, rather than a passion for living.

Shortly after that, he rang me again, distressed, and this time his very good friend had died whilst on a golfing holiday abroad. What he went through was monumental grief and I felt the heaviness and sorrow in his heart. In that weak moment, when he wanted a gleam of hope to get him through the day… gripped with fear and seeking strength, I raised him through the mire.

Not long after that, he rang me on his way to a mass after another friend, Billy, had died. "He smoked over thirty a day from the tender age of fifteen," he mourned. Like a pot calling a kettle, he implied that Billy was the end of his own ruins.

And then another death; his son's best friend had committed suicide in America. Death is relentless.

Although death is despairing, the death of a loved one can be a revelation that changes our perspective on life and goals. He was frightened that death was hovering in his midst and he thought he was walking through 'the valley', as his own health was worsening, despite exhausting everything that medicine could do. It was as though he desired death, because his present world was truly filled with the atmosphere of death. A rich man struggling at every level, hopping from one therapeutic intervention to another, he was always in need. This time, he had shingles, a sign of decreased immunity usually associated with old age and stress. Considering what I knew, I advised him to have an HIV test also, and he said they would have picked it up in his countless medical tests. It was imperative that I mention this. He felt impotent and powerless and was not lively anymore. He had lost his social power. I then noticed that his memory was starting to go; he would repeat things over and over and claim that I hadn't told him something that I had.

You would think that comfort doesn't mean a lot coming from a regular person, but I filled an emptiness that constantly threatened to consume him. When he was desperately thirsty, even if just for a minute of heart-warming laughter, he would ring me, in the hopes of quenching his thirst. I became a perpetuation of strength, a fountain of hope, providing enrichment that even his millions could not buy him. His most delighted phone call went like this...

"Guess what, Sandra. I have a lot to tell you."

"You sound so happy. Have you just won the lottery?" I asked.

"My son is on the mend and so am I."

He sounded overjoyed. I was happy he was happy.

I felt his agonising journey. Even in his darkest moment, my light came to him.

No one is above mistakes and indulgences. Tragedies are common, not only to the common people. Although cocaine is regarded as a 'privilege drug', what is once, twice, thrice used to drown sorrows, stress relief or seen as a coping mechanism for anxiety, often leads to addiction. Alas! The pestilence of addiction.

I made him smile on days he was struggling to simply breathe and make it through the day. He became my worry, day and night. This was not the time to scream that he is the end of his own ruins. I felt responsible for him and hoped that those who cared for him did so with patience and kindness without telling him to "man up; you have inflicted these deep wounds upon yourself". I wanted him to assure me he was in good hands, looked after by a family who would strengthen his faith and build his hope. When someone's lifestyle has been so gluttonous and extravagant, it is easy for loved ones to lose patience.

To massage their ego and be glorified, those of his class often want to hear how smart they are. But on the brink of collapse with a drug addiction and desperate for a rescue plan, he was dying to hear a different message – a message from me. A message of hope with love and understanding, that all the money in the world couldn't buy him, even from his highly paid consultants. I became sensitive to his voice and needs. Each time he rang, I always knew straight away if he was merry or paralysed with fear. One day he left me a voice message which didn't even sound like him, because he could hardly speak. He had been sedated and was just recovering. In his feebleness, dialling my number was the only strength he had. It felt like there was but one step between him and death, and it frightened me. He too was convinced this could be his end, but I told him to fight on until he is certain that he has finished his race. Fear eats the soul and death is chiefly provoked by giving up.

"Always know, one hundred per cent, that you have a special place in my heart." When I finally spoke to him after hearing that voicemail, with infinite sadness in his tone, he said he was in a wheelchair and in excruciating pain; he couldn't walk. "The doctor asked me to rate my pain on a scale of one to ten, and I told him it's eleven. Cassandra, I'm in torturous agony and I don't know what to do. I need to speak to you. That's what keeps me sane." When someone understands you, they are your balance. His testimony of excruciating pain gave me pain. I could feel him screaming for relief and I hated to hear him hurting.

'Cassandra' was my performance name in the brothels and on the call-girl website where he first found me. If you think there is nothing in a name, you are wrong. Him calling me Cassandra stung like a bee. "I am not Cassandra, the hooker," I told him. "My name is Sandra, and I'm your friend."

He did not dispute that, and it sank to the depth of his soul; he has never called me Cassandra since. He knew that if his spirit was alive, his body would live. But how do you keep your spirit alive? By hearing more of the right stuff.

Meanwhile, I was out of money, and the only thing I had of value to pawn for cash was the piece of jewellery he had given me. When I finally had enough cash to buy it back, I had to pawn it again in another desperate measure to make ends meet. This time there was no getting it back as I missed too many payments. Thinking about this makes me teary; I treasured my necklace. Asking the millionaire for money was impossible and tormenting. He would go on about Brexit and its effects on his business. Some Masters will have a table spread with food. They will feast and watch you suffer with hunger. They will deny you even the breadcrumbs that fall from their table.

It's important to beware of self. Me, myself and I: selfish, self-centred, self-sufficient, self-confidence, self-exaltation. You need saving from yourself. Self has pride and robs you of so much. Cast out the self-life; self is the root of all this trouble in the world today. I have no moral outrage and my caring attitude never changed. I always told myself, 'Perhaps he's a good guy who has made bad decisions from time to time.'

"I wish I could just die and rest from the world of toiling and trouble," he would say.

"Death and life are in the power of the tongue, so watch what you say. Words are powerful; don't break down the defences with careless words and give way to the spirit of death. Stop closing your own casket with your own words. Speak life," I would tell him.

"Don't you think I'm trying?"

"Maybe not hard enough," I said. "You wouldn't speak so recklessly if you were trying. Only say those words when you know you are ready to die."

The tide was turning and not in his favour. He always carried a Holy Rosary in his pocket because it had some joyful, sorrowful and glorious mysteries attached to it. It was a spiritual weapon, a shield from danger and a miracle agent, because it is believed that you are preserved from eternal fire when you die wearing it. Illness causes fear and anger, whether it's your own health or someone who is close to you. He would get angry about taking his son back and forth to the best consultants, with no success.

"I'm not scared for myself anymore, but my son can't die before I do. That's what frightens me, Sandra; I feel crippled. He's critically ill!"

Rich or poor, no parent should have to shoulder the burden of outliving their children.

For his betterment, he knew it was time to slow down. I say this facetiously but also earnestly. His life was like a script written by a drunken mad man, in shambles. He went for daily six-mile walks on doctor's orders, which was restful and refreshing for him. Usually he would ring me during those walks, and it felt like I had literally accompanied him. During one of his walks, a white feather landed on him. Delighted, he explained that it was a divine intervention. "It's an angel of faith and a hedge of protection. Feathers appear when angels are near." He seemed calm, relaxed and pondered on everything I told him.

When he didn't ring me, it meant he was walking with family and I would miss our chats. We have all been entrusted with a specific assignment in life that cannot be stopped by any force. Being an escort is not a tragedy for everyone. It has been my platform to dispense hope, tender love and care. My assignment is not to the entire world; I am completely unnecessary to some people, but I was necessary to a man who needed hope. I didn't tell him what he wanted to hear, but the truth is that no man is hopeless or useless until he lies down and the undertaker puts soil on top of him. No matter how far gone you are, so long as you are in the land of the living, you are not beyond saving. In doing so, I met his needs in a tremendous way.

Was he a snob or out of touch with reality? Uncertainly. One thing that was certain was his cocaine addiction. It had such a tight grip on him that he knew he was in captivity and thirsted for liberty. Love covers a multitude of defects, so I did not class it as a moral failing. When you love someone, you factor their social, behavioural and economic environment into their situation to better understand them because love is patient, love is kind and love is long-suffering. He thought the drug binges would subside with age, but it worsened; even rehabilitation didn't help much. Didn't he have licenced therapists? Still, on his difficult days, he needed a soul to cling to and it happened to be me.

In May 2016, I sensed his deep and desperate desire for help when he rang me and said, "Sandra, I was there in England for a retreat. I'm lost." He didn't have to explain that it was drugs. He knew that I knew what I knew, but still I screamed at him for the rest of the week because he didn't come to see me before he returned to Ireland. His wellness mattered to me and he knew I wanted what was best for him. We are all in need of different things. This man was truly in need and it was not for more money.

We spoke on video sometimes and he was comfortable to see me using the kettle for a month to boil water for my bath when my boiler had broken down. Clearly lacking compassion, he knew my problems first-hand, but he lashed out when I dared ask for him for anything at all. he was fully aware that his oasis… the person who lifts him up… lives in extreme deprivation, under enormous stress with a disabled child, on a council estate in a deprived area of Britain.

The inability to experience the suffering of another as one's own… is a moral failing and the reason the world is in turmoil? When I emphasised my son's health and well-being, he would say, "Don't use the weak to ask me for things. You are strong enough."

I took him in my arms and crowned him with my love. I shielded and protected him. Overcome by sudden passion, and traveling to the deepest parts of his being, perhaps I was intrigued also. He was a troubled VIP, a destitute millionaire. When his intellect failed him, when his own faith, power and riches were not sufficient, when other tycoons around him failed to reach him at his very core, because they are all so full of themselves, driven by greed and a thirst for glory; he knew that in me, he had a sincere friend.

We all have that part of us we don't share; too deep and dark to go there ourselves most days. But the right person hears you differently and stays with you in that darkness. He looked up to the person whom the world looked down upon and found sanctuary in my heart. That simple thing in life, the ordinary listener from a common background, was the extraordinary instrument for the most important part of his being, to lift him up. I have none of the silver and gold. In fact, the last of my gold I pawned away, but I brought sustaining love to the table. Nothing about love is meaningless. Every aspect of it is beautiful.

Enduring hardships, waiting to see the next client so that I could top up my gas and electric metre. On the other end of the line was a multimillionaire, constantly asking and thriving on my live sex videos as I earned my pennies from other men to make ends meet. He noticed that in some videos, I was giving a man a blowjob with a condom, and in other videos, I wasn't.

"Sandra, how do you decide which dick needs a condom and which one doesn't?" he asked.

I laughed and said, "I always do a visual assessment. Some dicks are not even tempting to touch, let alone eat, so I would rather suck the condom rubber. In comparison, like a piece of art, some dicks look so delicious and succulent that my mouth dives on it. In defence, eating is an art!"

That aside, how many children go to bed hungry while the world watches, and their conscious doesn't eat at them, because it's a harsh society? Hardest pill to swallow: if they wanted to end world hunger with extreme ease, they would. But pathological cruelties exist, and the weak become weaker, the powerful more powerful. For choosing to ignore their privilege because they can, they are not heroes to any degree.

Empathy is a myth to some. In their world, they serve only themselves. Born into a life in which they are simply entitled, there is a visible line between the seen and the unseen. We can only exude love and patience, because we exist to aid one another. When he was crushed and in a feeble state; depressed and ill, he rang me many times because there comes a time when even the mighty feel oppressed. They too, cry for help and long for safety, often seeking an instrument that adds strength, peace, joy, or even just a smile.

The last time I heard from him, he was suffering various ailments with no end in sight… showing signs of retiring as he had just had a pacemaker implanted, after suffering a heart attack.

With all his feebleness and fears… bound by his own chains, I loved him the way he was. Above all, I made every effort to weaken those chains. I loved him too much to leave him the way he was.

Chapter 35
Willpower

Our ability to consistently and knowingly make the wrong decision is infuriatingly tiresome. The strength of the human mind is incredible for the good, the bad and the ugly; the grind never stops. In the end, when your head and your heart are at war, which side wins, and is it up to you?

The continuous effort to keep the enemy at bay is exhausting. Keep trying. Keep fighting. It will be frustrating, but you are worth the many attempts to stay balanced. We all hit bumps in the road and life will give us a million reasons to turn around. Just put one foot in front of the other, then repeat, until you find that one reason to take one more step forward. The head has so many tabs open and every day we are all working at it like soldiers in a battlefield because life truly is a wrestle! A vicious battle! A raging war. We are not fighting with real swords because it is not a physical battle. It is a battle of the mind. Don't be a turtle without a shell. No soldier fights a battle without wearing or carrying something for victory and protection. There is nothing beautiful about life. We need strategy and creativity to make it beautiful!

The mind is the battlefield and seeks to consume us each day, like a deep dive on solid rock. It so powerful and we all know how it plays up and constantly fluctuates, when the skull seems to be nothing but a goblet of anxieties. What if there was a helmet to protect it, because that is the target of the enemy. Well, you are the helmet. Learn how to not give a fuck, and life will serve you better!

The heart is the most vital and vulnerable organ, and nothing breaks more than a heart. What if there was a breastplate to cover the heart and guard it with all diligence! You are the breastplate of your heart. Guard it unapologetically.

Knowledge is power; school only taught us how to consume content. What if it taught us how to cope with the real world or how to quench the fiery darts in this raging war called life. One can be book smart but god damn stupid. Survival and our life itself taught us the reality. It's simply called LIFE!

What if there was a shield to quench the insults and negativity from those who want to crush and break you to the point of despair. You hope for sympathy; there is none. You hope for comfort; you find none. Because when you look deeper, everything is real but not everyone is true. Trusting is what got us in this mess… remember?

We all want to stand firm and be strong but whatever your status, no one is exempt from the trials and tribulations we face. Victory and protection are not always guaranteed to the mighty, or the wealthy. It is merciful that no one is immune to the brutal, fiery darts of depression. It doesn't have a face and it can creep up on anyone at any time. Each day, with my legion of clients, I witnessed how it slays the soul and poisons the mind, wasting both life and pasture. Everyone is surviving on an anxious planet.

Again, I observed that we are all struggling and fighting against something, usually in the form of gluttony, and it doesn't pertain only to an over-indulgence of food or drink. We enter gluttony when nothing is done or taken in moderation. Any trigger literally blows up to a binge – always all-out and excessively, usually at the cost of health and dignity. Like a consuming fire, any addiction is there to steal, to kill and destroy everything. You wish to shake off the shackles of addiction! You wish to snap out of that depression.

The strains within us. Many are fighting a raging war every day… against anxiety and depression; the only art they know is to wake up and survive themselves. Some days are worse than others in trying to find balance. Others are bound by addiction to drugs and nicotine.

For those struggling with liquor, the booze and shots are calling them frequently. There is no such a thing as 'just one drink' for an alcoholic. That one sets the fire ablaze. Compulsive gamblers constantly fall short and frequently give in to the temptation of the slot machine, roulette, bingo, poker. The warnings 'gamble responsibly' or 'smoking kills' mean nothing when that demon takes dominance. Don't listen to that voice that tells you, "You are not your own master; this shall be a battle to thy death".

We are too often both the *sin* and the *sinner*; putting ourselves in situations that are going to hurt us. Many are not even hungry, but food – and I mean lots of it – is calling their name constantly, leading to a binge followed by a feeling so repulsive that they could chop their tongue off, but because of hypocrisy at its finest, that food addict will easily taunt a drug addict. I see preachers controlled by food, judging and condemning those bound by an addiction to drugs and alcohol. There is a bigger log in his eye he must remove before he sees the speck in someone else's. Both have gluttony. Wherever you are most vulnerable, whatever is most relatable to you, whichever shoe fits, just wear it and remember it's the same force. So, we are all under one umbrella called gluttony. When gluttony has a hold on you, you want to move forward, but that force takes you down, not to zero but worse off. If you are not going in circles, you are stuck in madness.

After I met some big players, influential in the social, political and financial world, they may be a little out of touch with the common man but that does not mean that the world is assembled around them. They may be privileged from cradle to grave but that doesn't mean every segment of their life is glorious. In the end, we are all sensitive spirits making sense of all the chaos. Enslaved by a big giant, every morning, they wake up wanting freedom and fighting that giant for it. It was a truly stirring insight that even they, the upper class, from the upper drawers, have their own share of misfortune. Suffering from debilitating depression, they too are constantly trying to extinguish the fiery darts in one way or the other. You think they are on solid ground; I have seen them in liquid mud… struggling. Trying to stay perfectly balanced on a tight rope, the temptations and human weaknesses that the rest of us are wrestling with in this highly alienating world have not bypassed them. In keeping up with appearances, they seem happy and healthy but inside they are screaming and perishing. They have no other strength but to keep on concealing the giant turmoil of pain with pretence until it consumes them to depression. We all fall short and give in to various desires. We are all quietly treating something, working through something and trying to keep it together.

Some people talk about willpower but what is willpower? To win the battle and still fight the war?

The ability to eat cleanly and be disciplined for nine days and then on the tenth day you have a binge and take in more calories which nullifies your whole effort?

The ability to be substance-free for a week and then have an uncontrollable cocaine binge?

Every day, it's a new effort and a new hope for a new era, but you still wake up afraid of the unknown, other days a little less afraid.

Where can you go to buy a clean slate? Slowly tiptoeing into the day, each day is a tightrope walk. You wake up and inherit your own mess and you're lost within the day, because the storm is within you. It's a horrendous battle. Struggling with desires, you try to find new pathways to resist temptations. Somewhere deep in the pit of your stomach, you hold a sense of fear… a knowing that at any moment, your willpower will only fail you. You know that when you give in, it hits you hard like a train on a rail-track.

At sunrise, you start off vibrant and the day starts shaping up so well. You are on track but by sunset, you are derailing, fading and withering away to the temptation of the binge, the drink, the gambling, the drugs, the smoke. Something always snatches away your effort. Slipping into your bed at night, knowing that your actions didn't align with your desires, you think to yourself, *wasn't today meant to be productive?*

The more you say, "Never again," the more you worry, fear and fret and that willpower fails you massively. With all the numerous temptations, something drags you down. It's a roller-coaster of instability, if not a deadly game of hide-and-seek with yourself and it wrecks your life. For a day or two when you seem to have it under control, even though you feel supremely talented in your willpower of steel but hold on, don't boast yet. You are still scared to move an inch because you know that the stability is only temporary – any move will derail you. Daily, as you hide the pain and harness your emotions, you are struggling badly at trying to keep it together.

If not tormenting, what then is willpower if the willingness to lose weight, stop the addiction, the drugs, the gambling is already present within you, but to do that which you are willing to do, you find you just cannot do it? The longing is one thing, but you find yourself doing the opposite. The more earnest and intense the desire to quit drugs, junk food, nicotine, alcohol, the more you fail. If only the willing and the doing were easily matched! If I could have a superpower, alas! I would choose the power of both – to will and to do.

Everyone has their own 'poisoning paradise'. My wrestle with gluttony and willpower was with none other than food. My journey for weight loss… gain… loss… that rollercoaster in the desperate desire to 'fix' myself. We eat every day, after all, and they say knowledge is power, so I decide to arm myself with lots of it only to find that the more I know, the less I know… the more I struggled. It seems like we know exactly all the wrong things that we shouldn't be eating but we can never figure out the right things that we should be eating. Nothing beats feeling in charge, yet there was always a predator devouring my effort.

There was a lot of discussion that being thin translates to more confidence and more business and happier clients. I thought my miracle was just a weight loss away, and so I worked at it because there was a promise… more profit and prosperity. One breakthrough causes another breakthrough. Weight loss has its own rewards… showing off skill, dedication and discipline, you feel like you could take over the world. I didn't want to be like those who put the weight back on, and even more. Well, that was when the corrosion and inflammation of the mind started. The rollercoaster and insanity of applauding myself for putting out a fire I started.

Keeping up with unrealistic realities gets even more difficult. Then we resort to desperate measures, all to feel slim and 'desirable'. I have been through radical, hostile and unsustainable diets; eating thorns and thistles and yes, I lost a lot of weight, but it didn't come with a risk warning. Overly aware of ourselves, our unquenchable need to belong backfires in a huge way… drives us insane and enhances depression. I became emotionally and mentally a slave; at the centre of my life was weight loss and weight gain, it almost consumed me. It's strange how what was supposed to lead to happiness, health and the perfect body eventually led to a garden full of anxiety. With all the debates surrounding weight loss, I fell into the trap of fad diets and like many others, I swore off certain foods and became fixated on righteous eating. Clean eating. Organic. Handpicked. Grass-fed. I have been a fat-traitor, carb-traitor, wheat-traitor… A diet-traitor. In the long run, on that rollercoaster, I was engulfed by orthorexia; it was about clean eating or not eating it at all. The numbers on the scale defined me, it created fear and anxiety. I became vile to myself, terrified. "Seriously, I woke up? Again?" Morning comes with dread. You think darkness has come to stay. Just because an A-List celebrity has endorsed a diet and given it wings does not make it healthy.

Anyway, I freed myself from the prison that I had created for my own mind. And body. I went back to what was healthful.

There is no instruction manual. If we are trying our best for wellness and support one another to stay balanced, that's what matters. We can get through this together and I am always going to be here for you.

Chapter 36
The Greatest of All Time

Junior was the son of an iconic celebrity and they visited England. As his father toured the country and went down to London, he was with me, cooking lasagne and smoking marijuana. He left his hotel and asked if he could come and stay with me. Initially, he said, because he does not like hotel or restaurant food. He loves home-cooked food.

I had a big, round cold sore on my lip which I tried to disguise as best as I could. I was just recovering from swine flu which had hit many people in that year, and I had taken treatment for it. The first time I met him was in a hotel in Manchester city centre and we went back to his hotel. He believed that African urine is healing for the mind, body and soul, so I had to urinate in a cup, and he gulped it all down with pleasure. Each time he saw me walk to the bathroom, he reminded me to take the cup with me.

After a few days with him, I realised the reason he had checked out of the hotel was because of his stepmother, with whom he did not see eye-to-eye. He expressed to me their hatred for each other and a few times he broke down and cried. Crying was allowed in my presence. You may be the son of the Greatest of All Time but if it hurts, you cry. He revealed a lot of things including how he feels that his father is alive yet dead, because his stepmother builds a wall that cannot be climbed over. When he tries to penetrate that wall, they argue.

We had many heart-to-heart talks. He said of his stepmother, in taking advantage of his father's illness, she wanted the son out of sight so that he would be completely forgotten. "I can't look after my father; she won't let me. I can't even sit near them on the plane; she won't let me. I can't tour with my father; she won't allow it. She hates me, and I hate her. I can't remember when the last time was when I spent a minute alone with my father. She avoids it at all costs. She is such a distraction, so destructive. All that I long for is just a minute with him, but it will never happen before he dies."

Society believes a cry of a man is emotional nudity. Hence, they don't want to undress themselves to that level. There are moments when they want to shed a tear or two, but their eyes and ego just won't give in, because they want to man-up, deal with it or get over it. The stigma doesn't end. Tears can, in fact, be a sign of strength because you let go of the things that are hurting you, it emotionally builds you and strengthens you. You get mentally healthy when you don't hold things back, and with good mental health, you achieve greatness. To cry is to accept you are hurting. It doesn't make you weak. It makes you strong. It makes you human. It's okay if your significant other cries in front of you. Do men even send a crying emoji? People refuse to believe that men cry. They say it's unacceptable unless someone dies. Wait, are they not human too? Yes, that's okay too.

Basically, he moved in with me for two days between 26 and 27 August 2009 and I cooked lasagne each day. For the first time I heard of oregano. He was so frustrated that I don't have some herb called oregano and I told him I had never heard of it. "How in the world can you have a kitchen without oregano? My grandmother swears by it and she says it's not a perfect lasagne without oregano." We went to the nearby supermarket and got some. He used almost half a tub of butter as well as the cheese; I was mind-blown and the calories in it meant that I wasn't even going to taste it, but the American man coaxed me into having just a mouthful. I had had never eaten so much fat. I had just embarked on a weight-loss journey. I watched him as he savoured every bite.

He went to the studio and did a photo shoot with a guy called Phil, and later he told me he was writing a memoir on the hardships he has faced, more especially since his father suffered from Parkinson's Disease since 1984, there was no room for him in his father's life. Also, he said he wanted to go to London to meet the queen before he returned to America. "With your father?" I asked him.

"No, I will go alone."

I told him, "Dream on. You may be the son of the greatest, but you are not just going to press the Buckingham Palace doorbell and sit down with the queen for a chat and more lasagne." He looked disappointed.

Chapter 37
Police in Our Sheets

Life had improved. I started to study law with the Open University, had some good grades, and one evening of 10 September 2010, my friend and I decided we should learn to go out sometimes. After all, my son had gone for respite to help me get some rest. Rather than sit in and catch up with the cleaning, we decided to go to Manchester. We were not familiar with the bars. We ended up in a bar off Deansgate. We bought soft drinks and chatted away.

We took some pictures as a reminder of our rare night out and other strangers decided to join in without an invite. We didn't mind.

After about ten minutes, a man who was smartly dressed in a waistcoat came from behind the bar and approached us. He asked us where we were from, and we said Gracious. He said, "No, I mean originally. Your ethnic origin."

We said, "Oh okay, we are from Malawi."

"Where is that?"

We told him Africa and all hell broke loose.

"I am not comfortable with you sort of people in my pub." He pushed us towards the door as he repeatedly shouted abuse.

Many people looked on in horror, because they saw us come in and knew that we had done nothing wrong. When they dared speak, the landlord shouted:

"You are the ones encouraging them. Stop it or I will bar you!"

Pushed outside on a cold and rainy night, in tears we rang the police and gave them the details. The man in the waistcoat came out again and said, "Are you two still here?"

We said, "Look we are out of your bar. Outside is a public place. We are waiting for the police."

"You are wasting your time," he said. "Stand on the other side of the road because I don't even want you this side."

One of the men came out to express his disgust and shock. The landlord shouted back at him that he would be banned from the pub.

We told him to go in because the police wouldn't be long.

After a few minutes, we saw one police officer walking down the street towards us and we felt a sense of relief, little did we know that he would cause the biggest scene because he had no humanity and common sense. We told him what had happened, that we were not being destructive, just black as we were, but he said, "I don't believe you. I know him well. His wife is a similar colour to you. How can he be racist? Tell me how he can be racist."

Somewhere along the way, someone, please tell the white officer that having sex with black people does not absolve one of racist behaviour. You cannot fusion racism with, "But I have black friends."

We pleaded with him to get witness statements because many other customers were stunned and aghast at the cruelty, when the landlord said it was within his right to have only whites in his bar. All the officer did was speak to the landlord, sided with him… then he came back out within five minutes and told us to leave.

One of the men whispered to us and confirmed that the callous pub owner and the police officer were very good friends. What chance did we have? In his uniform, right under our nose, how shockingly sad that in such horrendous circumstances, he failed miserably in his duty of care, because he chose to protect the fragile ego of a spineless, racist coward. Anyone who says racism doesn't exist has never come down from their high horse and seen how others can be treated.

I contacted Halpern Solicitors who took the case on. We explained how we were ejected from a bar, on grounds of our race and sex, contrary to sections 1(1)(a) and 20 of the Race and Relations Act 1976 and section 1(1)(a) and 29 of the Sex Discrimination Act 1975. After a counter claim in the Manchester County Court, case number 11Q13416, he eventually accepted unlawful discrimination and humiliating us with his words and actions, which deprived us of the social evening that we had arranged to spend. He accepted the charges after he struggled to make his fictional story authentic. People are only sorry when they get caught. The truth prevailed.

Oh, the horrors of discrimination! We didn't want sympathy, just fairness… but the actions of the police at the scene failed to protect the integrity of what Britain stands for. I complained about his actions to the Independent Police Complaints Commission (IPCC) who immediately passed the matter to the Professional Standards Department (PSD) and said I would hear from them REF (2012/005998) – but it has been years without word. Last time I checked, I was told to get over it, the computers are not working, and that the information may be lost.

The police constable got away with this conduct and will probably never know that the pub landlord, his loyal friend whom he shielded, accepted in a court of law, his unlawful actions that night. He can now hang his head in shame with this shake-up.

Whatever happened was nowhere near serving and protecting a citizen. It was truly frightening and destroyed my confidence in the police. If you want to know the truth, ask the downtrodden, for we can't afford pretence.

My last call to the police was disheartening. The silent heartbreaks of the muted postcode. An officer clearly said to me, concerning my vulnerable son, clearly irritated and dismissive, "We are very busy people. We have got work to do. You have invited this danger upon yourself, so be it. We will report this to other agencies." The devastation I was left with is unimaginable. Other agencies meant Social Services, but this time it was not necessary, and it was not about safeguarding Alfred. The pitiful attempt to reframe the issue as negligence on my part fell well short of standards expected of them. Blaming me was the easy option for them. It was demeaning, but the great unwashed are rising. They band together, combine skills and are taking care of each other even more. The community solved the issue and tackled the bully who was threatening to stab my son.

The injustices are astonishingly sad, and they should be deeply ashamed of themselves. Who schools and polices them when they lack the ability to serve and protect without discrimination? Those in high places, from the upper drawer, are served better. The great unwashed have had a lot of harrowing experiences. The mindset of the police is distorted beyond belief. The consequences of the failures are devastating. This inequality doesn't only let us down… It harms us badly, when there is no one to hear us and no one to listen when harm is in our way, because we are treated with utter suspicion. The citizen must come first in everything that they do, and their task cannot be executed with prejudice. Clearly, the police assume that everyone in this postcode is a daft troublemaker not worthy of being heard and undeserving of their time, protection and safety. I steadfastly believe that there is no greater disability than looking narrowly down on people, and this mindset needs a total overhaul.

Indeed, it is a poor, disadvantaged population and may not be their preferred postcode. There are no mansions around here, but it is not a breeding ground for criminals and unruly lowlifes. We are not a crime waiting to happen, so please don't put us on 'critical alert'. We just want to be treated as citizens and asking to be humanised. The police should rise to that level where they treat everyone equal and not mark certain areas and their residents as spam. After my experiences, I call for a change that will lead to safety and improve people's lives NOW for the good of everyone. This prejudice and bigotry must be combated. It's a toxic mindset with consequences more complex than most could ever imagine. We may be low down in society, but we are not sleep-walking through life; we are switched on and we need them too.

I can't believe I have to say this, but what does it take to feel safe and get justice when such discrimination of postcodes is on the rise? The police and some top chiefs may demean us during the execution of their duty, nonetheless, in their social time, a good few find themselves in this grime ghetto, getting some pleasure between our sheets and legs… under our covers… Oh yes, it all happens here. Beneath those uniforms are some kinky fuckers. Surely, we can't be that bad then? We must be worthy of some protection? Let us strike a deal and perhaps meet halfway, shall we? Work hard, play hard, and please protect us accordingly, in the exercise of that duty. We are what you WANT, to stretch our buttholes and suck your dicks. You are what we NEED in times of trouble.

When the police are so incompetent…with a prejudice bone, they disgracefully opt for the effortless way out. They dismiss a case and discount it as a family issue. 'Families' have killed each other on British soil. You, the police force, are faced with a multicultural generation, myriad social norms and deeply held beliefs. The first time the authorities noticed that I had been physically abused, he undermined them and proudly boasted "back off, she is my wife… I can do what I want." Remember this; some cultures are entirely incompatible, but we are here now. It is disturbing that certain cultures force marriage, force sex, are supportive of violence, physical punishment is the norm. Killing can be a matter of honour. Beating women and children is accepted as discipline. Female genital mutilation is promoted.

When someone cries out to you, they have broken a barrier, so consider the it courageous because they must really need you. Please don't be bystanders in such calamities. Terrified, I just wanted a hand away from the danger I was running from.

Chapter 38
A Smooth Criminal

Wishful thinking can only take you so far and faith without action is dead. Indeed, one must be seen to be doing something that potentially paves the way for that dream, but if everything must be hard fought to find and achieve, does that include love?

It's TIME and CHANCE and it can happen to anyone; being in the right place at the right time and spotted by the right person. Others have hit the jackpot and find themselves in the 'White House' or even the 'palace' somewhere, not because they are intelligent, wise or skilful. They may have fought harder, but time and chance happened to them.

Even though the number one *rule* in this utmost pleasure-business is "flirt but don't fall in love", escorts rarely admit that we do enjoy love and affection, sometimes desperately. We know better than to mix business with pleasure but bonds form naturally, with a chemistry so undeniable. If we made so many people happy, do we deserve happiness? We have a dream to be found by Mr Right, and this is the job that enables new possibilities. Perhaps the movie *Pretty Woman* gives a hooker an abnormally optimistic dream to strike gold? It is not the explosive sex that gets a man hooked. It is not because the hooker can suck dick without her hand on it. It is because they have found an intimate and emotional connection. That is the part that makes it hard to walk away. As well as the sex.

As much as I try to resist the strong attraction and protect myself from affection, all it does is leaves us both wanting more. In a few cases, I have built castles in the air because of that desire for a fairy-tale ending, to be crowned with love. I just want to be adored.

I believe in seed time and harvest time, so after all the troubleshooting, giving support to so many men, I longed for my harvest. I was not trying to be sold to the highest bidder… I wanted much more than just settling down with a man. I long for a man I can love and respect. Rather than finding the right man, I wanted to be the right woman found. I am strong. Looking for somebody stronger. Otherwise I am happy to grovel on in hardship and still enjoy my brief illicit encounters. I thought that someone out there deserved me and was just waiting for me to be ready for him, with my imperfections and vast previous experiences. Yet also, I trouble myself with longing because I have no idea if there is even such a thing as truth anymore.

To some, being an escort may be a hopeless route to find love, but don't dismay; love can be found in hopeless places. You can stumble into love in the least romantic places and under some pretty shocking conditions. No matter how down and dirty you feel about yourself, how unglamorous the setting or how traumatic your past or present is, love has a way of finding you. True love, as it turns out, writes a new story for every couple. It is not only in libraries and supermarkets that people find their significant other. Typically, some escort bookings branch off into a regular client, some into a friendship and others into romance. If you are lucky enough to find that, just let yourself love and be loved.

Not always knowing who you are going to meet on any given day adds to the experience and makes the job even more interesting. The perks of the job... there is always a fair bit of passion and romance thrown in. I longed for love, affection and intimacy. Through my interaction with many clients, I have met some wonderful men but there was always someone who melted in my heart; I referred to them as my VIP. You start to miss them, count down the hours, minutes and seconds before you see them again.

This time I discovered a rare gem, a man that had exceptional qualities. It started off as an overnight booking at a hotel in Deansgate, Manchester. When he rang me, he requested a GFE 'Girl-Friend Experience' because it was on the list of the services that I provided. As the name suggests, it includes more personal activity such as deep French kissing, cuddling and hugging. An onlooker at first glance is supposed to assume that the client is my lover because I am behaving like a girlfriend. Acting like I really want to be there, I am expected to look in his eyes with tender love and care as I caress his hand as we wine and dine, like lovers do. I thought he was the man to have and to hold.

Was I in love or purely in love with the idea of being in love? It was 2015 when I thought I had met Mr Right, but I was wrong. George was an English man. A consultant who always dressed supremely well. There was an instant spark and he charmed me with what I thought was thoughtfulness and class. He told me he was a widower; what a plausible lie! Premeditated heartbreak. Before long, he had me believing that he was the man to decorate my life and restore my faith in love and commitment. I realised it was a new error rather than a new era. He was well versed in feeding an escort just what she wanted to hear, with the expectation of luring her into romance. A pathological liar who made me believe that he was a widower and emotionally expressed that his wife died of skin cancer some years ago, hence he was lonely and ready to mingle with that one girl, and I was the chosen one. "She was buried in Spain next to her mum and dad," he would say as he held back a tear and I rebuked myself for bringing up the topic.

Grief is the loneliest journey. I thought I was helping him to process the change in his life. How could he lie of such, to lull me into a false sense of security and convince me that I am 'The One'? He even blamed the National Health Service for being reckless in his wife's illness and 'death', but I told him don't even go there; I defend the NHS with every fibre of my being and would never jump on the bandwagon of those who say otherwise. Where would I be without it? He had every infusion of compassion from me. I thought he captured the essence of grief so painfully well. I thought his deceased wife was a lucky woman to have been loved so deeply and purely during her lifetime – but she wasn't dead after all. He was the only man I met who played a fantastic stepfather to my son. I thought he was a 'confirmed bachelor' ready to take on the responsibility.

May 2015: Life took on a new meaning; I was in love with love. I enjoyed the theatres with George and that was way out of my comfort zone. Matthew Bourne's *The Car Man* at the Lowry Theatre in Salford Quays was an excellent starter for me, a phenomenal world of dance thriller which I never knew existed. Away from my work, I struggled to discover other interests. On its first tour in eight years, it was certainly one of the most outstanding performances I have ever witnessed with my own two eyes. As I watched the sensational creativity of the dancers and choreography, somewhere between horrified and excited, I realised how much I had been alienated from the rest of the world with my job as an escort, and it felt like I was on a whole different planet. In my set of circumstances, my creativity was in sex and I was programmed by that culture and system. Hence, this awesome performance was so relatable. It was a genius production of sex, desire and sexual cravings played out on one stage in the most moving yet effortless and faultless way. The magnificence of *The Car Man* stirred my soul, sent my spirits soaring high and is certainly a piece of art which will stay with me for a lifetime.

To Kill a Mockingbird, the story of racial injustice, was an awesome memory staged at the same theatre. I enjoyed it because, like most of the audience, I had read the text in high school, in my own case back in Malawi. Fond memories of my favourite English teacher Mrs Matinga kept pouring in because she had excellently explored the character so well and drew us in. This time around, having experienced some racial injustice as an immigrant in Britain, the play brought chilling echoes throughout.

I have never been one to use the 'race card', so not only do I feel embarrassed and sad as it diminishes the actual horror of racism when people misuse it, but I find it to be an all-too-common, often misunderstood concept, extremely destructive to blacks, whites and others. I like to know I qualify, and I am able, rather than being chosen or admitted for the sake of some diversity quota. Give me equality, not preferential treatment because of my colour. It's not tragic that I'm black. Inequality is rife, but this time under the guise of diversity. When I experience hardship, my colour is not the first and only thing that leaps to mind and it puzzles me when people's psyches are so deeply ingrained with the issues of race.

This play resonated as a painful reminder that the problem is on-going. Others have been wrongly suspended, expelled, arrested, imprisoned and killed for being black. I ask you earnestly, search your heart, if you are contributing to the on-going racism, in the social, political or economic world, the establishment, the state; and benefiting from structural racism, I ask you yet more earnestly to please stop. Prejudice in any form gets in the way of success, opportunity and progress, and it harms others badly. We will always remember the historians who shed light on the truths of racial discrimination, so that this prejudice may not continue. Beyond remembering, we must always do our part.

This play brought back my own painful experiences with racial oppression. It was touching and reflected on those moments where it was so apparent, obvious and painful that they hated and excluded me because of my colour. When that neighbour moved out and said she just could not live near *Negros*. When a mother scolded her two children for playing with my black son, a mother's prejudice ruined our children's fun. Amongst other incidents, I couldn't help but remember that landlord who demanded that my friend and I leave because he hates black people. It is deeply saddening that my list of experiences could go on and on, but I don't let my pain change me for the worse. I let it mould and humble me to be a better person.

George had assumed that I would be familiar with the Royal Exchange Theatre in the heart of Manchester and was shocked to learn that I hadn't even heard of it. With charm and sarcasm, he said to me, "But you know every brothel and swinging venues in Manchester and the surrounding areas, don't you, darling?"

"Indeed," was my reply.

After a lovely meal in Deansgate, we made our way to St Ann's Square where the theatre was situated. This time it was a nine-hundred-plus-page novel, crammed into a two-hour production. *Anna Karenina* by Leo Tolstoy. Anna's husband was a cold fish with wealth and excellent social and professional connections, a wife everybody adored and a high-spirited son, but all these things came to nought because his life was prescribed by a strict schedule of work, dinner parties and reading. The evenings he spent with his wife were philosophical discussions, rather than emotional. The narrative of this play fit in well with some wealthy clients I have encountered – cold, heartless and greedy. Clueless what joy is, their life was simply a machine, successful but emotionless.

Anna acts outside the social rules prescribed for her and cheats on her husband, Karenin. Shockingly, he doesn't yell at her, but decides that it would be too humiliating for him to have a public divorce, so he asks her to still be with him and simply act as his wife, despite living separate lives, to preserve his reputation and position in society. There is no secret under the sun and Karenin became a laughingstock like most are today, in highly controversial circumstances behind closed doors.

This interesting play was the last theatre trip I enjoyed with George. It was awesome while it lasted.

Calculative and manipulating, cash was always king for George. He avoided using credit cards to avoid being caught at home. After several months, alarm bells started ringing. First, when I forgot my lipstick in his *BMW* and that seriously rattled his cage. I wondered what the outburst was all about. Then I left my large pair of earrings in the glove compartment after I removed them during a long drive from the Lake District. It was an unpardonable offence and again, I wondered what the fuss was all about, considering it was now my fiancé's car! Yes, he had put a ring on my finger!

One discovery led to another, only to find out that his wife wasn't dead after all and there was even another black escort in the exact position as I was. She was from West Africa and had the exact engagement ring that I had from him. We spoke at length and didn't reduce each other to tears, even though we were hurting and bitter. We both had high hopes. How he juggled and multi-tasked his consultancy work, being a husband, a grandfather and a fiancé to both of us must have been exhausting mentally and physically, but he must have classed it as genius. He got us the same clothes and handbags and accessories, maybe to save himself time or to decide who wore it best; only he knows!

All the awkward moments started adding up and fit in the painful jigsaw. Every lie brought us closer to goodbye. How dare I leave lipstick and earrings in the car he used with his wife? No wonder he had tantrums when he saw me uploading my good life pictures on social media updates. "Please delete them because my two daughters are still healing from their mother's death, so let us do this properly."

Where death is concerned, there is always sympathetic understanding, but I told him, "Don't worry. My profile is not open to the world. It is more family-orientated." He had a look to prove it.

These hookers are loyal but when you play games with their heart, you die by your own sword.

Chapter 39
The Presidents Club

Empires may fall, but the phrase "boys will be boys" has endured. By any other name, across any city, there will always be a rebirth and great awakening of the Oxford University Bullingdon Club. It is in these clubs that men of privilege and wealth lock the world outside and manifest who they truly are – rampant and rowdy boys. There is no room for the pretence they must deal with daily in the current fragile climate and I love what my clients have told me about them so far. That excited and overwhelmed look in their eyes when they reflect and speak of it. If this was really a free world, many would love its renaissance and some of us 'hostesses' wouldn't mind getting on all fours for a bit of filthy fun and cash.

2018: Looks like it was the mother of all men-only clubs, attended by the very rich: The Presidents Club Charitable Trust was shut down within hours of the *Financial Times* story being published amid widespread criticism, but its anachronistic existence has shone a light on the culture of money, power and above all, the selfish theory of entitlement.

Let's stop acting surprised. By any other name, a well-prepared, men-only, hard-drinking dinner with ostentatious displays of wealth surrounded by half-naked women is a lustful and stimulating playground often leading to a potential one-night stand. The art of turning it into a fundraising event is a strategic move. The Presidents Club's media attention became relatable to me. Like those in the corporate entertainment industry, I followed closely the outcry for social change after hostesses, who were instructed to wear matching underwear, were allegedly groped and sexually harassed at the charity dinner.

They were not a trap for anyone to fall into. Nevertheless, following its exposure, others stepped down from their positions and many reputations were severely tarnished. As if men of education and position are not allowed any amusement!

Good money suddenly became bad money; so tainted that it resulted in sick children at the Great Ormond Street Hospital, an important and special charity, returning the much-needed cash. The charities were the victims in all this insanity!

I live in a world that others don't understand; just like others live in a world that I don't know about. We can accept and appreciate that we are totally ignorant of each other's world and that our definition of happiness is not the same.

Now that these elitist entertainments had finally 'existed' and emerged to the public, the pathetic hysterical outrage about the Presidents Club was, to me, evidence that those who are not aware of another world, twist, attack and demonise with ignorance and moral policing. The character assassination was horrifying. Opinions: hastily written by people who were not fully informed. Man-hating, honourable feminists especially, were leaping to conclusions and reacting to headlines and previews simply because the present-day venomous feminist is irrational and advocates inequality against men. Oh, the endless drama and pettiness! Fun and frolics conflicts with their moral stance. They forget that attractive men also act as 'hosts' and work in strip clubs, but it is never classed as 'inappropriate entertainment'. It's a case of heightened hypocrisy and the on-going agitation is annoying.

People wondered how many rich, high profile men were going regularly to events like these and purporting in public to be something totally different. The brutal answer is this: many… and it is not coincidental that these events have passed off unremarked for decades. Everybody is mischievous! What occurred in the 'locker room' stayed there and they reminded each other to be vigilant on all fronts with regards to confidentiality.

Those who found this to be demeaning, making a stand for morals, utterly condemned the event as 'totally gross' and 'totally unacceptable' as others followed suit. Reading the many startling and ignorant comments, was it a catastrophic attempt to turn men into monks? It was an assault on freedom to get kinky. Like the Presidents Club charity dinner, I have been there, have experienced that and have mopped up the aftermath in disgust, shock and sorrow. But the money I made wiped the tears away. Sometimes it's not the love of money that is the root of all evil, but the lack of it.

Believe me, I know a thing or two about these events, so sit down; don't interfere with things you have no clue about. Hostesses, waitresses, strippers, models and escorts, we are all in the same boat to some varying degrees; as willing participants, open to offers and happy to use our assets. If that seems so wrong, we don't want to be right. I saw so many delighted men under one roof and all had one thing in common, wealth, power and the selfish theory of entitlement inherent in them. Everybody dressed supremely well, mostly attendants from the white-collar executives, banking sector, current top businessmen and according to the organiser, some influential powerful political figures, I and many other women chose to work at this men-only event, not to be reduced by the men but to be lifted by earning some money. We were not under duress; but that is a conversation you are not ready to have. Many women whom I spoke to told me of the other events that they had previously attended and emphasised that I had 'missed out', economically rather than socially.

Was this, once again, an unfolding calamity to clamp down on our pleasures, art and mind? Is a woman's autonomy still a heated debate, or does each person, as a free agent, have the final say on themselves? I am resolutely against anyone deciding what adults can and cannot do with their bodies.

Truth be told, no one was forced to attend, and no women were manipulated into working there, as concluded by the anti-choice brigade. Fun and frolics conflicts with what they want people to be. Let others be who they are, without comparing yourself to them. Happy to showcase our skills, we were all well prepared and old enough to understand our position in this commercial life choice. To be happy is one of the greatest forms of success. We have complete freedom to choose what to work as and we were not there automatically… That's what is important on all levels. Getting laid was reasonably predictable at these events, so it was only sensible that I had brought with me my condoms, lubricants and well-charged toys, in case I needed some extra reinforcement. Whether or not the event sat well with our values, we were there not to add glamour, but as instruments for their quality adult entertainment; that is what we had signed up for, as all these men knew that 'tonight is the night'. Looking around the room were grins from the hosts as the guests and the women were all in one accord, relishing the moment. No one left early because the icing was always towards the end of the event. The suspense of discovering if this would turn into a random, all-out orgy or just a tease kept them all there until the finish line. Many stayed in the hotel…

There were no table manners because dining involved a bit of play, as most men could not keep their hands to themselves. Neither did we expect them to. Every action brings a reaction, and this was a perfectly designed package; we were hired to flirt, dressed provocatively in mouth-watering, willy-tormenting hold-up stockings, stilettos, suspenders and all things bright and revealing the intentions. It was a kinky set of affairs. I looked desirable in a lovely Basque which defined my figure. Thighs clad with stockings; the stares and a few wolf-whistles were part and parcel of it all. Towards the end of the dinner, a comedian arrived to catch the moment. His speciality was innuendos, dirty jokes and he was well versed with every word in the sex industry, even more than the sex workers, to give the men the perfect kick-start to what was to come. They brought in an influential comedian who made everyone laugh until they fell out of the boat on dry land. He conquered as we seduced. He certainly knew just how to manipulate the men's minds with sexual innuendos and propel them into giving for charity. If it takes such a tactful and kinky strategy to get this class of people to stretch out their hand and give 'generously' to the vulnerable, to those in need, so be it. I dare say the vision of sex and giving aligned perfectly.

With little concern for charity, they surely got a lot of compensation for their donations! His utterly masterful jokes in a room full of half-naked girls overheated the men and generated their excitement into giving more, which was a win for everyone. Instead of actively helping the needy, some rich people enjoy their privilege alone… unless they have a chance to fuck, which, in this case they were guaranteed. For oppressing their environment based on wealth, they are not heroes to any degree.

The strange-but-true connection of all things sex caused even the tight-fisted hand to give generously. Everyone's creative juices created some magic at a gentleman's evening which brought men together as they raised money for charity. Whether it is simply amazing, or horrifying, is a matter of opinion, but the amount of work and organisation that goes into planning these events, which are nothing short of kinky… is phenomenal. For many years, the game shooting industry was the good old network that used to reach out to men with this passion who kept it discreet because in it they found freedom to explore. After meeting at the top shooting grounds, they ended up here for fun and frolics, and improving their shooting… if you like.

If any man would say of this event that he was there but didn't enjoy it, or that he felt obliged to be there, he would have a challenging time proving that he was not hypocritical. The environment suited all. No one seemed clueless as to what was going on. No one stormed out. I was just mesmerised to see so many happy men having an evening that not even their wives knew about, according to those I had a chat with.

Strategically, and for convenience, considering I was a major part of the entertainment, my room was booked just opposite the room in which they had their dinner. The first room at the top of the stairs at a leading Manchester hotel was where the event took place. The place usually held meetings, conferences and weddings, but this time it was something different. Women strictly excluded, rich men, fine wine, stimulated with alcohol and women including myself, in beautiful lingerie, all rolled in to one. What's not to love? I was within reach and at first, they queued up like they do in banks, before it turned into an orgy whilst others sniffed cocaine. Next to my room were more girls offering sex, but my friend and I were the only black girls, so the men had that choice to either go to the enticing ebony room where we had porn ready on my laptop, or the cream room. It was after the sex that most men felt the whole event was worth their time and their giving.

Others were left with the imagination, but many affluent, smartly dressed men came into the room and paid. Some sniffed cocaine as they watched. There was no set price for sex. I was overworked and underpaid but because there were so many men, it all added up.

What I found deeply disturbing and infuriating was that these men, all incredibly rich, put so little money in the 'honesty box' for the incredible sex they had. They assumed that their donating had bought them the happy ending, the best part of the event that they looked forward to. Tight-fisted to the core, they ranked poorly in their generosity. When money is the only scaffolding that sustains you, you are destined to collapse. It was disappointing, but the sex made their 'giving' worthwhile. It was alarming how the 'sophisticated' society gives you what costs them nothing and consider it genius when they get away without paying. They do whatever they can get away with, within society. I should have been wiser and put a price on the sex instead of expecting their goodwill.

When you're a star, the hookers let you do anything? Presumptuous and entitled men with posh accents heaving over me, the tough task masters, came for a second helping of sex without topping up the cash. Their expectation of everything, all-inclusive, meant that they wanted to get as much in as possible. One clearly said, "I finished too quick," and I reported him to the event organiser for expecting a 'buy-one-get-one-free' service. Totally devoid of manners, they owned the night and expected generous returns, by hook or by crook. Hence, they complained to the host when I didn't yield to their demands. The kinky theory of double penetration is a man's fantasy and always seems possible until several attempts prove otherwise. It's simply a massive figment of their fragile imagination. Penis size, erection type, body shape and size, flexibility; many things factor into it; even my black magic fails me. There are some fantasies that money cannot buy. I was supposed to be professional, so they expected no games or gag reflex. Swallow and don't spit, squirt when I say so, remember I have paid. I was under enormous pressure and I had to educate most of these men about using condoms and they hated that even more. Most of the men said I am supposed to be on the birth control because they hate condoms. "I want to leave my sperms inside you," said one. "I don't like the discomfort of these things… Look, my dick goes limp," shouted another. I told them to take it or leave it and that didn't go down well. Seeking to take risks with my health as well as their own just showed a gross sense of entitlement.

They looked at how high and how great they were and felt condensed when I didn't dance to their tune. They used some racist words a few times and one of their own, who saw that this was not exciting to watch, told them there was no need for that. Those frustrated with erectile dysfunction still had a go and asked me if I had Viagra. Rattled and infuriated, they reported me to the hotel manager who was also having an exciting time surrounded by three lap dancers. He was told that I was reluctant in giving them what they wanted, after all the giving and the donations they had just made on the fundraising event. Rather than implore them, he leaped to the defence of the entitled rich men and in the most humiliating way. I should have simply just allowed them to indulge as they pleased, without question. Damned shame I didn't! So, the dispute had reached an impasse, and, oh well… I was given an indefinite ban from the hotel.

Like a big cult, privilege blinds some people until they know no bounds. They are so absorbed with fame and fortune; they think they can just grab a woman by the pussy whenever they want. They throw some racist words around knowing they will not be held accountable for their actions. Toxic masculinity? What the hell is wrong with these people? They know you are deeply offended but they just hope that you are desperate enough. You have no time to throw tantrums because you are too occupied with alleviating your poverty.

This was the circle of selfishness that caused a rich man to burn a £50 note in front of a homeless person, which also made national headlines in Britain. It would astonish only those who continue to think that the elite are always known for their chivalry and manners. The sad truth is that some people need instructions on how to be a decent person. Many I have met have had values that are rotten to the core. They must realise their ways are selfish, with no regard for the rest of us. Where wealth abounds, the sense of entitlement abounds even more.

The organiser was the first one to have a free go at me and my friend as a test drive before everyone else, so he timed it as the high calibre guests wined and dined. He believed that he was somehow entitled because he had scratched our back to invite us to the event to earn some money, so we felt obliged to scratch his back too. Whether it was a reasonable expectation or a selfish sense of entitlement, he had done me a massive favour, giving me work that I desperately needed. Surely, a pat on the back wasn't a sufficient gesture of gratitude.

People deploy money for their own advantage, usually at the expense of the have-nots and there is no compromise. With sadness and in many ways, I have seen the seamless correlation between ego, wealth and entitlement. Was I exploited, harassed or objectified? Must I wait to get to a place of luxury and privilege, before I rise to condemn the thoughtlessness of the powerful and the disgusting nature of their world? If they are floating, everyone else can drown. If it profits them, the planet can burn.

The disease of an entitled mind and the calamities it brings…